AN EXPOSITION OF GENESIS

Iohannes Oecolampadius

AN EXPOSITION OF GENESIS

translated & with an introduction by

Mickey Mattox

REFORMATION TEXTS WITH TRANSLATION
NO. 13
KENNETH HAGEN, GENERAL SERIES EDITOR

FRANS VAN LIERE, EDITOR OF BIBLICAL SERIES

www.marquette.edu/mupress/

LIBRARY OF CONGRESS CATALOGING-IN-PUBLICATION DATA

Oecolampadius, Johann, 1482-1531.
An exposition of Genesis / Iohannes Oecolampadius ; Translated & with an Introduction by Mickey L. Mattox. — First [edition].
pages cm. — (Reformation texts with translation ; no. 13)
Includes bibliographical references and index.
ISBN-13: 978-0-87462-713-8 (pbk. : alk. paper)
ISBN-10: 0-87462-713-3 (pbk. : alk. paper)
1. Bible. Genesis I-III—Commentaries—Early works to 1800. I. Mattox, Mickey Leland, 1956- , Translator. II. Oecolampadius, Johann, 1482-1531. In Genesim enarratio. Selections. III. Oecolampadius, Johann, 1482-1531. In Genesim enarratio. English. Selections. IV. Title.
BS1235.53.O3313 2013
222'.1107—dc23

2013004063

Johannes Oecolampadius (oil on wood panel) Scottish School, (17th century) / Edinburgh University Library, Scotland / With kind permission of the University of Edinburgh / The Bridgeman Art Library

∞The paper used in this publication meets the minimum requirements of the American National Standard for Information Sciences—Permanence of Paper for Printed Library Materials, ANSI Z39.48-1992.

MARQUETTE UNIVERSITY PRESS
MILWAUKEE

The Association of Jesuit University Presses

CONTENTS

ACKNOWLEDGMENTS

I wish to thank the general editor, Kenneth Hagen, for including this work in Reformation Texts with Translations. The Biblical Studies series editor, Frans van Liere, worked patiently with me throughout the editorial process and contributed a great deal to making this a better text. Aaron West and John L. Thompson both checked the entire Latin transcription as well as the English translation, and saved me from many an embarrassing mistake. Mr. West also helped with some obscurities in citations from the Hebrew language and literature. Over the last few years, my Marquette teaching assistants—David Luy, Phillip Anderas, and Luke Togni—also helped edit the text. Anderas in particular assisted me with ferreting out some of the biblical allusions. My Marquette colleague Mark F. Johnson assisted with a few odd Latin idioms. To all these friends and colleagues I am grateful. Responsibility for any inadequacies that may remain in the text is mine alone.

I also thank the staff of the Herzog August Bibliothek (HAB) for their assistance with this project. I first saw this text during a stay at the HAB in 1992. The Lesesaal there, and even more so the brilliant and eclectic assemblages of scholars gathered there provided a stimulating working space. Lastly, I thank Marquette University for its support of this project in the form of a Summer Faculty Fellowship, as well as a travel grant, which made possible my research in residence at the HAB.

Mickey L. Mattox

Festival of St. Teresa of Avila, Virgin and Doctor

IOHANNES OECOLAMPADIUS, BIBLICAL REFORMER

In the Swiss city of Basel in 1536, an enterprising publisher, Johann Bebel,[1] brought out a new biblical commentary entitled *An Exposition of Genesis,*[2] which offered readers a learned exposition of the Bible's first and arguably most evocative book. The commentary had been written—or, more accurately, spoken—by Basel's own late university professor and pastor, Iohannes Oecolampadius (1482-1531). The diminutive volume[3] Bebel offered his customers was what in the Latin language would have been labeled an *opus imperfectum*—an "incomplete work"—for it treated only the first sixteen of Genesis' fifty long chapters. Nevertheless, the publisher had every reason to expect considerable interest in the new book.

In the first place, the early chapters of Genesis, which told the story of creation and fall, had always captivated the minds and imaginations of Christian readers.[4] Even more importantly, in the 1520s Oecolampadius had gained recognition as one of the leading church

1 For Bebel's career as a printer of the works of various Reformers, see *Contemporaries of Erasmus*, ed. P. G. Bietenholz and Thomas B. Deutscher, Vol. 1: A-E (Toronto: University of Toronto Press, 1985), pp. 112-13. For larger projects, including perhaps the present one, he worked together with other Basel printers, particularly Andreas Cratander.

2 *D. Io. Oecolampadii in Genesim Enarratio*, (Basel: Bebel, 1536). "Enarratio" is a difficult term to translate. One might choose "lecture," or even the plural "lectures." However, the sense of the singular noun *enarratio* in the title of this particular work is better conveyed by singular English "exposition."

3 It was published in *octavo* size, i.e., small enough to be carried in a coat pocket.

4 For a broad sampling in sixteenth century Genesis exegesis, including Oecolampadius, see John L. Thompson, *Genesis 1-11*, Vol. 1 in the Reformation Commentary on Scripture: Old Testament (Downers Grove, IL: IVP Academic, 2012). See also Mickey Leland Mattox, *"Defender of the Most Holy Matriarchs": Martin Luther's Interpretation of the Women of Genesis in the Enarrationes in Genesin 1535-1545* (Leiden, Boston: Brill, 2003).

reformers of the early sixteenth century, and as a learned expositor of Holy Scripture, particularly the Old Testament.[5] Scriptural exposition, moreover, was very much at the center of the religious conflicts that defined the sixteenth-century, nowhere more so than in Basel in the 1530s. Books like this one were in high demand.

The present volume offers an English translation of the crucial first three chapters of this *Exposition*, with the translation and the original Latin text on facing pages. It includes the brief epitaph in praise of Oecolampadius that greeted sixteenth-century readers on the book's first page, as well as the dedicatory letter with which Wolfgang Capito (1478-1541), a fellow reformer in south Germany and Switzerland, commended the work to its first readers. Next, there is the "epiclesis," an "exhortation" to Holy Scripture with which Oecolampadius began the lectures. The exposition of Genesis 1-3 follows. To help readers better understand the text offered here, both its interpretation of Scripture and its historical significance, I offer below a brief a brief biography of Oecolampadius, important information about the historical context and intended effects of the *Exposition*, and an analysis of its exegetical and theological content.

THE LIFE AND REFORMING WORK OF OECOLAMPADIUS

As with so many other sixteenth-century reformers, the name by which this learned man is known to history is a Latinized Greek version of his given, German name. Johann Husschyn, or Hussgen, or Heussgen, was born in 1482 in the south German village of Weinsberg, located in present-day Württemberg.[6] The German name combines *Haus*

5 Note the remarks, for example, of Stephen G. Burnett, in his "Reassessing the Basel-Wittenberg Conflict: Dimensions of the Reformation Era Discussion of Hebrew Scholarship," in *Hebraica Veritas?: Christian Hebraists and the Study of Judaism in Early Modern Europe*, ed. Allison P. Couldert and Jeffrey S. Shoulson (Philadelphia: University of Pennsylvania Press, 2004), 181-201; on esteem for Oecolampadius as an expositor, see pp. 188-9.

6 For the life of Oecolampadius, see Ernst Staehelin, *Das theologische Lebenswerk Johannes Oekolampads* (Leipzig: M. Heinsius Nachfolger, 1939). The best biographical introduction in English is still Gordon Rupp, *Patterns of Reformation* (Philadelphia: Fortress, 1969): "Part I: Johannes Oecolampadius: The Reformer as Scholar" (pp. 3-46). Oecolampadius's

and *Schein,* which together mean "house lamp," so that later in life he adopted the scholarly name "Oecolampadius," adapted from the Greek words for house (*oikos*) and lamp (*lampas*), with a masculine Latin ending, i.e., "-dius." In 1499 he matriculated as a student in the University of Heidelberg, where he took his Bachelor and Master of Arts degrees in 1502 and 1503, respectively. In Heidelberg he also developed a network of scholarly friends and supporters—including Jakob Wimpfeling (1450-1528), who founded the famous humanist library at Sélestat in the Alsace—who were interested in the Christian humanist movement that was sweeping northern Europe at the time.[7] Focused on classical learning and languages, Christian humanism would contribute much to diverse movements for church reform—both Protestant and Catholic—during the long sixteenth century.

In 1506 Wimpfeling helped the young Oecolampadius secure a position as tutor to the sons of the Elector Philip of the Palatinate. By 1510, however, Oecolampadius had left the Elector's employ, after which he was ordained a priest and accepted a position, endowed by his own family, as preacher in the German city of Weinsberg. This preachership was of the new type that had become common in later medieval Christendom, the so-called "people's priest" (*Leutpriester*), in which citizens of large cities and some better-off towns provided funds for a priest whose specific duty would be to offer edifying sermons. From his earliest days as a church worker, then, Oecolampadius was called to put his learning to the service of the faith and piety of Christian lay people. So it happened that in 1512, at the urging of Wimpfeling and others, Oecolampadius published a series of sermons "On the Passion of the Lord," which inaugurated what was to become a distinguished publishing career.

In the following years he was busily improving his abilities to proclaim the message of the Bible. In 1513 he matriculated at the university

---

correspondence, together with further documents pertinent to his life and deeds, is collected in *Briefe und Akten zum Leben Oekolampads,* ed. Ernst Staehelin, 2 vols. (Leipzig: M. Heinsius Nachfolger, 1927-34).

7 For an introduction to Christian humanism in relation to the sixteenth-century reform movements, consult, inter alia, Lewis W. Spitz, *The Renaissance and Reformation Movements,* 2nd rev. ed., 2 vols. (St. Louis: Concordia Publishing House, 1987); Jean- Claude Margolin, *Humanism in Europe at the Time of the Renaissance,* trans. John L. Farthing (Durham, NC: Labyrinth Press, 1989).

in nearby Tübingen, where he came into contact with the humanist scholar Johannes Reuchlin (1455-1522). With Reuchlin's encouragement, he began to study and eventually mastered both the Greek of the New Testament and the Hebrew of the Old, a rare feat in his day. For instruction in the latter, he turned to the Hebraist Matthaeus Adrianus (dates unknown; active 1501-1521), the author of the sixteenth century's first Hebrew grammar.[8] Eventually Oecolampadius developed an expertise with the text of the Old Testament that earned him a reputation as one of its most important expositors.

He found work in Basel with the printer Johann Froben when he followed his friend Wolfgang Capito (1478-1541) there in 1515.[9] Working as an assistant to the celebrated humanist scholar, Desiderius Erasmus of Rotterdam (1466-1536), he helped with the publication in 1516 of a Greek New Testament, the first of its kind, with explanatory notes and commentary. At nearly the same time he enrolled yet again as a student, this time in the theological faculty of the University of Basel, from which he received the licentiate in Theology in 1516 and the doctorate in 1518. In 1518 he was also appointed cathedral preacher in Augsburg, and his linguistic prowess bore early fruit in the form of a well-received Greek grammar printed by Andreas Cratander, who served thereafter as publisher and editor for Oecolampadius's works. At the same time, through his ongoing work with Erasmus, particularly the Index volume he prepared in 1520 for Erasmus's nine-volume edition of the works of St. Jerome, he developed a considerable knowledge of the church fathers. He was particularly interested in Greek patristics—writers like John Chrysostom and Basil the Great—for which he had been well prepared by his study of the Greek language. Clearly, the young scholar was by this time well on his way to an outstanding academic career. Reuchlin even tried to have him appointed professor of Hebrew at Wittenberg. Instead, he took work as a confessor at the cathedral church (Münster) in Basel.

8 On Adrianus, see *Contemporaries of Erasmus*, Vol. 1, pp. 9-10. For his influence in the sixteenth century, see Burnett, "Reassessing the Basel-Wittenberg Conflict," pp. 183-6.

9 For the Reformation in Basel, see Amy Nelson Burnett, *Teaching the Reformation: Ministers and Their Message in Basel, 1529-1629* (Oxford: Oxford University Press, 2006). According to Burnett (p. 26), Froben published "the first collection of Luther's Latin works in 1518."

Oecolampadius surprised everyone in April 1521 when he entered the Brigittine "double house" (i.e., with both men's and women's branches) at Altomünster. This monastic community was ruled by an Abbess, and his friend Felicitas Peutinger had entered the religious life there only a short time before.[10] At Altomünster, Oecolampadius apparently sought solitude for study in order to resolve his remaining hesitation to identify with the increasingly radical movements of church reform, particularly those associated with Martin Luther. His eventual answer came in the form of a short treatise published in 1521, "Judgment on Doctor Martin Luther," in which he announced his determination that the Roman case against Luther was wrong, and that Luther was closer to the truth of the Gospel than were his Roman opponents. At last Oecolampadius was clearly on the side of the evangelical reform, even if the city of Basel itself was still years away from the adoption of a reformed church order. For a few months during this period he also served as a chaplain to a group of knights under the leadership of the outlaw Franz von Sickingen (1481-1523), a one-time student of Reuchlin whose interventions in 1519 had freed the latter from the clutches of his enemies among the Dominicans, particularly the inquisitor Jakob Hoogstraaten.[11]

In November 1522 Oecolampadius returned to Basel, where he soon provided the evangelical movement with "a prominent and highly educated leader."[12] In spring 1523 he began a series of university lectures, which he had a right to do by virtue of his doctorate, on the prophet Isaiah. These lectures were hugely popular and formed the basis for his commentary on Isaiah, published in 1525, which greatly increased the already high esteem in which Oecolampadius was held,

---

10 Miriam Usher Chrisman notes that Felicitas later left the convent in defiance of her family's continuing loyalty to the Catholic faith. See her *Conflicting Visions of Reform: German Lay Propaganda Pamphlets, 1519-1530* (Boston: Humanities Press, 1995), p. 152. For Capito's reaction, e.g., to Oecolampadius's entry into the religious life, see Kittelson, *Wolfgang Capito: From Humanist to Reformer* (Leiden: Brill, 1975), p. 55-6.

11 For this episode, see David H. Price, *Johannes Reuchlin & the Campaign to Destroy Jewish Books* (Oxford/New York: Oxford University Press, 2011), pp. 198-200.

12 Burnett, *Teaching the Reformation*, 26.

at least for a time, even in far away Wittenberg.[13] At the same time, he was still busy with his work on the church fathers. In September 1523, he completed a Latin translation of John Chrysostom's Greek sermons on Genesis, which he had begun at Altomünster. Published by Cratander, these sermons are important for present purposes because they constitute Oecolampadius's first sustained scholarly attempt to work through the interpretation of the book of Genesis.[14] As was so often the case with sixteenth-century books, this translation was soon plagiarized. In 1524, the Paris publisher Jean Petit made his own edition of the text available for sale. In 1525, Cratander answered with the incorporation of the work into an edition of the complete works of John Chrysostom.[15]

Over the space of two short years, then, three editions of Oecolampadius's work were made available, which suggests that it found a ready market. More importantly for present purposes, his Latin translation lived a secret life long after these printings had been forgotten, as it made its way into the mainstream of sixteenth-century editions of the church fathers. As Alexander Ganoczy notes, it was incorporated into a larger edition yet again in 1530, this time Erasmus's expanded and improved edition of Chrysostom's works published in Basel by Froben. The 1536 edition of Claudius Chevallon also contained a pirated edition of Oecolampadius's Chrysostom translation, although without attribution, since Chevallon published for a Catholic audience and would not have wanted to mention the name of such a notorious evangelical.[16]

In the years following his final return to Basel, Oecolampadius also became ever more deeply involved in the leadership of the reform

---

13 According to Heinrich Bornkamm, Luther and Johannes Bugenhagen "gladly made use" of Oecolampadius's commentary on Isaiah, published in 1525. *Luther in Mid-Career 1521-1530*, trans. E. Theodore Bachmann, (Philadelphia: Fortress, 1983), 577. Cf. Burnett, "Reassessing the Basel-Wittenberg Conflict," pp. 188-9.

14 *Divi Ioannis Chrysostomi, Archiepiscopi Constantinopolitani, in totum Genesews librum Homiliae sexagintasex, à Ioanne Oecolampadio hoc anno versae* (Basel: Cratander, 1523).

15 For the publication history of the *Homiliae*, see Staehelin, *Lebenswerk*, 183-5.

16 Alexander Ganoczy, *Chrysostomus: Ein Beitrag zur Hermeneutic Calvins* (Wiesbaden: Franz Steiner Verlag, 1981), 6-7.

movement, not only in Basel itself but on a broader international stage as well, where he formed an alliance with the more famous reformer of Zürich, Ulrich Zwingli (1484-1531). Like Zwingli, he had developed a spiritualist understanding of the Eucharist, about which more will be said below. In 1525 he was appointed to a chair in theology at the University, and he served as preacher in the St. Martin's church. Reform was in the air. The mass was understood in late medieval Catholicism as a propitiatory sacrifice whose benefits could be applied to the faithful departed still suffering the pangs of purgatory. Masses were therefore said even in the absence of a congregation gathered to participate. In 1525 Oecolampadius refused to say mass when there were no parishioners present, a clear rejection of both Catholic teaching and practice. In 1526 he participated in a disputation held at Baden, where he and other reformers debated their Catholic opponents, including the famous Johannes Eck. Nevertheless, his scholarly work continued with the publication of a new three-volume set of translations of the writings of Cyril of Alexandria in 1528.

Finally, in April 1529, after years of internal wrangling and increasing tensions between the reformers and their traditionalist opponents, and spurred on by outbursts of iconoclasm in the city's churches, the town council adopted reform in the form of a Reformation Ordinance. The Ordinance set out both the rationale and the method of reform, including guidelines for biblical preaching, the re-arrangement of church services, new rules for the celebration of the sacraments, and so on. The council assumed responsibility for the religious well being of the city; Catholic clergy who wished to remain were required to take an oath of citizenship, as well as to attend evangelical lectures and sermons. Catholic rites were prohibited.[17] Representatives of an alternative type of reform, the so-called Anabapists, or "re-baptizers," were expelled from the city under threat of execution if they should return.[18] For his part, Oecolampadius was transferred from the St. Martin's church to the very Münster he had once served as confessor. Change

17 "With the Reformation, then, the number of clergy serving Basel's church dropped from over four hundred to about a dozen." Burnett, *Teaching the Reformation*, 27.

18 Hans Ludi von Bubendorf was the first Anabaptist executed in Basel, by beheading, in January 1530. See Christian Neff, "Ludi, Hans (d. 1530)" in the *Global Anabaptist Mennonite Encyclopedia Online*. 1957. Web. 25 April 2012. http://www.gameo.org/encyclopedia/contents/L850.html.

came to the university too, as in 1529 two professorships were established, one in Old Testament, the other in New, with Oecolampadius installed in the former, and the pastor of the St. Peter's church, Dr. Paul Phrygio (1483-1543), in the latter.[19]

In the midst of this whirlwind of ongoing religious strife and rapid social change, Oecolampadius followed the reformers' teaching and decided to marry. Though his nuptials would be seen by his Catholic opponents as yet another sex scandal among the reformers, he acted on principle and in 1528 took to wife Wibrandis Rosenblatt, the twenty-six year old widow of another church reformer, Ludwig Cellarius (d. 1526), by whom she already had a daughter. Together, she and Oecolampadius had three children, to each of whom they gave a Greek name: Eusebius ("Pious"), Irene ("Peaceful"), and Aletheia ("Truth"). The story of Wibrandis herself is an interesting one. A native Basler, following Oecolampadius's death in 1531 she became the wife of his friend, Wolfgang Capito. Capito too, however, predeceased her. Thus in 1542 she married yet another reformer, the famous Martin Bucer, whom she followed to Protestant England in 1549 when he accepted the position of Regius Professor of Divinity at Cambridge University. Upon his death in 1551 she returned to Basel an honorable widow four times over, the mother of eleven children by four different fathers. She died there during an outbreak of the plague in 1564.[20]

With the official adoption of reform, Oecolampadius became "the dominant figure and, for the next few months, he was for Basle what Zwingli was for Zürich, and what Calvin would be for Geneva."[21] As Gordon Rupp's words suggest, however, his time was short. In the two and one-half years between the city's adoption of reform and his own death he was astonishingly busy. In October 1529 he met at Marburg with Luther and Melanchthon in an effort to resolve their differences over the Lord's Supper. The Colloquy had been arranged by the reform-minded young prince, Philip of Hesse (1504-1567), in an effort to provide theological unity as the foundation for a political and

---

19 Kittelson, *Wolfgang Capito*, p. 214.

20 For a brief sketch of this important sixteenth-century woman, see Edwin Woodruff Tait, "Bride of the Reformation," in *Christian History* 84 (Fall, 2004): pp. 43-5. For further detail, see Roland Bainton, "Wibrandis Rosenblatt (1504-1564)," chapter 7 in his *Women of the Reformation in Germany and Italy* (Minneapolis: Augsburg, 1971), pp. 79-96.

21 *Patterns of Reformation*, p. 38.

military alliance between reformers in south Germany and Switzerland with those in Wittenberg and beyond. The failure of this effort would epitomize for generations to come the crucial difference between what would become the "Reformed" branch of Protestantism over against its "Lutheran" counterpart. Crucially, Oecolampadius and Zwingli defended their understanding of the Lord's Supper against Martin Luther and Philip Melanchthon. The two Swiss reformers had adopted a symbolic or memorial view of the bread and wine used in the ritual of the Lord's Supper. On this view, the bread and the wine represent, but do not become, the very body and blood of Jesus Christ. When Christ said at the Last Supper, "This *is* my body," he meant only the same sort of thing that he meant when he elsewhere compared himself to a vine or a door. He meant, in other words, not that he *was* a vine, or that he *was* this cup and bread, but that he was *like* a vine or a door, *like* this cup and bread, in a symbolic way.

The Wittenberg reformers, on the other hand, stood fast with a literal understanding of the "words of institution," i.e., "this *is* my body." Indeed, an extensive argument between Luther and Zwingli had preceded the meeting in Marburg, and each side had defended its position with vigor. Thus, while they were able to reach theological agreement on nearly everything else, they differed on this one crucial matter. The Swiss reformers thought they had the better biblical argument, and Oecolampadius had been able to enlist a considerable patristic witness in its support. Luther for his part believed deeply in Christ's real presence in the Lord's Supper, and all on the Lutheran side could see that agreement with the Swiss on this issue would only further distance them from the Catholics, with whom they still had hope of reconciliation. The Marburg Colloquy thus ended in failure, leaving earliest Protestantism politically divided and vulnerable to its enemies.[22]

Meanwhile, tensions continued to rise between the Swiss cities that had adopted reform and those that had not. Shoring up the perceived orthodoxy of the reform movement, Oecolampadius wrote against the Spanish anti-trinitarian Michael Servetus, and he further defended his understanding of the Lord's Supper against Philip Melanchthon in a lengthy treatise. In the spring of 1531 he was busy traveling

---

22 For an English translation of the exchanges between Luther and Oecolampadius at the Marburg Colloquy (1529), see Luther's Works, vol. 38: *Word and Sacrament IV*, trans. Martin E. Lehman (Philadelphia, Pa.: Fortress Press, 1971), pp. 3-89.

through the territory around Basel in an effort to assess the progress of reform. Afterwards, he went on to the German city of Ulm, lecturing on the Bible and helping with reform efforts there. The pace was almost frenetic. Back in Basel in August, he and others began their public lectures on Genesis and Matthew, in alternating weeks, in accord with the new Reformation Ordinance. In late October, however, they received the disheartening news of Zwingli's death in battle. Just a few weeks later, Oecolampadius himself fell ill, and by the end of November Basel's great reformer lay dead, his work on Genesis, along with everything else, cut short.

In the sixteenth century, events such as these were seen not merely as this-worldly occurrences with temporal consequences, but as happenings charged with cosmic significance that offered a glimpse into both the unfolding of God's plan for human history and into the fearsome judgment that awaits every human being beyond this life. The sudden death of two of the most prominent leaders of this controversial reform movement—which claimed to have God on its side—in such rapid succession and on the heels of the failure of the Marburg Colloquy, could not escape the notice of their contemporaries. Indeed, both Protestant and Catholic opponents of the Swiss reform movement readily interpreted this shocking turn as evidence of God's judgment. For his part, Luther forthrightly attributed Oecolampadius's sudden illness and death to the devil's attack.[23] The Basler's friends, on the other hand, rushed to his defense. In Zürich, for example, Heinrich Bullinger (Zwingli's successor) bemoaned the impudence of "lord Luther" even to suggest that Oecolampadius had been tormented by the devil and then died as a result. "Just look," he cried, "at what that monk dares to say now!"[24] In this episode we see displayed all the pathos, and much of the tension, intrinsic to an age of bitter religious controversy, apocalyptic angst, and deepening Christian division. The section of the *Exposition* translated here, however, derives from happier times, when both Zwingli and Oecolampadius still lived,

23 Cited in Staehelin, *Briefe und Akten* II, 753-4: "... dass Emser und Oekolampad und dergleichen durch solche feurigen Pfeile und Spiesse des Teufels so plötzlich gestorben seien." Cf. WA 38.197.

24 Ibid., 754: "Oecolampadium, virum sanctissimum illum, praedecessorem tuum in istis furiosis rixis palam praedicat a satana strangulatum periisse. Vide, quid monachus iste audeat!"

and their hopes and plans for the reform of church and Christian society seemed on the cusp of fulfillment.

HISTORICAL CONTEXT OF THE EXPOSITION

In his studies at Heidelberg and Tübingen Oecolampadius had acquired the linguistic and historical skills prized by humanists and church reformers alike. And at Weinsberg he had become adept in the practice of preaching for piety, i.e., preaching and biblical exposition in the service of the lay peoples' desire to live a richer and more authentic Christian life.[25] In his reforming years in Basel, those skills proved essential, especially in the matter of the interpretation and application of the Bible. Basel's Reformation Ordinance had specified that on workdays at three in the afternoon there would be a biblical exposition. This exposition was patterned after the so-called *Prophezei* that had been instituted in Zürich. The determination publicly to read and exposit the Bible is perhaps puzzling. What did the reformers and the city fathers hope to accomplish?

The answer to this question may be found in the heady brew of scholarly and religious ideas that were fermenting among the network of like-minded scholars and churchmen within which Oecolampadius had become situated even as early as his student days in Heidelberg. With a view toward the specific issue of the interpretation of Scripture, this scholarly/religious network has been dubbed the "école Rhénane d'exégèse."[26] According to Bedouelle and Roussel,

25 In this regard, Oecolampadius may be seen as a representative of the so-called *Frömmigkeitstheologie*, "theology of piety," that was so influential in the late middle ages and early Reformation. To this topic, see Berndt Hamm, *Frömmigkeitstheologie am Anfang des 16. Jahrhunderts. Studien zu Johannes Paltz und seinem Urkreis* (Tübingen: Mohr Siebeck, 1982); idem, "Was ist Frömmigkeitstheologie? Überlegungen zum 14. bis 16. Jahrhunderts," in *Praxis Pietatis: Beiträge zu Theologie und Frömmigkeit in der frühen Neuzeit*, ed. Hans-Jörg Nieden and Marcel Nieden (Stuttgart: Kohlhammer, 1999), pp. 9-45.

26 For the "école Rhénane d'exégèse," see *Le temps des Réformes et la Bible*, ed. Guy Bedouelle and Bernard Roussel (Paris: Beauchesne, 1989), pp. 215-33. For his part, Rupp speaks of a "*sodalitas litteraria Rhenana* of the Rhineland, with its links with the humanists of Paris, LeFévre and his friends, with the cities of south Germany, Switzerland and distant Vienna, with north Italy, and with numbers of scholarly correspondents scattered

this "Rhineland school of exegesis" was constituted by a dense set of relations, parallel activities, and an accumulation of works with common traits produced by biblical scholars in south Germany and Switzerland, particularly Strasbourg, Basel and Zurich. They include among its members many of the scholars mentioned above, as well as Conrad Pellikan (1478-1556), a one-time Franciscan and Hebraist who, like Oecolampadius, had studied with Adrianus and become a reformer; Sebastian Münster (1488-1552), in Basel after 1529, a master grammarian whose translations of the Old Testament would be much criticized by Martin Luther; Simon Grynaeus (1493-1541), Oecolampadius's collaborator in the reform in Basel; and the Hebraists Jean Rabus and Elie Schadée in Strasbourg. According to Bedouelle and Roussel, this "school" was strongly influenced by Erasmus, which is not surprising given the latter's long residence in Basel, and it focused particularly upon the Old Testament. The relations between these figures were not those of masters and disciples, but more like a working group. One sees evidence of their commonalities in the prefaces and prologues to their works, as well as their posthumous editions of one another's works. They formed a common front against both the Anabaptists and spiritualists, and they also kept their distance from Luther and the "groupe de Wittenberg," especially on the doctrine of the Lord's Supper.

More importantly for present purposes, Bedouelle and Roussel argue that men like Bucer, Zwingli, Oecolampadius, and Capito were, in effect, inventing a new type of urban church. They wanted to apply the Bible, particularly the Old Testament, to all aspects of Christian society, an effort Bedouelle and Roussel characterize as the "moralization of public life."[27] In short, they wanted to further "Christianize" a nom-

among universities, printing houses and princely courts." Rupp also notes Oecolampadius's distinctive position in this group. "The Rhineland circle was of great moment for Oecolampadius: it joined Wimpfeling and Reuchlin of the older generation with Melanchthon, Brenz and Bucer of the new. Between the two generations—an older humanism fretfully loyal, and the young men soon to be in the van of rebellion—stood Oecolampadius, who like Zwingli and Vadianus of St. Gall, was within months the contemporary of Martin Luther." See *Patterns of Reformation*, p. 4.

27 *Le temps des Réformes et la Bible*, p. 219: "La stratégie qu'ils devaient mener dans un environment urbain n'est pas sans rapport avec leur goût pour l'Ancien Testament. Les écrits prophétiques suggèrent des norms et des exemples pour preparer les decisions du Magistrat et 'moraliser' la

inally Christian society through the dense application of Scripture.[28] This was a high calling indeed, one for which they were qualified by virtue of their work as doctors of Holy Scripture. Oecolampadius's translation work on the church fathers—including his work on John Chrysostom's sermons on Genesis—should be understood in this context.

So what exactly did Oecolampadius and like-minded scholars believe sixteenth-century students of the Bible could learn from John Chrysostom? What scholarly zeal propelled him in the gargantuan task of bringing those Greek sermons over into Latin? As he informed his readers in the preface to the 1523 edition, Oecolampadius believed that Chrysostom had modeled a better way of reading the Scriptures. "The allegories of Origen, Didymus and Cyril seem most fragrant," he warned his readers. Conversely, he praised Chrysostom's focus on *historia,* the *sensus genuina* of Holy Scripture. This *literal* exegesis had the power to build up the reader and edify the church in divine truth.[29] Small matter, then, as Oecolampadius candidly admitted, that Chrysostom had sometimes overestimated the *liberum arbitrium,* or "free choice." The essential matter, Chrysostom's synergism notwithstanding, was the recovery of the genuine, historical meaning of Scripture, and in that effort he was a reliable guide. Indeed, that is a good summary of just what readers would find in Chrysostom's homilies: a theological interpretation of the patriarchal histories that focused not on the more exotic figural implications of the text, but on the meanings that could be discerned in the literal sense, i.e., the story level of the text.[30]

---

vie publique. Pour edifier 'le peuple' et détourner son agressivité vers des combats spirituels : les Psaumes." The south German and Swiss practice was paralleled in Wittenberg in the sermons Luther gave on Matthew and Genesis beginning in 1519. To this, see Bornkamm, *Luther in Mid-Career,* pp. 229-230, with further references.

28 For the Reformation as Christianization, see Scott H. Hendrix, *Recultivating the Vineyard: The Reformation Agendas of Christianization* (Louisville/London: Westminster John Knox Press, 2004).

29 *Homiliae,* a2^{v}.

30 For an English version, see the translations of Robert C. Hill: *Homilies on Genesis 1-17,* Fathers of the Church no. 75 (Washington, DC: Catholic University of America Press, 1999); *Homilies on Genesis* 18-45, Fathers

Ganoczy has shown that Chrysostom's attention to the literal meaning of the text—which in the case of Genesis was mediated to sixteenth-century readers through Oecolampadius's translation—proved helpful to John Calvin as he sought to return biblical exegesis to what he saw as a more solid footing.[31] Perhaps Martin Luther was also aided by Chrysostom's readings of the patriarchal histories. The *Homiliae*, in Cratander's 1523 edition, were available to Luther in the Wittenberg University library.[32] Moreover, one frequently discerns parallels between Luther's and Chrysostom's ways of reading the biblical histories, even if there is no solid evidence to prove that this was the case.[33] Nevertheless, Oecolampadius's work on Chrysostom's sermons on Genesis mediated a voice to sixteenth-century readers that matched neatly with the widely-expressed Protestant and humanist intention to return biblical interpretation to the Scripture's own, literal meaning. There is, however, a certain paradox here, for the reformers' movement back to the Bible was facilitated by—and in fact went hand in hand with—the painstaking work of recovering the *testimonia patrum*, in this case the exegetical testimony of St. John Chrysostom.[34] The deeper scholars like Oecolampadius took their readers into patristic tradition, the more deeply they saw themselves moving into the biblical text itself.

---

of the Church no. 82 (Washington, DC: Catholic University of America Press, 1990).

31 Alexander Ganoczy, Stephan Scheld and Klaus Müller, *Calvins Handschriftliche Annotationen zu Chrysostomus* (Wiesbaden: Steiner, 1983).

32 See Sachiko Kusukawa, *A Wittenberg University Library Catalogue of 1536* (Binghamton, NY: Medieval and Renaissance Texts and Studies, 1995), catalog number 127 (p. 19).

33 On this question, see the Mattox, "*Defender*," pp. 127-8. See further Hans-Ulrich Delius, *Die Quellen von Martin Luthers Genesisvorlesung* (Münster: Christian Kaiser, 1992), p. 21.

34 For the church fathers in the sixteenth century, see *Auctoritas Patrum: Zur Rezeption der Kirchenväter im 15. und 16. Jahrhundert*, Leif Grane, Alfred Schindler, and Markus Wriedt eds., 2 vols. (Mainz: Philipp von Zabern, 1993); *The Reception of the Church Fathers in the West: From the Carolingians to the Maurists*, ed. Irena Backus, 2 vols. (Leiden: Brill, 1997); *Die Patristik in der Bibelexegese des 16. Jahrhunderts*, ed. David C. Steinmetz and Robert Kolb (Wiesbaden: Harrassowitz, 1999).

CONTENT OF THE *EXPOSITION* ON GENESIS 1-3

Oecolampadius's own exegesis of Genesis, the *Exposition* of 1531, should also be seen in this reforming humanist context. No longer did he merely look to Chrysostom's sermons to identify the edifying *sensus genuina Scripturae sacrae*. Instead, he stood and identified that meaning himself, publicly proclaiming it to the young men in Basel's public school in the afternoon lectures called for in the Reformation Ordinance of 1529. Actually, it was not a single lecture, but three, and the biblical text to be examined would alternate weekly between the Old and New Testaments. The Old Testament lectures began with Genesis, the New Testament with Matthew. The lectures offered an impressive public display of piety and erudition. First, either Sebastian Münster would read and comment on the text in Hebrew, or, in the case of the New Testament, Simon Grynaeus would do so in Greek. Next, Oecolampadius would offer a learned exposition of either the New or the Old Testament text in Latin. Finally, pastor Paul Phrygio would preach a sermon on the text in the vernacular German.[35] As mentioned above, this rather ambitious program imitated similar lectures, the *Prophezei* that had previously been instituted in Zurich and Strasbourg, and it was a crucial step toward establishing reformation at the very center of public life in this important Swiss city.

The lectures began on Monday, 7 August 1531 with great energy and hope, but, as mentioned above, they ended in early November amid defeat and confusion.[36] Over those two short months, Oecolampadius had been able to deliver some thirty-two lectures on Genesis, continuing up through chapter 16 verse 16. The text published some five years later was based on handwritten notes taken down, apparently verbatim, by the student Johannes Gast,[37] and later assembled

35 *Briefe und Akten* II, No. 904. Cf. Staehelin's account in *Lebenswerk*, 580 ff.

36 See Burnett, *Teaching the Reformation*, pp. 80-1.

37 The notes on which the published volume was based have been compared to another set of notes, this one by Balthasar Voegelin. According to Staehelin, the two are so thoroughly in agreement as to suggest dictation, a fact that suggests a rather stiff and formal public delivery. *Lebenswerk*, 580. As one might guess, the lectures on Matthew have a similar history. Oecolampadius lectured through Matthew 10:27. Based on student notes, again taken by Gast, the lectures were published by Cratander in 1536 under the title *Enarratio in Evangelium Matthaei*.

for publication by Capito, who came into possession of the literary remains of Oecolampadius when he married the latter's widow, Wibrandis Rosenblatt.[38]

The laudatory epitaph that prefaced the work praised Oecolampadius as a man who had given the city of Basel a gift as great as those provided by the founders of Athens and Sparta. In so doing, the publisher announced the greatness of Oecolampadius. Simultaneously he signaled the lofty aspirations of Basel itself, i.e., to achieve the stature of those classical cities not on the basis of mere human law or military prowess, but by its own biblical, and thus godly, order. In his preface to the *Exposition* Capito underscored Oecolampadius's capacity for inculcating sound faith, and with that, biblical order. He informed the reader that in the first place Oecolampadius had hoped that his "no less pious than learned" interpretation of Scripture should, at the least, take nothing away from the "sound scope of faith," and that he strove to meet this goal, in an obvious echo of Oecolampadius's own praise of John Chrysostom, by attending to the *sensus genuina* of Holy Scripture. Clearly, this was to be neither an academic analysis of Scripture, nor an exercise in personal spirituality. To the contrary, Oecolampadius intended his work to enable the "*rudes*" (i.e., the unlearned) to understand and judge the things of Holy Scripture for themselves, and thus to wonder at the goodness of God in giving it.

The *paraclesis* or "exhortation" with which the work began suggests a venture every bit as auspicious as the epitaph proclaimed, when Basel's leading reformer invited his listeners to accompany him into the inner sanctum, the "holy of holies," i.e., Holy Scripture itself. Reminding his readers of the terrible consequences that had befallen those biblical figures who had failed to show proper respect for holy things, he inculcated a reverence for the text itself as holy, and its diligent study as a means of attaining to holiness. In this it offers something of a contrast to the more famous *paraclesis* Erasmus had written to preface the New Testament he had published in 1516 with Oecolampadius's help. Where Erasmus invites the reader into the text of the New Testament in order to learn the teachings of Christ,[39] Oecolampadius exhorts

38 See Kittelson, *Wolfgang Capito*, p. 193.

39 For this text in English, see *Christian Humanism and the Reformation: Selected Writings of Erasmus with His Life by Beatus Rhenanus and a Biographical Sketch by the Editor*, 3rd ed., trans. John C. Olin (New York: Fordham University Press, 1987), pp. 97-108.

one to adopt the humility and zeal—to be "adorned in the mystical garments of righteousness"—requisite to enter the sacred place, there to experience the radiance of divine glory revealed in Holy Scripture.

In his exegesis of the biblical text itself, Oecolampadius offers a continuous commentary that includes both theological explanation and moral exhortation. When we recall that the text in Hebrew would already have been read out and commented upon by Münster,[40] this is not surprising, since questions of grammar and the like would already have been examined. The lectures on Genesis 1 include a Christian refutation of Hellenistic speculation about the origins of the world. Oecolampadius rejects Plato's notion of the world's eternity, and he defends the Christian doctrine of creation *ex nihilo*. The latter shows for Oecolampadius the power and control of God over all things, which means that the Christian can trust in the providence of God to guide even a fallen world to its fulfillment and perfection. Nevertheless, Oecolampadius elsewhere shows himself indebted to Platonic notions of the Good and of participation in the divine. As he observes in his comments on Gen. 1:14-19, "It is a characteristic of the good that it should impart itself. The most excellent God imparts himself to all things..." He understands participation, however, in a robustly Christian and trinitarian way, i.e., that participation in God happens when believers are sealed by the Holy Spirit into the Son who is himself the true image of the Father, "so that the beauty of the whole Trinity is in us."[41]

The lectures on the creation also reveal Oecolampadius's premodern, Ptolemaic cosmology.[42] Thus, in his comments on Genesis 1 he relies on the notion of the spheres of creation when he interprets the separation of the waters from the firmament on the second day. So while Oecolampadius criticizes the ancients and their worldview in certain respects, at the same time he himself inhabits it quite comfortably. Oecolampadius also offers here a concise summary of the teaching to be found in the text. God is at the same time the beginning, the middle

40 Staehelin, *Briefe und Akten* II, no. 904: "una hebdomada in veteri praeleget Munsterus, textum enarrandum Hebraice, iuxta grammaticen." Letter to Martin Bucer, 5 Aug. 1531, two days before the lectures actually began. See also Staehelin, *Lebenswerk*, 583 ff.

41 Comments on Gen. 1:26.

42 Nicholas Copernicus's groundbreaking work, *De revolutionibus orbium coelestium*, was not published until 1543.

and the end. The central teachings of Scripture, clear to behold there in the text of Genesis, are three: one, God created all things *"propter hominem,"* i.e., for the sake of humankind; two, God has saved fallen humankind through his Word, the incarnate Son; and three, God now gives in the Son *"ineffibilia bona,"* goodness beyond measure. In short, Oecolampadius led his *"rudes"* into the text of Genesis—Hebrew, Latin, and German!—with high expectations on every side.

Perhaps the most intriguing discussion in Oecolampadius's reading of Genesis 1 pertains to the image of God. In his comments on Genesis 1:26, he puts on display the broad learning that qualifies him to lead the reform movement in Basel. The text speaks of the creation of humankind in the "image and likeness" of God, a phrase that had been much discussed in the long centuries of Christian tradition. Oecolampadius situates himself initially within the mainstream of this tradition by finding in the plural noun, "let us make," the "clearest testimony" of the Trinity. In the same section, he engages in a direct but not polemically charged attack on Jewish exegesis, mentioning the interpretation of the text offered by the Jewish expositor Ibn Ezra—who discerned here a reference to the angelic hosts, and not to a trinity of divine persons—and explaining why, in his opinion, it does not hold up to scrutiny. Throughout the commentary, Oecolampadius generally engages Jewish learning constructively, borrowing from it what he finds helpful and rejecting what he does not.

Examining the question of the "image and likeness" of God, he puts his massive patristic learning on display. First, John Cassian and Basil of Caesarea are brought in to reprise their refutation of both the "ineptitudes of the anthropomorphites," who thought God had a body, as well as the opposite error of the Manichees, who rejected altogether the goodness of the body. Thus far, Oecolampadius has the fathers on his side. Afterwards, however, Oecolampadius explicitly critiques St. Augustine's notion that the image is located in the "mind, reason and will." He also associates this opinion with the *"recentiores,"* complaining that it does not seem to touch the substance of the matter. Far different, according to Theodoret, is the one God—Father, Son and Holy Spirit—than any three-ness that can be identified in human nature. Oecolampadius is somewhat less expansive here than we might wish, but his point seems to be an apophatic one, i.e., that there simply can be no comparison between a creaturely "trinity" and the divine Trinity itself. To point to the natural faculties in humankind in order

to identify the divine image, he seems to think, is a category mistake, confusing finite human attributes with the ineffable substance of deity.

A better opinion, Oecolampadius argues, may be found in Cyril of Alexandria, who says that the creation of humankind in the *imago dei* means precisely that we are made in that "true and most certain image of the Father," that is, "in the Son," meaning that any talk of the "divine excellence" of the human soul can only signify our participation in the Son through the Holy Spirit. In sum, he replaces the Augustinian "trinity in man" with an equally venerable, and equally trinitarian, reading of the divine image. Oecolampadius then fleshes out and defends his interpretation by appeal first to Eusebius of Caesarea and then to Origen of Alexandria. Specifically, these two writers confirm the likeness of the "immaterial and incorporeal" soul, "intelligent and rational" in its essence, to the divine Creator from whence it comes. Working from the Greek text, Oecolampadius takes from these authors the use of the Greek term *eikon*, and he employs it in the following discussion. Adducing for support I Corinthians 15, he anticipates what is to follow in Genesis 3 when he says that humankind bears at the same time the "earthly image, according to the flesh," and the "heavenly image" given by the Spirit. This leads into a discussion of holiness, for while free choice has been lost in Adam, the Holy Spirit now renews believers in the image of God and leads them on toward good works. Works show our character, he says, for they reveal whether one has the dignity of the character of God, because life eternal consists in the knowledge of Christ, himself the image of the Father, given in the Holy Spirit.

Indeed, Oecolampadius's extensive deployment of the eastern fathers in these public lectures is striking. He draws on Cassian, Basil, Theodoret, Cyril, Eusebius, Chrysostom, and Origen. To be sure, his exegesis is still identifiably Latin and western. But his explicit disagreement with Augustine and the *recentiores* is noteworthy. By *recentiores* one would presume he meant the medievals, including such standard exegetical authorities as the *Glossa Ordinaria*, Nicholas Lyra, Hugh of St. Cher, Denis the Carthusian, and so on—in short, the exegetical tradition to which most western interpreters would have turned instinctively in preparing a lecture such as this *Enarratio*. By contrast, in Oecolampadius's own exegesis, the interpretation of the "icon of God" of Genesis 1:26 is suffused with elements of eastern patristic thought in the form of a trinitarian reading of the icon of God focused on union with Christ through the Holy Spirit.

In his treatment of the creation of the woman in Genesis 1 and 2, and later in his examination of the fall in Genesis 3, Oecolampadius identifies an original created equality between male and female, or at least something very close to that. Linking Galatians 3:28 ("There is [in Christ]... neither male nor female...") to Genesis 1:27, Oecolampadius claims that the text includes "male and female" so that the reader should know and be certain that women have not been excluded from the dignity of creation in the image of God. "Still," he says in his comments on Gen. 1:26, "we read here that God also created the female with the male. Granted that he was superior after she had sinned, nevertheless she was created in equal dignity with the man. Just as even now man and wife are one in Christ, neither is this woman inferior to that man." The woman was subordinated to the man only on account of sin; beforehand she was his equal. His conception of Eve's original positional relationship to her husband, moreover, seems to bear none of the marks of Augustine's notion of her original submission, but instead lines up well with Chrysostom's sometimes-equivocal affirmations of her original created equality.[43] Once again an eastern Father, this time one he knew very well, works his way into the center of Oecolampadius's exegesis.

In his interpretation of Genesis 2, Oecolampadius further demonstrates his commitment to the Scriptures as "reliable history," not just allegory. Unlike some other Christian readers, then, he imagines paradise as a real place, a restful and refreshing garden of created delights. Still, he insists that the ultimate rest for the human being lies not in any created thing, but in God alone. The tree of life described in this chapter thus presents Oecolampadius with an interesting problem, one that has its background in the controversy over the Lord's Supper, more specifically in John 6 where Jesus, in a verse dear to both Oecolampadius and Zwingli, insists that the "flesh counts for nothing" (NIV), i.e., that salvation—which *is* life in God—can only be imparted spiritually, not physically. Likewise, he insists that the tree of life had no intrinsic power to impart life. Only the Spirit can do that.

---

43 On Chrysostom's interpretation of Eve, see John Lee Thompson, *John Calvin and the Daughters of Sarah: Women in Regular and Exceptional Roles in the Exegesis of Calvin, His Predecessors, and His Contemporaries* (Genève: Librairie Droz, 1992), 75-79; Mattox, "Defender," 43-48. See also David C. Ford, *Women and Men in the Early Church: The Full Views of St. John Chrysostom* (South Canaan, PA: St. Tikhon's Seminary Press, 1995).

Considering the creation of Eve, Oecolampadius skillfully refutes ascetic readings of the text that had turned it against marriage and procreation, making Adam the paragon of the married life. Paradise as Oecolampadius imagines it would have rung with the sounds of the children of Adam and Eve happily at play. This interpretation cannot be incidental to a reforming moment in which clerics like Oecolampadius had embraced the married life as godly. The imagined beauty of the original human pair is reflected poignantly in Oecolampadius's comment on Gen. 2:25: "Innocence is happy without clothes." In that paradise, the benevolence of God was visible at the briefest glance, and the human pair had been graciously created with the gift of perfect justice.

Here, interestingly, figural interpretation comes to Oecolampadius's aid. With what did the original human pair clothe themselves when they heard God walking in the garden in the "cool of the day" (Gen. 3:12)? Echoing an ancient allegorical tradition, he says that the "fig leaves" they wore when confronted by God after they had eaten the forbidden fruit were nothing other than the "frivolous excuses" they offered the divine inquisitor. His reading of this text also reflects its traditional use as a paradigm for the sacrament of confession and absolution. God in his interrogation brings them to confession, announces the punishment of the snake, but then lifts them to hope in the announcement that through the seed of Eve the human race would one day crush the devil's head. The point of the narrative, then, is the divine mercy that awaits every sinner who sincerely confesses.

In sum, the *Exposition* is very much a Christian biblical commentary, and one that has a good deal in common with other premodern commentaries on Genesis. In that sense its delivery was a religious act, intended to speak from faith to faith. At the same time, however, viewed within the context of the tri-lingual daily public lectures out of which it came, it was also a political act, a means through which reform was to be promoted in church and society in newly reformed Basel. The tensions displayed in Oecolampadius's engagement with the exegesis of the church fathers reflect not only the determined appropriation of the past typical of the theology of the early reformers, but also the critical willingness to break with the past intrinsic to the adoption of evangelical reforms in cities like Basel. On the one hand, Oecolampadius engages rather freely in criticizing the exegetical wisdom of the church fathers. But on the other hand, he also attempts to identify a kind of golden thread in patristic exegesis to which his own

interpretation will connect. In the process, he leaves no doubt that the reformers are establishing Basel as a properly Christian society both in continuity with its own authentic Christian past and in compelling discontinuity with previous false faith and practice.[44] The voice of this learned humanist ringing forth in the "public school" would have had the effect of assuring Basel's citizens that in spite of all the dizzying change and social upheaval steady hands were at the wheel, and that the church reforms they had so recently adopted were consistent with the divine truth as given in Holy Writ.

For that task, few early sixteenth-century theologians were as well equipped as Oecolampadius. Even fewer could have brought the voices of the eastern fathers to the support of the cause of reformation so readily as he did. Cool breezes from the east blew steadily, if eclectically, through the *Exposition* and into the streets of Reformation Basel. In the exegesis of learned westerners like Oecolampadius, the voices of the Jews, too, were sounding out right alongside those of the eastern fathers. Examination of the text in the Hebrew language was also beginning to play its part. When the new studies of the eastern Fathers and of the Hebrew text were combined in the work of the western church reformers with the widespread demand for the renewal of church and society through the application of Scripture to public life, they made for a potent mixture indeed. Moreover, the attempt to read the Scriptures responsibly in the original languages with a view toward the original text and its reception in the traditions of Christian exegesis, east and west, is still very much with us today. The work of Oecolampadius translated here thus reminds us not only of the difficulty and complexity of that task, nor even of its long history, but of its necessity for the life and faith of Christian people in every age.

NOTES ON THE TEXT

The text used for this translation is the copy of the 1536 edition by Johann Bebel held by the Herzog August Bibliothek (HAB), in Wolfenbüttel, Germany: Signatur H: C 21.8° Helmst. 1. In translating this text I generally chose a more literal approach as opposed to a

44 For a recent study of the appropriation of patristic authority in the sixteenth century that stresses the innovativeness of the reformers, see Esther Chung-Kim, *Inventing Authority: The Use of the Church Fathers in Reformation Debates over the Eucharist* (Waco, TX: Baylor University Press, 2011).

sense-for-sense rendering. This seemed important in order to retain something of the atmosphere and feeling of dictated lectures given in a classroom. The result is an English text that is sometimes stiff and stilted, but one that hews closely to the original and thus gives a more accurate impression of a work that was first delivered orally as a series of lectures in the classroom.

Where it seems necessary in order to avoid confusion, I have inserted text in brackets to clarify the meaning of the Latin text. Page numbers in the original text are indicated in brackets in the Latin transcription. Where Oecolampadius uses the Latin term *homo* (human, man), I have generally chosen the English "humankind" or "the human race," except where the reference is clearly to a particular male human being, i.e., Adam. In some cases of general reference to human beings where the Latin is singular, *homo* is translated as "the human being" or "man." "Spirit" and "Word" are capitalized where they seem to refer to the Holy Spirit and the Son of God. Biblical citations where they appeared in the margins of the original work have been noted in the footnotes accompanying the Latin text. These are not repeated in the footnotes to the English translation. For the many occasions on which Oecolampadius quotes, refers, or alludes to biblical texts without citation in the original work, I have added footnotes to the translation using standard abbreviations for the biblical books. It should be noted that Oecolampadius's usage of biblical turns of phrase in the commentary is extraordinarily dense, so much so that the notes offered here cannot claim to have specified them all. I have generally not attempted to track down citations for the many cases where he refers to the works of an impressively wide range of church fathers and ancient writers, e.g., Plato, Aristotle, Origen, Chrysostom, Theodoret, Augustine, Philo, and so on. That happy task I leave to the interested reader. I have also added both paragraphing and bracketed biblical verse numbers to some lengthier sections of the English translation in order to ease the reader's task.

[IV]EPITAPHIVM IOAN. OECOLAMP.

CECROPIJS QUOD ANTE SOLON CORDATUS ATHENIS, AUT TIBI BELLIPOTENS SPARTA, LYCURGUS ERAT, DIUINIS LUBEAT RECTE MODO LEGIBUS UTI, OECOLAMPADIUS HOC BASILEA TIBI.

[2R]LECTORI

En candide Lector annotatiunculas in Genesews librum, a pio uiro Ioanne Oecolampadio in schola publica, frequenti auditorio praelectas, & accurata diligentia a studioso quodam conscriptas: quiq; iam ante tam in Euangelium Ioannis, quam in Prophetas minores non poenitenda dedit: tum etiam, si dominus ei uitam concesserit longiorem, alia non minus docta & pia in communem reipublicae Christianae utilitatem daturus est, idq; constanti fide promisit. Arbitratur enim studiosos hoc unico facto posse demereri. Sperat deniq; etiam rudes in adyta sacrae scripturae sine ulla molestia per hunc suum laborem non solum posse induci, sed & admirabili quadam dulcedine trahi. Breues quidem sunt fateor annotatiunculae, sed nihil a scopo sanae fidei, quod non satis laudari potest, aberrantes. Plus fructus pius Lector in his habebit, quam in plerisq; commentationibus, quae nostro tempore absq; iudicio diuulgantur, & quae fere plus a scripturae rectitudine & intelligentia abducunt, quam genuinum sensum aperiant. Qua de re docte & prudenter D. Myconius venerandus senex in suo epistolio in

AN EPITAPH FOR IOHANNES OECOLAMPADIUS

WHAT WISE SOLON ONCE WAS TO THE CECROPIAN ATHENIANS, OR AS LYCURGUS, WARLIKE SPARTA, WAS TO YOU, THAT SHE MIGHT BE PLEASED TO USE DIVINE LAWS RIGHTLY THIS, O BASEL, OECOLAMPADIUS WAS TO YOU

TO THE READER

Behold fair reader brief annotations on the book of Genesis, read out by that pious man Iohannes Oecolampadius in the public school before a crowded lecture hall, and written down with care by a certain studious fellow.[1] He had already given two commentaries by no means displeasing on both the Gospel of John and the Minor Prophets. What is more, if the Lord had conceded to him longer life he would have brought forth other works no less learned and pious for the common benefit of Christendom, and this he promised in steadfast faith to do. It is agreed that the studious can fulfill their obligation by this one achievement.[2] He hoped at last that through this his work even the unlearned could without any trouble not only be led into the holy of holies of Sacred Scripture, but even be drawn [into it] by a certain wonderful sweetness.

These annotations are indeed, I acknowledge, brief, but they depart not at all from the mark of sound faith, which cannot be praised enough. The pious reader will find more good fruit in these annotations than in most commentaries that have been published in our time without proper judgment, and so lead one away from an accurate understanding of Scripture almost more than they explain the genuine sense. In his prefatory letter for Oecolampadius's commentary on the

1 I.e., Johannes Gast. See the Introduction, above.

2 I.e., to promise that it should be done.

prophetas minores praefixo, admonuit. Quod autem supremam manum pius Oecolampadius non imposuerit huic operi, fatum diuinum in causa fuit. Quem autem thesaurum, si tota Biblia percurrisset pius homo, post se putas reliquisset? Ex ijs paucis caetera conijcere si[2v] ne dubio poteris, si tibi ullum in diuinis iudicium est. Scio etiam si ea diligenti animo euolueris, quod non solum in illius pii prophetae admirationem rapieris, sed & uoluptatem cum aedificatione spiritus maximam hauries. Neque satis grata illa brevitas a doctis laudabitur unquam. Praeterea te celare eius indefessum studium et in praelegendis & inseruiendis fratribus nolumus: praelegit enim ad eum usq; diem, quo lecto se alligauit: interim pijs & religiosis uiris nihil detrectans officij in admonendo ad pietatem, illis inquam qui die noctuq; ei adsistebant, morbi istius causam aut rimantes, aut summo obsequio se ad omnia quaeque astringentes. Verum quid ago, cum Grynaeus doctiss. ad amussim omnia illa depinxerit in Epistola, quam D. Vuolfg. Capitoni inscripsit: hanc lege, & admiraberis. Vale, & fruere his in Domino, ad Christianae religionis augmentum.

Minor Prophets, the venerable old man Doctor Myconius reminds us about this matter in a learned and prudent way.[3] But as for the fact that Oecolampadius did not complete this work, divine destiny is responsible [because he died young]. If that pious man had made it through the whole Bible, what a treasure do you think he would have left behind for us?

From these few remarks you will no doubt be able to guess the rest, if you have any judgment in divine matters. For I know indeed that if you think through these things with a diligent mind, you will not only be caught up with admiration for that holy prophet,[4] but also drink in the greatest delight and with spiritual edification. Nor will that pleasing brevity[5] ever be sufficiently praised by the learned. In addition, we do not want to conceal from you Oecolampadius's untiring zeal both in lecturing to and serving his brothers, for he lectured to them right up to the day he went to his sick bed for the last time. Nothing deters devout and religious men from their duty to admonish others to piety, which he did, I say, for them even as they cared for him day and night, trying to determine the cause of his illness and seeing to all his needs with the greatest devotion. But what am I doing, since the most learned Grynaeus[6] has already depicted with precision all those things in the letter he wrote to Dr. Wolfgang Capito?[7] Read this letter, and you will be amazed. Be well, and enjoy these things in the Lord for the increase of the Christian religion.

---

3 Oswald Myconius (1488-1552), who succeeded Oecolampadius as cathedral pastor following the latter's death. This seems to be a reference to Oecolampadius's *Annotationes Piissimae Doctissimae'que in Ioseam Ioëlem Amos Abdiam &c.* (Basel: Cratander, 1535). Johannes Gast was also responsible for the notes on which this publication was based. Amy Nelson Burnett notes that Myconius was a close associate of Zwingli, as well as Bullinger. See her *Teaching the Reformation: Ministers and their Message in Basel, 1529-1629* (Oxford: Oxford University Press, 2006), p. 31.

4 I.e., Moses, the presumed author of Genesis.

5 The "brevity" Capito refers to here is apparently that of Scripture itself, i.e., its fullness of meaning.

6 I.e., Simon Grynaeus (1493-1541), Oecolampadius's fellow reformer in Basel.

7 *Briefe und Akten zum Leben Oekolampads*, Vol. II: 1527-1593, ed. Ernst Staehelin (Leipzig: M. Heinsius Nachfolger, 1927-34), pp. 730-736, Letter No. 968.

[3R] D. IO. OECOLAMPADII PARACLESIS IN BIBLIA

Accedimus dilecti, non ad paupertinos, & prophanos privati cuiuspiam heri penates,[1] sed ad sacrosancta divinissimi adyti limina: in quod, non modo temere irrupisse, sed & indigne ingredi, nulli impune fuerit. Inhabitator enim loci huius, de scriptura loquor, est deus zelotes, ignis consumens, gloria domini exercituum, maiestas summa, vel ipsis angelis tremenda. Non omnes fert tanti numinis excellens fulgor. Male excipiuntur incircuncisi corde & immundi, alienigenae. Graviter plectuntur arrogantes Ammonitae & Moabitae. Diras poenas luunt Dathanitae & Abyronitae seditiosi. Lapides expectant quotquot pecuinis animis feroces, qui transitis suis terminis, huc contendunt. Talibus quidem religiosus iste locus interdictus est. Accipit autem ve-

1 In Roman religious practice the Penates were the guardian or patron deities of a household. Thus, Oecolampadius speaks of a household shrine of a citizen of ancient Rome. This seems to hint at a criticism of the Catholic devotion to the saints as well.

AN EXHORTATION INTO THE BIBLE BY DOCTOR IOHANNES OECOLAMPADIUS

We draw near, beloved, not to the sorry and profane household shrine of some private citizen of Roman times, but to the most holy threshold of the divine inner sanctum,[8] into which, not only intruding heedlessly, but even entering unworthily will for no one go unpunished. For the one who dwells in this place—I am speaking about the Scripture—is a jealous God,[9] a consuming fire,[10] the glory of the Lord of Hosts, the supreme majesty, dreadful even to his own angels.[11] The excelling radiance of such divinity tolerates no one. The uncircumcised of heart,[12] the impure, and the foreign-born are hardly admitted.[13] The arrogant Ammonites and Moabites are severely punished.[14] The quarrelsome Dathanites and Abironites suffer fearful penalties.[15] Fierce stones await all the beastly-minded who transgress their own limits and rush in here.[16] But this sacred place has indeed been forbidden to such men. It admits,

---

8 The allusion here is to the "holy of holies." See, inter alia, Ex. 26:34.

9 Ex. 20:5.

10 Deut. 4:24, Heb. 12:29.

11 Perhaps this is an allusion to Isa. 6.

12 An allusion to the "circumcision of the heart" mentioned by Paul in Rom. 2:29.

13 This seems to be an allusion to Israelite purity requirements for entry in the Temple. See, e.g., Num. 1:51; Heb. 9:1-9.

14 Cf. Deut. 23:3.

15 Note the fearsome judgment meted out to Korah, Dathan, and Abiram in Num. 16.

16 Stoning was the punishment for those who approached the holy place unworthily. See Ex. 19:13, Deut. 21:18-21.

ros Israelitas, doli expertes, placido ingenio, sequaces, sacerdotes, vocatos a domino, sanctificatos, mysticis iustitiae vestibus honestatos, & cum sacrificio ac munere comparentes. Tales inquam accipit religiosus sacrarum scripturarum locus. Pape, inquis, quale hoc exordium, quo auditores non tam invitas ac introducis, quam deterres ac a[3v]mandas? Quis enim haec audiens, quamvis sibi bene conscius, id dignitatis sibi arrogare ausit? quis ita suae parvitatis immemor, tam perfrictam induet frontem? quis ita periculorum contemptor salutis suae prodigus erit? Ad salutationem angeli nemo non trepidat. Si igitur persuasum, haec esse uiui dei eloquia, et indigne, auscultantibus non defutura supplicia, qui periclitari non uult, pedem reducet. At ego vestro nomine, auditores optimi, bono animo sum: haec enim quae non sunt dicta ad desperationem immittendam, sed ad religionem erga sacras literas incitandam, animos non abiectos, sed alacres reddent, & socordiam quidem ac oscitantiam, id quod maxime precor, remorabuntur. Studii autem feruorem & indefatigabilem conciliare poterunt diligentiam. Neq; parum momenti habet, si sciatis quam gloriosus, quamq; beatus sit qui colloquio uos dignetur. Christiani estis, peculiaris dei populus, & per Christum episcopum animarum, & sacerdotem magnum, facti & ipsi sacerdotes ac reges. Submoto per sanguinem eius velamine, liberum ad contuenda quae intus sunt arcana, aditum accepistis: iam idonei mystae qui in reconditiora penetralia intromittamini. Non uos ex male dicta ista fece Allophylorum spuriorum, Moabitarum Ammonitarumq; processistis, sed liberi Isaaci, & promissionis filij, ad quos nihil aliorum maledictiones perti[4r]nent.

however, true Israelites, guileless,[17] gentle spirits, the teachable ones, priests, those who are called by the Lord, sanctified, adorned in the mystical garments of righteousness, appearing with sacrifice and offering. Such men, I say, the sacred place of the Holy Scriptures admits.

Dear father, you ask, what kind of an introduction is this, by which you do not so much invite and introduce your hearers, but frighten away and dismiss them? For who, with any awareness of himself, would upon hearing these things dare to arrogate to himself such a dignity? Who is so forgetful of his own smallness that he would put on such a false front? Who is so contemptuous of the dangers that he will throw away his own salvation? No one fails to tremble at the salutation of an angel. Once persuaded that this is the voice of the living God, and that punishments will not be lacking for those who hear unworthily, whoever does not want to be put to the test will retrace his steps. But in your case, noble listeners, I am of good cheer. For these things have not been said to cause despair but to incite reverence toward the sacred writings, not to cast down spirits but to restore good cheer, and they will indeed deter listlessness and inaction, for which I pray intently. They can also bring about fervor and untiring diligence in study. That is of the utmost importance, if you consider how glorious and how blessed is the one who deigns to speak with you.

For you are Christians, God's own people, and through Christ the bishop of souls[18] and the great high priest you yourselves have also been made priests and kings.[19] Since the veil has been removed through his blood,[20] you have received free access to contemplate the mysteries within, and have now been made suitable initiates who are admitted to the more secret inmost places.[21] You have not come from those accursed dregs of bastard foreigners like the Moabites and the

---

17 The allusion is to John 1:47, i.e., Jesus' recognition of Nathanael as "an Israelite in whom there is no guile."

18 I Pet. 2:25.

19 See I Pet. 2:9, 25; Ex. 19:6; Heb. 2:17, 3:1, 4:14, 9:11; Rev. 1:6.

20 Cf. Mt. 27:51.

21 Heb. 6:18; 2 Cor. 3:13-16; Eph. 2:18, 3:12; Rom. 5:2.

Indignos etiam nos tanto dei munere confitemur: nullus enim fuerit, qui deum demerebitur, & coram illo gloriari audebit. Sed ingens discrimen est inter prophanorum populorum, & Christianorum humilitatem. Illi deum uerum blasphemare, & suis idolis post ponere non uerentur, superciliosiq; sunt, & propter carnem spirant nihil. Nostram autem uilitatem, quam libenter agnoscimus, honestat incomparabilis apud patrem Christi gratia: nostram humilitatem exaltat eius, qui ultra omnes coelos euectus est gloria: nostram insipientiam non aspernatur sapientia illa coelistis: imo paruulis lautissimum illud, de quo sapiens loquitur, parauit conuiuium. Et quae sapientibus huius mundi pater abscondit, ea testimonio Christi, paruulis reuelare dignatur. Ad haec, sacrarum literarum dignitas, auidas summorum bonorum mentes accendit maxime. Nam si aliae artes laudatae magis expetuntur, quam desiderabilis est ea quam nemo satis laudare sufficit, & si cum aliis contuleris, prophanas eas & uanas esse conuincet? se autem solam & sanctissimam & incomparabiliter frugiferam: ipsa sola omnes omnium seculorum errores detegit, redarguit, refutat. Sola consummatam & ab omni hypocrisews fuco alienam uirtutem docet. Sola beatitudinis uitaeq; verae & aeternae spem solidam introducit. Sola abditos

Ammonites,[22] but the free offspring of Isaac,[23] sons of the promise to whom none of the curses on outsiders apply. We too confess that we are unworthy of such a gift of God, for no one will deserve the favor of God and dare to boast before him.[24] There is a great difference between the humility of Christian peoples and that of the worldly nations.[25] The latter are not afraid to blaspheme the true God, and to neglect him for their own idols. They are arrogant, and on account of the flesh they breathe nothing of the spirit.[26] The incomparable grace of Christ adorns our unworthiness, which we freely acknowledge before the Father. The glory of him who has been raised above all the heavens exalts our humility.[27] That heavenly wisdom does not spurn our foolishness. In fact, he has prepared that most elegant banquet for the little ones, about which the wise man speaks.[28] And those things, which the Father has hidden from the wise of this world, these [very] things, according to the testimony of Christ, he deigns to reveal to the little ones.[29]

Moreover, the dignity of the sacred writings greatly arouses minds keen for the highest goods. For if the other esteemed arts are much sought after, how desirable is that which no one can praise enough? And if you compare the one with the others, you will be convinced that the others are profane and untrustworthy, but only [the Scripture itself] is most holy and incomparably fruitful. For only Scripture itself

---

22 Oecolampadius alludes here to the origins of the Moabites and Ammonites in the incestuous relations between Lot and his daughters. See Gen. 19:30-36.

23 The son of Abraham, and heir to the promised inheritance of Abraham. See Gen. 18 ff. Cf. Gal 4:21-31.

24 I Cor. 1:31.

25 Note the close conjunction here between humility and the rejection of merit. The problem of merit in later medieval and Reformation theology is notoriously complex. For a brief but informative introduction, see Euan Cameron, *The European Reformation* (Oxford: Clarendon Press, 1991), pp. 79-87.

26 Rom. 8:5-9. Cf. Eccl. 3:19.

27 Eph. 1:20-21.

28 This seems to be an allusion to the words of Solomon, the "wise man," in Prov. 9.

29 See Mt. 11:25. Cf. Luke 10:21.

diuinitatis thesauros commonstrat. Aliae licet [4v] nec ipsae contemnendae, huic ancillantur, si in bonos animos inciderint: nunquam tamen eo perueniunt, ut tam sublime uolent, tantos prouentus asserant, tanta claritate rutilent. Iam cum in aliis nihil sine labore succedit feliciter, & multis conatibus disciplinae obtinentur, inuitante interdum paruo uel gloriae, uel rei familiaris commodo: quid non ferendum, & faciendum, quae noctes non lucubrandae, cui oleo parcendum, ut ea quae maxime sancta, plurimum honesta, supra omnem modum beata consequamur? Iam si degener animus quispiam, qui nec honesti, nec utilis boni cupiditate tangitur, proq; magno lucri compendio habet, relicto monte hoc, euasisse poenas: cum monuerimus, hac uia nequaquam elabi, sed in charibdim incidere non minus horrendam, iterumq; in iudicis manus. Scriptum est enim, Ignorans ignorabitur.[2] Et Prouerbiorum 28. cap. Qui declinat aurem suam ne audiat legem, oratio eius erit abominatio coram domino.[3] Terreat huiusmodi Hoseae dictum: Succisus est populus meus, qui est absq; scientia: quia tu sacerdos repulisti scientiam, repellam te ne sacerdotio fungaris.[4] Terreat etiam Esaias, propterea dicens captiuus ductus est populus meus, eo quod ei non fuit scientia.[5] Et id satis liquet, uel mediocriter cordato. Qui enim fieri posset non offendi eum, qui se a luce auertit, et tenebras sectatur? & eum qui uitam abrumpit, & [5r] mortem eligit? Sic autem agunt hi qui haec quae spiritus sunt, reijciunt. Porro qui uere poenas euitare, & multis bonis abundare uolunt, ij & verba dei magno studio quaerunt, & dignos se praebent auditores. Nec refert etiam si extra sepem colligantur ad conuiuium caeci, claudi, & inutiles uitio aliquo,

2 A marginal note here refers the reader to I Cor. 14[:38].

3 At verse 9.

4 A marginal note here refers the reader to Hosea 4[:6].

5 A marginal note here refers the reader to Isaiah 5[:13].

exposes all the errors of all the ages, disproves and refutes them. It alone teaches the highest virtue free from any hypocritical disguise. It alone brings firm hope of blessedness and of life, true and eternal. It alone makes known the hidden treasures of divinity. The other sciences, however, are not to be despised. They are ancillary to Scripture, if they fall upon good minds. Even so, they never arrive at the point where they fly so high [i.e., as Scripture], bring forth such results, or shine with such a rosy brightness.

Now since in the other sciences nothing succeeds well without hard work, and the disciplines are mastered only after much effort by one who has been attracted either by a bit of glory or to profit an estate, what then would we not bear or do, how would we not burn the midnight oil which we had saved[30] so that we might pursue those things which are most holy, most honorable and blessed beyond all measure? Now a degenerate soul—someone who is touched by the desire neither for honesty nor for usefulness, if he has abandoned this mountain[31] for the sake of great material gain, he should have evaded punishment; although we have warned him, that he by no means can escape in this way, but will fall into a charybdis no less horrible, and back into the hands of the judge. For it is written, "The one who does not know, is not known." And in Proverbs chapter 28, "The one who turns away his ear lest he hear the law, his prayer will be an abomination before the Lord." The saying of Hosea should frighten in the same way: "My people, who lack understanding, have been cut down; because you the priest have spurned understanding, I shall spurn you and you will not perform priestly service." Isaiah should also frighten us when he says, "My people have been led away captive because they had not understanding." And this is sufficiently clear, even to the moderately intelligent.

For who would not be shocked by one who turns away from the light and pursues darkness, one who rejects life and chooses death?[32] Those, however, who reject those things that are of the spirit, do so. But those who truly want to avoid punishment and abound in many good works will both search the words of God with great zeal and

30 Cf. Mt. 21:1-13.

31 Oecolampadius alludes to Mt. Sinai, where Moses received the Ten Commandments. See Ex. 20.

32 Deut. 30:15-20.

modo audiant ac obtemperent, & sic tanquam oues pastorem in pascua sequantur. Breui enim sic erimus omnes sacerdotes qui perpetuo in coelo uersabuntur, quiq; noctes & dies in lege domini meditabuntur, uncti oleo gratiae, ut & sacrificia offerant, & de sacrificio edant ac impinguentur: hoc est, ut toto corde se consecrent, & carne Christi, quae est panis coelestis, laute reficiantur. Et ut aperte dicam, duo in sacrarum literarum auditoribus necessaria sunt, nempe humilitas quae adorare diuina doceat, ac sobrie sapere, & alacritatis spiritus nihil laboris subterfugiens, uel periculi, quo gloria dei crescat. Neminem horum poenitebit : corticis amaritudinem, nuclei compensabit suauitas. Vera enim hinc scientia, uera exaltatio, uera animorum beatitudo, ueraq; quies & tanta bona, quanta nusquam aliunde sperare nedum accipere queas, homini dabitur. Tanta autem bona nobis concedi, vel inde liquet, si simul totius scripturae scopum spectemus, quem nescio an pleriq; attingant. Mihi sufficit, si inde uere edoctus fuero deum esse deum [5v] ac patrem nostrum, cui me, salutemq; meam recte concredere ualeo. Nam & tunc uere a deo edocti sumus, quum tria illa praecipua quae homini diuinitus dantur, quaeq; omnia in scriptura traduntur uberrime, recte perceperimus. Deus enim initium, medium, ac finem dat: condidit enim omnia propter hominem, hocq; pro primo bono numeramus: deinde per uerbum, id est, filium suum, eum quem condiderat, reparauit: atq; ita in Christo multa ampliora bona accepimus : concessurus etiam deus tandem ineffabilia bona quae nec oculus

prove that they are worthy hearers. And it does not matter even if the blind, the lame, and those rendered useless by some kind of injury are gathered to the feast from outside the fence,[33] only let them hear and obey, and thus like sheep follow the shepherd into the pasture.[34] For in a short time we will all be priests who will live forever in heaven, and who will meditate night and day on the law of the Lord,[35] anointed with the oil of grace so that we might offer sacrifices, and eat and be fattened from the sacrifice, that is, that we may consecrate ourselves with our whole heart and so be richly restored by the flesh of Christ, which is the bread of heaven.[36]

And to speak openly, two things are necessary for the hearers of the sacred writings: *humility*, of course, which teaches us to worship divine things and to think soberly, and *a zealous spirit* that shuns no exertion or danger by means of which the glory of God might be increased.[37] None of these will he disappoint; the sweetness of the nut will compensate for the bitterness of the hull. From here [i.e., Scripture] comes true understanding, true exaltation, the true blessedness of souls, and true rest. He will give such good benefits to man, benefits you would never be able to hope for much less receive from anywhere else. And that such great things are conceded to us is certainly clear if, at the same time, we keep in view the aim of the whole of Scripture, although I do not know whether very many can really do that. For me it suffices if from there I shall have learned that God is God, and also our Father, to whom I rightly entrust myself and my salvation.

For we have truly been taught by God when we have rightly learned those three main things[38] which are divinely given to humankind, and which are all abundantly handed down in Scripture. God gives the beginning, the middle, and the end. For He *created* all things on account of humankind, and we count this as the first good. Then, through the Word, that is, through his own Son, he also *restored* that which

33 An allusion to Luke 14:13-14.

34 Cf. John 10:27.

35 Ps. 1:2.

36 John 6:33, 51.

37 Emphasis added.

38 The "three main things"—i.e., creation (beginning), restoration (middle), and consummation (end)—are indicated by italics, which are added here for clarity.

audiuit, neq; in cor hominis ascenderunt, si ullum fontem boni ex illis creatis cognouerimus. In Mose quidem, & in hoc statim capite primo discemus, ut deus hominem & omnia propter hominem fecerit, sicut habes psalmo octauo. Nihilominus interim multa alia disci ac doceri hinc inde ex scripturis possunt. Hominem deus rectum condidit sed sua ignauia lapsus est. Deus data lege, ad se reuocauit. Pulchrum est itaq; uidere deum esse conditorem uniuersi, coeli scilicet ac terrae : qua doctrina statim stulta erit omnis Graecorum de rerum principijs tam uaria statuentium. Alij enim mundum aeternum, alij conditum dixerunt, & omnino se deum ignorasse docuerunt, tametsi ex conditione coeli ac terrae, ex uisibilibus istis agnoscere illum poterant, ut est Rom. 1.[6] Nihilominus interim multa etiam alia ex ijs quae prophetae narrant, in Mo[6r]se addiscere possumus, qui spiritu diuino locutus est. Et propheta recte appellatur, quandoquidem id doni prae alijs abundantius accepit. Adserit multa quae ad mores nostros formandos attinent, siue fides asserenda, siue errores obstruendi, siue exempla petenda, siue Respublicas instituendas, siue ingenia exploranda, ubique illa fuse Moses tractat.

Moses hunc librum scripsit in Aegypto, docens deum uerum deum esse aeternum: sicut dicit: Qui est, misit me. Reliquos autem quatuor in deserto. Populus sane Aegyptiorum erroribus abductus, etiam in Aegypto idola colebat, ut testatur Ezechiel cap. uigesimo: cui malo occursurus, originem rerum ac genesim diuino spiritu afflatus docet.

6 At verse 19-20.

he had created. So it is that in Christ we have received many greater goods. And *at last* God will even give us such indescribable goods as no eye has perceived nor have arisen in the heart of a human being,[39] no matter what source of good we know from among created things. Indeed, according to Moses, and as we will learn right away in the first chapter, God made humankind, and he made all things for the sake of humankind, just as you have it in Psalm 8. At the same time, many other things can also be learned and taught from the Scriptures here and there. God made the human being upright, but he fell by his own sloth. By giving the law, God recalled him to himself.

It is therefore wonderful to see that God is the creator of the universe, that is, of heaven and earth, by which teaching all that [false teaching] of the Greeks about the beginning of things that have been established, which is so varied, will immediately be [seen as] foolish. For some [of them] said that the world is eternal, others that it was made, and so they all showed that they knew nothing of God, even if they could acknowledge him from the creation of heaven and earth, i.e., from what is visible, as it says in Romans 1. Nonetheless, here in Moses, who spoke by the divine Spirit, we can learn many other things besides what the prophets tell. And he is rightly called a prophet, since he has received that gift more abundantly than others. Moses asserts a great deal that pertains to the formation of our morals, whether it be the faith to be asserted, errors to be opposed, examples to be emulated, the civil state to be established, or character to be developed; and he everywhere treats those things abundantly.

Moses wrote this book in Egypt, teaching that the true God is the eternal God. Just as he said: "He who is sent me."[40] The other four [books of the Pentateuch Moses wrote] in the desert. The people were certainly led away by the errors of the Egyptians, for in Egypt they even worshipped idols, as Ezekiel testifies in chapter 20.[41] In order to confront this evil, Moses by inspiration of the divine Spirit teaches what was the origin and the genesis of things.

---

39 An allusion to I Cor. 2:9.

40 Ex. 3:14.

41 An insistent focus on the evil of idolatry is typical of the early Protestant movement, particularly in South Germany and Switzerland.

[6v]

ENARRAT. IOAN. OECOL.

CAPVT I

In principio creauit deus coelum & terram. Terra autem erat informis & inanis, & tenebrae erant super faciem abyssi, & spiritus dei mouebat se super faciem aquarum.

Versus isti duo in genere nobis ea indicant, quae postea diligentius explanantur, quomodo a deo formata, sint disposita speciatim. Omnino in unum & eundem diem referimus ea quae hic narrantur, & quae mox sequuntur. Fuerunt quidam in hac sententia, deum omnia condidisse, uno die & uno momento. Neque necessitas ulla est quae nos sic urgeat, ut tam facile literam nobis patiamur e manibus auelli. Videmus enim hic diuinum ordinem, ut etiam in alijs quae divina scriptura nobis proponit. Imperfecta praemittit, ut perfectiora sequantur. Ita in foetibus humanis formandis videtis primo in materno utero imperfectos fœtus absque lineamentis, absque statura debita, &

CHAPTER I

[1] In the beginning, God created heaven and earth. [2] But the earth was unformed and empty, and darkness was upon the face of the abyss, and a wind[42] of God was moving over the face of the waters.

These two lines indicate to us in general matters that are afterwards explained more fully, how the things made by God were laid out according to their kind. We refer both the matters narrated here and those that soon follow to one and the same day. Some were of the opinion that God established everything in one day, and in a single instant. Nor is there any reason so pressing that it should compel us so easily to allow the simple meaning to be snatched from our hands.[43] For we observe here the divine order, just as we do in the other matters which the divine Scriptures set before us. It begins with the imperfect, in order that more perfect things may follow.[44] Thus, [for example,] you see that in the formation of human fetuses in the mother's womb, at first they are imperfect, without their features or proper size; only at the end do they receive their increase. In this way God consoles our

42 I follow Oecolampadius's suggestion below, that the Latin "spiritus" should be understood in this case not as "Spirit" (i.e., the Holy Spirit) as in much of the antecedent exegetical tradition, but simply as "wind." This is an interesting exegetical move that suggests Oecolampadius is not at such pains to see the Trinity intimated in this text as were some of his Christian predecessors.

43 I translate the Latin *litera* here with "simple meaning," rather than with the English cognate, "letter." The insistence that Scripture be interpreted according to its "simple meaning" is a hallmark of early Protestant exegesis. This insistence itself reflects, however, exegetical developments that had been underway throughout the later middle ages. As Christopher Ocker observes, later medieval scholastic hermeneutical theory had already underscored the full "spirituality of the letter." See his *Biblical Poetics Before Renaissance and Reformation* (New York: Cambridge, 2002); here, p. 219.

44 Imperfection, as Oecolampadius uses the term here, refers not to a defect in a thing, but to its as-yet incompleteness. Perfection, conversely, has the connotation of the fulfillment of a thing in its underlying reality and purpose. Thus, the first things made are not defective, but they remain as-yet incomplete.

tandem sua incrementa recipere. Sic deus consolatur nostrum pusillanimitatem, & longanimitatem docet, si non ista aeterna gloria ab initio fruamur quam deus suis electis dare paratus est. Dabit eam tem[7r] pore constituto, quando incrementa nostra sumpserimus, post hanc uitam. Alij etiam in dubium uertunt, an eadem die angelos creauerit. Non uoluit Moyses hoc loco mentionem angelorum facere, licet quidam per coelos anglicam creaturam intelligent. Malo simplicitatem literae sequi, quam ficta quaedam & incertae asserere. Plerique ex Graecis senserunt, ut Hieronymus ad Titum, & Hilarius narrant, quomodo angeli multis millibus annis ante conditum seculum creati fuerint. Nos illam sententiam nequaquam accipimus. Tempus cœpit, cum cœlum et terra cœpit. Et ita Aristotelem reijcimus, qui demonstrationes nescio quas habet, atque adeo si quis ad rationes scripturae conferat, uidebit nostros[7] superiore loco esse, adhibito fidei adminiculo. Audent quidam oblatrare: Multa, inquiunt, dicit Moses, et parum est quod asserit. Nos eadem obijcere possumus ipsis, cum ita tenuiter etiam sua probant. Nam aliqui testantur fidem esse ueterum, mundum conditum esse ab eterno. Caeterum in posterioribus maior erit occasio confutandi haec: & si excusserimus illas rationes, inueniemus plane illas esse inutiles, imo apparent hi deum nunquam recte scisse, atque adeo felicitatem homini summam tollunt. Quae fides nostra, nisi deum crediderimus conditorem & cœli & terrae, imo & nostri & omnium habere curam? Si ab aeterno omnia condita [7v] sunt, ubi

---

7 Reading "nostros" here for "nostos" as found in the original text.

faintheartedness and teaches us patience, even if at the start we do not enjoy that eternal glory which God has prepared to give to his elect. This he will give us at the appointed time, when we shall have received our full measure of growth, after this life.

Some also turn into doubt here whether the angels were created that same day. Moses did not wish to mention here [the creation of] the angels, even though some will interpret "heaven" as a reference to the angelic creatures.[45] I for my part prefer to follow the simplicity of the letter, rather than to assert things false and uncertain. Many of the Greeks are of the opinion—as both Jerome, in his letter to Titus, and Hilary relate—that the angels were created many thousands of years before the creation of the world. We do not accept this opinion at all. Time began when heaven and earth began. So we reject Aristotle, who has I don't know what [supposed] proofs; moreover, if one should compare them to the arguments of Scripture one will see that our authorities are from a higher place, because of the application of the support of faith. Some dare to bark out here: Moses, they say, declares many things but asserts too little. We can make the same objection against them, since they so feebly demonstrate their own point. For some maintain that it is the ancient faith[46] that the world was established from eternity. As for the other claims, there will be a better opportunity to refute them later. And if we have completely dismissed other arguments, we have found that they are clearly not profitable. Indeed it would appear that these men never rightly knew God, and therefore they take away the greatest happiness of humankind. For what is our faith, except to believe that God is the creator of heaven and earth, and indeed that he cares for us and for all things? If all things were established from eternity, where is the providence of God?

45 For an English translation of Augustine's influential reading of the creation of the angels in Genesis, see *The Literal Meaning of Genesis*, Vol. 1: Books 1-6, trans. John Hammond Taylor, S.J. (New York: Newman Press, 1982), pp. 132, and 136-41. A theological analysis is offered in Eugene TeSelle, *Augustine the Theologian*, (New York: Herder & Herder, 1970), esp. 209-11.

46 For Oecolampadius, as for most of the Reformers, the "ancient faith" is superior because it does not reflect the errors that were introduced in the middle ages. Hence in this place the strength of the argument for the creation of all things in one and the same instant would be its claim for antiquity. Oecolampadius seems to reject this argument on the grounds that it reads too much into the "simple meaning" of the text.

providentia dei? Sed ualeant hi cum suis excogitatis rationibus. Moses hic proponit nobis ea, ut sciamus omnia deum creasse, & conseruare omnia: quia omnia condidit. Omnes creaturae & res a seipsis non potuerunt habere originem. In hoc uidemus uires nostras omnes nullas esse, ideo merito omnem fiduciam in illum collocare conuenit. Plato quidem prae alijs uidetur magis nobiscum sentire, sed nec ille recipi potest: ponit enim deum exemplar & hylen, quasi artificem ad exemplar fabricantem, imo ponit ordine quodam tres deos, ἡ ἀγαθὸν νοῶ ψυχλωω. Sed ea omnia philosophis committimus.

In principio.) Id est, antequam aliquid fieret creauit deus coelum & terram. LXX. habent ἐποίησαν. Sed fecit idem est quod creauit. Facere, sine mora aliquid et perfecte effingere hic significat. Et opus facere, indicat plane summum opificem. Hebraei coelum duali numero proferunt השמים. Inculta Graeci exponunt ἀόρατος & ἀκατασκεύαστος, id est, inuisibilis & incomposita. Et uult dicere, Terra erat inornata arboribus & animalibus, & caeteris rebus. Non quod omnino fuerit inuisibilis: si fuisset homo, qui uidisset, non fuisset omnino invisibilis. Etiam qui blese loquuntur non omnino muti sunt. De hac re crastina die copiosius dicam.

[8r]

LECTIO

Fortassis heri primi duo uersis, quando quidem breuitate temporis praeoccupati fuimus, non satis intellecti fuere: igitur quae tunc abrupimus & non satis ex planauimus, nunc disseremus. Moses quidem datus a deo Hebraeis, qui laborabant in Aegypto, non solum corporali seruitute, sed etiam ob consuetudinem gentis infecti erant idololatriae

So farewell to them with their rational contrivances. Moses sets these matters before us here so that we might know that God has created and preserved all things, because he established everything. All creatures and things cannot have their origin from themselves. Thus we see that all our strength is as nothing, and so we are rightly directed to place all [our] faith in him [i.e., God]. Compared with the others, Plato at least seems mostly to agree with us. But he cannot be received either, for he provides God the pattern and the material, as if God were merely a craftsman working from a pattern.[47] In fact he places three gods in a certain order: the good, mind, and soul.[48] But all these matters we leave to the philosophers.

In the beginning.) That is, before anything came to be, God created heaven and earth. The Septuagint has here *epoiēsan*, "made." But "he made" is the same as "he created." "To make" in this case signifies to fashion something immediately and completely, and the work of "making" clearly indicates the highest workman. Heaven in the Hebrew language is twofold in number: *hashamayim* ["the heavens"]. The Greeks express disordered matter here with *aoratos* and *akataskeuastos*,[49] i.e., invisible and unformed. And it[50] wants to say that the earth was not yet adorned with trees, animals, and other things. Not that it was entirely invisible; if there had been a human being who would have seen it, then it would not have been completely invisible. After all, even those who stutter are not entirely mute. About this matter, I shall speak more fully tomorrow.

READING

Perhaps yesterday the first two verses were not sufficiently understood, since we were cut short by the lack of time. So we will now discuss what we then left off and explained insufficiently. Moses, indeed, was given by God to the Hebrews, who were laboring in Egypt, not only in bodily servitude, but also because they had been infected with the evil of idolatry on account of the customs of the [Egyptian] people. The

47 See the *Timaeus*.

48 Oecolampadius refers here to concepts actually set forth in the fifth *Ennead* of Plotinus (ca. 204-70 CE).

49 Oecolampadius cites here words used in the Septuagint Greek translation of the Hebrew *tohu vavohu* in Gen. 1:2.

50 I.e., the Greek translation "wants to say."

scelere. Curauit igitur beatus uir pro munere sibi iniuncto, ut primum nos a morbis animi liberaret, & a graviore seruitute, & etiam ex Aegypto scelerum, per potentem dei manum educeremur. Docuit igitur tunc Iudaeos fugere ab Aegyptiorum consuetudine. Eusebius de praeparatione euangelica, qui uetustissimos historicos diligenter legit, dicit Phoenices & Aegyptios sublatis in coelum oculis, solem & lunam & caeteras stellas, obseruatis motibus & ordinibus, adorasse: & quum deberent inde agnoscere suum creatorem, admirari magis coeperunt creaturas, imo pro dijs coluerunt. Alij deificauerunt benefactores suos: unde praecipuos deos habuerunt Osirim & Isim. Osirim solem putarunt, quem multi oculum interpretantur. Et lunam Isim: cui etiam cornua affinxerunt, ut in novilunijs uidemus, quia nonnihil alludit ad iuuencam, uel bouem cornutum. Hos pessimos Aegyptiacae gentis mores imitati sunt Iudaei. Vnde cum educti essent ex Aegy[8v]pto, moram in monte agente Mose, uitulum erexerunt, dicentes: Hi dij tui sunt qui te ex Aegypto duxerunt. Ab hac igitur peste uolebat illos liberare, & ostendit deum esse aeternum. Hoc studium Mosi in quo spiritus sanctus locutus est, occasione hinc sumpta, multis ab erroribus nos abducit. Scriptum est, quod omnia propter nos scripta sint, qui

blessed man therefore was concerned for the duty imposed on him, that first he might free us from diseases of the soul, as well as from that more serious servitude, that we too would be led out from the "Egypt" of wickedness through the powerful hand of God.[51] Therefore he taught at that time that the Jews should flee from the custom of the Egyptians.

In his *Preparation for the Gospel,* Eusebius, who carefully reads the most ancient histories, says that the Phoenicians and the Egyptians, having lifted up their eyes to the heavens, worshiped the sun, the moon, and the other stars, by observing their motions and ordered movement. And though they should have thence acknowledged their creator, they began more to regard creatures with wonder—indeed, they worshiped them as gods.[52] Others deified their own benefactors, whence they regarded Osiris and Isis to be special gods. They thought that Osiris was the sun, which many understood to be an eye, while Isis was the moon, to whom they even added horns (like we see in a new moon) because in some measure it is reminiscent of a heifer or a horned bull.

The Jews mimicked these worst customs of the Egyptian people. Thus when they had been led out of Egypt and Moses was delayed on the mountain they erected a calf, saying "These are your gods who led you out of Egypt."[53] Therefore he [Moses] wished to free them from this plague, and he showed that God is eternal. This zeal of Moses, in whom the Holy Spirit has spoken, leads us away from many errors if from here[54] we avail ourselves of the opportunity. For it is written, that all these things were written down for the sake of we who have come upon the end of the ages.[55]

---

51 Note that Oecolampadius reads here the history of Israel's bondage and deliverance in Egypt as a figure of the soul's bondage and deliverance from sin.

52 See Rom. 1:19-25.

53 See Exodus 32.

54 I.e., from this text of Scripture.

55 An allusion to I Cor. 10:11. More broadly, Oecolampadius reflects here the apocalyptic frame of mind characteristic of some early Protestants, who saw in the tumultuous events of their times signs of the end of history. Briefly to this issue, see Robin B. Barnes, "Review Essay: Varieties of Apocalyptic Experience in Reformation Europe," *Journal of Interdisciplinary History* 33:2 (2002): 261-74.

in terminos aetatum incidimus. Vnde ex illis primis uersibus maximam partem philosophorum refutare possumus. Primo ἄθεος illos qui omnino deum negarunt, ut Diodorus & Protagorus. Similiter facile refelluntur qui innumerabiles posuere deos ut Anaximander. Similiter alios qui deum corporeum finxerunt. Platonicos & Aristotelicos non absque magnis erroribus de mundo mentionem fecisse, nemo non novit.

Heri indicaui tenuia esse argumenta illorum qui de creatione mundi sua somnia adferunt: nam quae ipsi obijciunt, a nobis nequaquam recipiuntur, edocti ex diuinis literis aliud. Inter caetera argumenta dicunt, quod materia sit ingenerabilis. Quis autem Christianorum reciperet hoc? Incumbebat Aristotelem illud probare. Nam ita deum fecisse coelum absque omni sui mutatione, scriptura clare ostendit. Etsi initium coeperit mundi creatio, tamen nulla in deo facta est mutatio. Quod decreuit deus aliquando secum, hoc coepit aliquando perficere: non quod nouam operationem ipse habuerit, sed quod res quam se[9r] cum iam antea decreuit, coeperit esse sua uoluntate. Et ab aeterno habuit illam uoluntatem. Praeterea quod motus ingenerabilis sit, etiam explosum est a nobis. Qui coeli autor & terrae, etiam omnis motus & temporis. Praeterea non facimus deum obnoxium tempori uel creaturae. Vt incorporeus est, ita supra omnia. De deo, ut dignum est, sentire decet Christianos. Interim autem nos magnam spem & fidem concipimus, dum discimus ex nihilo fecisse deum coelum & terram, & statim parati sumus ad credendum alia dei miracula, qui uocat quae non sunt, tanquam sint. Qui recte hoc credit, ille scit deum se ex maximis periculis posse liberare. Is etiam corpus collapsum & in cineres dispersum facillime posse reparare, credet. Quod si quis rationi uelit obtemperare, ille posthac semper mancipium erit rationis suae, & nihil credere

Thus, on the basis of these first lines we can refute the great majority of philosophers. First "atheists," those who deny God altogether, like Diodorus and Protagoras. Just as easily rebutted are those who posit innumerable gods, like Anaximander. Likewise those who imagined that God had a body. And no one is unaware that the Platonists and Aristotelians never made mention of the world without great errors.

Yesterday I pointed out how tenuous are the arguments of those who set forth their fantasies about the creation. The arguments they put forward are not at all received by us, since we have been taught otherwise from the divine writings. Among other arguments, they say that matter is ingenerable [i.e., cannot arise from nothing]. But who among Christians could accept this? They insist that Aristotle proves it. But Scripture clearly shows that God made the heavens without any change to himself.[56] Even if creation commenced with the beginning of the world, still the creation itself caused no change in God. What God decreed at some point within himself, this he began at some time to carry out. Not that God himself had a new operation, but that the things he had previously decreed within himself began to exist by his own will, for he had that purpose from eternity. Moreover [the idea] that there is any ungenerated motion is also rejected by us. He who is the originator of heaven and of earth is also the originator of motion and time. Besides, we do not make God liable to time or created things. As he is incorporeal, so he is above all things. It is suitable for Christians to think worthily about God.

At the same time, we draw great hope and faith when we learn that God made heaven and earth from nothing, and we are immediately prepared to believe other miracles of God, "who calls things that are not as though they were."[57] Whoever rightly believes this knows that God himself is able to deliver him from the greatest dangers. He also believes that God is able easily to restore a body that has fallen into ruin and been scattered as ashes. But if any one wishes instead to comply with the demands of reason, he will afterwards forever be the prisoner of his own reason, unable to believe anything that reason has not determined beforehand. Hence this kind of a person will be able

56 Oecolampadius here insists on divine impassibility, i.e., the doctrine that God as God does not change.

57 A citation of the Vulgate version of Romans 4:17.

poterit, quod ratio non ante dictauerit. Proinde nihil huiuscemodi poterit persuaderi. Et hoc antea indicatum sit de aeterna prouidentia.

Mouebat se.) Vel motitabatur, aut ferebatur. Et indicat hoc uersu, ea quae a deo condita fuerant, fuisse ad huc confusa & indigesta, rudiaque. Postea uidebitis triplicem distinctionem. Hic autem est triplex confusio. Terra uasta & incomposita, una confusio. Altera, tenebrae super abyssum. In aquis istis erat magna tenebrositas, neque aquae erant perspicuae. Aër etiam nomine aquae [9v] continentur, quatenus particeps est humoris et liquoris. Abyssum aquam multam uocat, quae non potest propter suam profunditatem perspici. Non est interruptio terrae. Terra infimo loco inculta: aquae similiter tenebrosae erant & inamoenae aspectu. Tertia, cum dicit, Spiritus dei: quem intelligo plane uentum. Vehementia aquae agitabat etiam aquas ipsas, ita ut omnia hinc inde confunderentur. Proinde illa quae principio ita condita erant, opus maiori illustratione habebant. Posteriora id indicant, quomodo deus omnia digesserit. Quidam allegorias adducere uoluerunt de spiritibus immundis, & contrarijs potestatibus: sed omnino dimittamus istas ociosorum hominum inuentiones, nisi errare placet. Deinde de spiritu Dei plerique intellexerunt hunc locum, non solum recentiores, sed & ueteres Theologi tum Graeci, tum Hebraei: attamen non reijciunt hanc expositionem, spiritum dei uentum nominari. Quidam ponunt regulam hanc: cum spiritui adijciatur dei, tunc intelligi debere spiritus sanctus: hoc tamen non est certum. Nam in psalmo 147

to be persuaded of nothing. And this should be disclosed beforehand concerning eternal providence.[58]

Was moving itself.) Either was being moved, or was being carried. For in this verse he indicates that those things that had been made by God were still disordered, chaotic, and undeveloped. Afterwards you will observe a threefold distinction; here, however, there is a threefold confusion. First, the earth was empty and unformed, a disorder. Second, darkness was over the abyss. In the waters themselves there was a great darkness, and neither were the waters clear. The sky too is included in the name "waters," insofar as it shares in fluidity and liquidity. The abyss he calls a great water, which cannot be seen through on account of its great depth. There is no break in the land. The land was jagged even at its low point; the waters likewise were dark and disagreeable in appearance. Third, when he says "Spirit of God," I understand this simply as wind.[59] The violence of the water was stirring even the waters themselves, so that all things in this way and that were jumbled together. Hence those things that were made in the beginning had a larger representative function.

The works that follow show how God arranged all things. Certain men want to bring in allegories about unclean spirits and opposing powers, but we dismiss these altogether as the inventions of idle men, lest it seem right to err. Then many understood this text as pertaining to the Spirit of God, not only more recent theologians but also the older ones, both Greeks and Jews. Nevertheless, they do not reject our exposition, that the Spirit of God is called wind. Certain men put forward this rule: wherever to the word "spirit" might be added "of God," there the Holy Spirit should be understood.[60] Nevertheless, this is not certain. For in Psalm 147[:18] we find the contrary, where it is said:

---

58 Oecolampadius seems to offer this sentence as an aside. He means that the question of "eternal providence," i.e., predestination, should be approached with a humility informed by God's incomparable power to make and even remake the human being. Reason thus submits to revelation.

59 See note 7, above. As Oecolampadius reads this text, the wind is one of the three elements of confusion that prevailed before God imposed order on the original chaos.

60 Perhaps Oecolampadius has in mind here the letter of St. Athanasius to Serapion, "On the Holy Spirit." For a translation, see *The Letters of St. Athanasius Concerning the Holy Spirit*, trans. C.R.B. Shapland (London: Epworth, 1951).

contrarium inuenimus, ubi dicitur: Flabit spiritus eius & fluent aquae. Et Iob cap. 9. Spiritus dei in naribus meis: id est, quandiu est flatus meus, non assentior uobis. Proinde non facile ulli sunt redarguendi: ego malo simpliciter pro uento exponere. Bene etiam dictum est, fouere: tamen mouere magis [10r] congruit, ut uidemus in mari tempestuoso, quando uehemens uentus fertur esse, quanta maris importunitas sit, & quas tempestates excitet uiolentia uentorum. Ita & hic apparuit talis confusio. Quia igitur omnia ista nondum satis ordinata, non mirum omnia sic uideri. At tamen ex creatione tantarum rerum satis omnipotentia dei manifestabatur. Nunc sapientia dei ea, quae in pondere & mensura creauit, disponit. Praeterea hic animaduertendum, plerosque ex hoc principio trinitatis quaerere mysterium, quod plane neutiquam est contemnendum. Sed illud non satis apte hoc in loco adstruitur: nam dum per principium, filium & Deum patrem & spiritum sanctum colligunt, uidentur uiolentius sensum quaerere, cum possent alia ratione commodius. Cognoscimus uerbo aptata esse secula, ut in epistola Hebraeorum habemus.[8] Sed rationem triadis pulcherrime inueniemus etiam in primo die. Nam mox sequetur: Dixit deus, & statim illud apparet. Ad quod utique Ioannes Euangelista allusit, & felicissime citauit. Item: Et uidit deus lucem quod bona esset, id est approbauit. Voluntas dei tertiam personam insinuat. Ita interim summa ista arcana satis feliciter nobis commendantur.

---

8 A marginal notation here refers the reader to Hebrews 1[:10].

"His wind will blow, and the waters will flow." And in Job 9:[61] "The breath of God is in my nostrils," that is, "as long as my breath remains I do not agree with you." Just as no one of them[62] was easily to be convinced, I prefer simply to explain it as "wind." It [i.e., the spirit] is well said "to keep warm." But "to move" fits better, just as we observe how great is the relentlessness of the sea when the wind is violently stirred up on a stormy sea, and that the violence of the winds causes such tempests.

Here too there was great confusion. Because all these things were not yet sufficiently ordered, it is no wonder that they looked like this. Still, just from the creation of such great things the omnipotence of God is sufficiently shown. Now the wisdom of God sets in order those things he created by weight and measure.[63] Here also it should be noted that many seek [to establish] the mystery of the Trinity from this beginning, an effort, which, to be sure, should by no means be condemned. But that is not supported suitably here in this text. When, for instance, they infer the Son and God the Father and the Holy Spirit through "the beginning," they seem to seek the sense violently, although they could do so in other more appropriate ways. We know the world was formed by the Word, as we have in the letter to the Hebrews.[64] Quite happily, however, we will find the mention of a threefold relation even on the first day. For next it follows: "God said, and immediately it appeared," [an assertion] to which John the Evangelist surely alluded[65] and cited most gladly. Likewise, "And God saw that the light was good," that is, he approved it. The will of God implies a third person.[66] Thus, happily enough, those deepest mysteries are [here] commended to us.

---

61 The correct reference here appears to be Job 27:3. This is apparently Oecolamadius's own translation of that verse.

62 I.e., no one of Job's interlocutors.

63 See Wisd. Solom. 11:21. This deuterocanonical text is also called Wisdom, or Book of Wisdom.

64 Heb. 11:3.

65 I.e., in John 1:1-3. The evangelist, in other words, alluded to Genesis 1:3.

66 Oecolampadius seems to mean that the willing approval expressed in the phrase "God saw that it was good" implies differentiation internal to the Godhead, i.e., the distinction between the Father, the Son, and the

Dixitque deus, fiat lux, & facta est lux.

Fuit lux, uel facta est, utrunque recte dicitur: quia tanta inordinatio erat, & omnia sepulta in tenebris, ideo [10v] dixit deus, Fiat lux: & exponunt illud fere omnes simpliciter pro poliuit. Psalmus habet: Dixit deus & facta sunt, mandauit & creata sunt. Placuit igitur deo opus suum. Potuisset beatus Moses uti uolendi uerbo, neque enim hoc uerbum deest Hebraeis: sed maluit dicere, Dixit. Quod utique non est factum sine causa: nam plane uerbum est apud deum, quod Ioannes fideliter nos docuit, dicens: In principio erat uerbum, & uerbum erat apud deum, & deus erat uerbum. Ne putetis autem illud esse temporale uerbum: iam antea dixi deum non hoc modo operari. Deus ab aeterno haec ordinauit. Quicunque loquitur, alteri loquitur: deus quia loquitur, alteri cuipiam loquitur. Ab aeterno angeli non fuere, igitur habuit uerbum secum, id est, suam sapientiam. Non ignoro quid obstrepant Iudae uel Iudaizantes, qui cum fateri ipsi cogantur diuinam naturam, nequaquam tamen sibi esse perspectam dicunt: quod & omnes fatemur: sed ea quae deitatis sunt examinari[9] uolunt, quasi essent

9 The printed text here has "exanimari," i.e., "to be cut off, or deprived of life." I read here instead "examinari," i.e., "to be examined," which seems to make more sense in context.

[3] And God said, "Let there be light," and light was made.

There was light, or it was made; either way it is rightly said. For great was the disorder, and all things were hidden in darkness, so God said, "Let there be light." Almost everyone expounds this simply as "he adorned." The Psalm has: "God spoke and they were made; he commanded and they were created."[67] Thus, his own work pleased God. Had he preferred to do so blessed Moses could have used the word "willed,"[68] for the Hebrews do not lack this word. But he preferred to say, "He said." Certainly he did not do so without cause, for plainly the Word is with God, as John faithfully teaches us, saying: "In the beginning was the Word, and the Word was with God, and God was the Word."[69] Nor should you think that this is a temporal word, for as I said before God does not work that way. God ordained these things from eternity. Whoever speaks, speaks to another; because God speaks, he says something to another. The angels did not exist from eternity; therefore he had the Word with him, that is, his own wisdom.

I do not ignore what the Jews or the Judaizers cry out,[70] who, although they are compelled to confess the divine nature, nevertheless do not claim that they have examined it—which we all also confess.

Holy Spirit. His rejection of exegesis that finds the Trinity in the phrase "in the beginning" is thus offset by the exegetical claim that the divine dialogue of Genesis 1 itself suggests a triadic structure, at least when read in the light of the New Testament (i.e., Hebrews 1 and John 1). The connection of "will" with the Holy Spirit seems to echo Augustine's notion of the Trinity as being, knowing, and willing.

67 Psalm 33:9.

68 I.e., "God *willed* and they were made."

69 A reference to the Gospel of John 1:1, a crucial intertext for the Christian reading of Genesis 1.

70 For sixteenth-century controversies over the Christian appropriation of Jewish biblical exegesis, including the claim that such an appropriation amounts to a "Judaizing" of the text, see Stephen G. Burnett, "Reassessing the Basel-Wittenberg Conflict: Dimensions of the Reformation Era Discussion of Hebrew Scholarship," in *Hebraica Veritas?: Christian Hebraists and the Study of Judaism in Early Modern Europe*, ed. Allison P. Couldert and Jeffrey S. Shoulson (Philadelphia: University of Pennsylvania Press, 2004), pp. 181-201. More broadly, see *Jews, Judaism, and the Reformation in Sixteenth-Century Germany*, ed. Dean Philip Bell and Stephen G. Burnett (Leiden: Brill, 2006).

similia illis quae ante oculos proponuntur. Dicunt uerbum illud esse plane deum, quod & nos fatemur: sed non habere aliquam subsistentiam in deo, hocque probare non possunt. Valeant hi, nobis testimonia sufficientia per Christum sunt. Alia etiam ratio est, cum dicimus, Iratus est Deus: & alia, gauisus est: non oportet ob id aliam personam ponere. Euangelistae commen[11r]darunt uerbum esse apud Deum, & non inter hypostases esse ut discordent. Quod si nunc de externa creatione loqui uoluerimus uidete ut attemperarit nobis suum sermonem. Loquitur nobiscum tanquam rex potens. Sed dicit: In seipso habet uerbum.

Lux.) A luce pulcherrime exorditur, qui est ipse lux, quique habitat lucem inaccessam. Neque est lux corporea, sed mentalis, quae mentes illustrat, quae ueritatem docet. Condidit Deus lucem, ut opera eius fiant conspicua.

Facta est lux.) Iterum uides omnipotentiam dei. Absque ulla mora opus fuit statim absolutum ad nutum dei, & ad unicum dictum, ut in psalmo habemus: Verbo domini coeli firmati sunt.

Et uidit deus lucem quod esset bona & distinxit deus lucem & inter tenebras.

Videre deum, est approbare. Iam ab initio Moses haereticos quosdam repellebat, qui corporalia mala esse dicebant & ut Manichaei, quique deum bonum & deum malum dixerunt. Et illam corpoream machinam, quam deus bonam dixit, illi malam pronunciant. Depulsi sunt hi haretici ab orthodoxis, propterea nolo in refellendis illis tempus perdere. Fecit deus, ut sic appareret lux, & dum ipse uidit esse bonam, uere bona est, nemo igitur illam culpet. [11v]

Distinxit.) Discreuit uel separauit. Statim ornatum rebus addidit, & distinctionem quoque. Tenebrae istae erant absentia lucis. Fecit igitur discrimen inter diem & noctem, idque in utilitatem humani generis, postea producendi. Vt enim nobis dies est necessarius multis modis,

But they want matters of the deity to be examined as if they were just like those things that can be placed before the eyes. They admit that Word is clearly God,[71] which we also confess. But they say that the Word does not have any subsistence in God, and this they cannot prove. Farewell to them; through Christ there are sufficient testimonies for us. Another reason [they bring forth] is that when we say "God is angry" or "God is glad" it is not proper on that account to set forth another person. But the evangelists assured us that the Word is with God, and that there is no discord among the divine persons. If we wish to speak now about the external creation, note well that he accommodates his speech to us. He speaks with us much like a powerful king. And he says that he has the Word within himself.

Light.) It begins with a most beautiful light, who is himself the light, and who dwells in light inaccessible.[72] Nor is light corporeal, but mental, a thing which enlightens minds,[73] which teaches the truth. God created light, so that his works might be made clear.

Light was made.) Here again you see the omnipotence of God. Without any delay, the work was done immediately, at the nod and the singular utterance of God, just as we have in the Psalm [33:6]: "By the word of the Lord the heavens were established."

[4] And God saw that the light was good, and he separated light and darkness.

For God to "see" means to approve. For from the beginning Moses pushed back certain heretics who said that bodily things are evil, and also the Manichaeans who said that there is both a good god and an evil god. So that bodily frame, which God called good, they call evil. These heretics were driven out by the orthodox, and for that reason I do not want to waste time on refuting them. God brought it about that light should appear, and since he himself saw that it was good, it truly is good, and therefore no one should find fault with it.

He separated.) Discerned or divided. Immediately he added adornment to things, as well as distinction. That darkness was an absence of light. Therefore he created the distinction between day and night, and afterwards made it useful for the human race. For as daytime is

71 I.e., that the word spoken here, "let there be light," is spoken by God.

72 I Tim. 6:16.

73 John 1:9.

ita etiam noctes propter quietem admodum sunt necessariae, necnon propter alias causas.

Vocauitque deus lucem diem, & tenebras uocauit noctem: & fuit uespera, fuitque mane dies unus.

Deus appellationem istis rebus indidit. Et diem habemus qui nos excitet ad opera: Noctem quae aliquo modo retrahat ab operibus, & quietem concedat. Graeci ponunt νύκταν και ἡμέραν, diem & noctem. Vnde ipsi accipiunt interpretationem τὸν ἥμερον, tanquam mansuetum: die enim omnia mansuetiora sunt quam nocte. Etiam in nocte qui laboribus fatigatus est, quodammodo reficit vires suas & reparat ad futurae diei laborem. Ita ipsa nomina utilitatem rerum nobis commendant. Neque opus ut hic aliquid de naturali die dicam, & artificiali, apud alios potestis id requirere.

Et fuit vespera.) Hebraei dicunt uesperae, finem diei praecedere noctem, & sequi diem. Imo dies completus fuit, & peruenit ad uesperam, & nox ad summum mane: & ita ego intelligo. Condidit deus lucem: utique lux [12r] perseuerauit, & secuta est nox, ut deo placuit. Non est opus hinc, ut magnas moueamus controuersias. Certum est, fuisse aliquam diem, etsi iam sol in coelo non esset, nihilominus deus illustrauit diem absque illo sole & lumine. Potuisset Moses dicere, dies primus: sed dixit, unus: & id etiam in Euangelio habemus de una die, quam possumus dicere primam diem.

necessary to us in many ways, so also the nights are extremely necessary for rest, and indeed for other reasons.

[5] And God called the light day, and the darkness he called night. And it was evening and morning, day one.

God gave a name to these things. And we have the day, which stirs us to works, and the night, which in another way draws us back from works and grants [us] sleep. The Greeks use here "*nyktan kai hēmeran,*" day and night.[74] Thus they accept the interpretation of day as *ton hēmeron,* that is, gentle, for by day all things are gentler than in the night. Even now whoever has been made weary by labor somehow in the night renews his bodily powers and revives for the labor of the next day. Thus, the names themselves commend to us the usefulness of the things [they refer to]. There is no need that I should say anything here about the natural and artificial day;[75] you can ask the others about that.

And it was evening.) According to the Hebrews, evening is the end of the day that precedes the night and follows the day. Indeed the day was complete and came to evening, and night was completed in the morning, or so I understand the matter.[76] God created light. Certainly the light continued, and the night followed, just as it pleased God. Here there is no need that we should stir up great controversies. It is certain that there was a day of some sort, even if the sun was not in the heaven. Nevertheless God illuminated the day even apart from that sun and its light. Moses could have said, the "first" day. But he said "one," as we have it also in the Gospel concerning day one,[77] which we may call the first day.

---

74 Oecolampadius's text has the Greek terms for "day and night" reversed. The citation of the Greek text should have ἡμέραν καὶ νύκτα.

75 The problem here seems to be that sun and moon are not created until the fourth day. Thus, the question is what kind of light is spoken of on the first day.

76 Oecolampadius is attempting to understand the biblical locution "evening and morning," which seems to make the evening the beginning of a day.

77 Perhaps this is an allusion to Christ's resurrection on "day one" of the week, i.e., on the day after the Sabbath. See Matthew 28:1.

Et dixit deus: Fiat firmamentum in medio aquarum, & faciat distinctionem inter aquas & aquas. Et fecit deus firmamentum, distinxitque inter aquas quae erant sub firmamento, & inter aquas quae erant supra firmamentum, factumque est ita.

In isto secundo die legimus deum fecisse firmamentum aquae. Per aquas autem intellige non solum elementum, quod nunc uocamus aquam, sed etiam aërem. Supra audistis in tres partes omnia diuisa esse, & quomodo pulchra rerum distinctio a Mose obseruata sit. Nam in medio aquarum, aquas quasdam solidauit, & fecit firmamentum, quod cohibeat aquas superiores & inferiores, ne hae ascendant, & illa descendant. Ex aquis quae supra firmamentum sunt, coelum est crystallinum, quod uocant, aquae concretae. Neque est imaginandum, quod sit aqua densa ut nostra: nam illa aquae perspicui[12v]tas est in eo spacio, quod est super firmamentum, siue uim ad refrigerandum, siue non habeat, mea non refert. Neque contendimus de hac re, quia etiam aliorum non satis sunt solida argumenta, qui multa de his rebus in medium adducunt. Firmamentum autem dicimus octauam sphaerum, quae septem sub se continet sphaeras.

Distinxit.) Separata fuit una pars aquarum supra, secunda super firmamentum, tertia infra, quae aquae postea amplius coarctatae sunt in suum locum.

Et uocauit deus firmamentum coelum, & fuit uespera, fuitque mane dies secundus.

Firmamentum illud, pars coeli, siue unum coelum dicatis, siue plurimos, non refert, quia ad eandem naturam pertinent. Et iterum expono diem secundum, ut superius diem primum. Quantum ad historiam attinet, primo indigesta, sapientia dei digerit in suum locum: unde deus iure potest admirationi esse, propter opera tam potentia. Nemo

[6] And God said, "Let there be a firmament in the middle of the waters, and let there be a separation between the waters." [7] And God made the firmament, and he separated the waters that were below the firmament from the waters that were above the firmament, and it was done.

On that second day, we read that God made a firmament of water. "Waters," however, is understood not only as the element that today we call water, but also the air.[78] Above you heard that all things were divided into three parts, and how a beautiful separation of things was observed by Moses. For in the middle of the waters, he somehow solidified certain waters and made a firmament, that it might contain the waters above and below, lest these below should ascend or those above descend. Heaven is crystalline, made out of the waters above, "solid waters," as they say. Nor should it be imagined that it was a dense water like ours, for there is a transparency of water in that space which is above the firmament, and it does not matter to me whether it has the power to make cold or not. Neither do we contend about this matter, because there are not sufficient solid arguments even from those who adduce many things about this in public. The firmament, however, we call the eighth sphere, which contains within itself the seven spheres.

He separated.) One part of the waters was separated at the highest point, a second upon the firmament, and a third below, which waters afterwards were more fully secured in their own place.

[8] And God called the firmament heaven, and there was evening, and there was morning, the second day.

That firmament was a part of heaven. Whether you use the singular or the plural matters not, because both terms pertain to the same nature. And again I exposit the second day like the first day above. As far as history is concerned,[79] what was at first disorganized, the wisdom of God arranges in its own place. Hence God may rightly be admired

78 In the discussion that follows here, Oecolampadius assumes the Ptolemaic cosmology. The eighth sphere is the "firmament of stars," while the ninth is the "sphere of crystal." For a compelling introduction to medieval cosmology and the broader worldview informed by it, see C. S. Lewis, *The Discarded Image: An Introduction to Medieval and Renaissance Literature* (Cambridge: Cambridge University Press, 1964).

79 By "history" here, Oecolampadius intends the literal meaning of Scripture.

enim illa melius potuisset digerere, quam digesta sunt. Et omnia illa in solatium maximum humani generis facta sunt, ut postea audietis. Coelum habemus, quo ascendit Christus iuxta carnem, dans spem coelistis conuersationis omnibus in se credentibus.

LECTIO

Didicimus superius uel ex primo uersu summam potentiam dei, qui ex nihilo coelum terramque [13r] condidit: reliquum est ut discamus etiam summam illius sapientiam atque bonitatem. Vt autem innotescat nobis diuina sapientia, scitote sapientis esse ea quae imperfecta sunt perficere, & ea quae perfecta sunt ornare, ac illustrare. Caeterum deus potuisset primo momento omnia simul absoluere, & perfectissima facere, sed noluit,& hac ratione, ut sapientia sua manifestior fieret, nobisque magis cognobilis. Audistis, terram fuisse uacuam, & tenebras super faciem aquarum: quo uersu quaedam imperfectio significata fuit: ex quo licet cognoscere, deum sponte creaturas fecisse, non coactus ab ullo, uel angelorum, uel mortalium, cum nullus adhuc esset. Nam si primo finxisset creaturas perfectas, hi qui deum necessario uolunt omnia condidisse, obstinati mansissent in suo errore. Audiuimus quomodo statim primo die, ne diu laterent opera eius, obscuritatem remouit. Desiderabatur claritas inter caetera, & eam tenebrositatem remouit, ponendo lucem, & distinguendo inter lucem & tenebras. Praeterea confusio erat aquarum, id est, aëris, & elementi aquae. Nam nomine aquarum accipimus elementa tenuia. Turbabantur aquae illae, flante uento domini. Itaque secundo die fecit deus expansionem, uel interstitium quoddam, quod firmamentum dicimus. Aquas perspicuas eleuauit super firmamentum, alias sub firmamento esse voluit, etiam sic [13v] auferens quod imperfectum esse uidebatur, & ut suo uerbo iusserat, ita factum est. Porro terra adhuc nondum erat repurgata ab aquis, neque suum ornatum acceperat, obtecta scilicet aquis

as much on account of his works as of his power. For no one would have been able better to arrange things than they have been arranged. And all things were done for the greatest solace of the human race, as you will afterwards hear. We have heaven, into which Christ ascended according to the flesh, giving the hope of a heavenly way of life to all who believe in him.[80]

READING

We learned above even from the first verse about the great power of God, who made heaven and earth from nothing; it remains that we may also learn about his highest wisdom and goodness. In order that the divine wisdom may be made known to us, however, understand that it is characteristic of wisdom to bring to completion that which is incomplete, and to adorn and embellish things that have been completed. God could have brought all things to completion and made them most perfect all at once, in the first instant, but he did not wish to for the reason that his wisdom should be more obvious and more intelligible to us.

You heard that the earth was empty, and darkness was over the face of the waters. In that verse a certain incompleteness was signified, from which one may know that God made creatures voluntarily, not coerced by any other, either of the angels or mortals, since there was none there [to do that]. For if he had at first produced completed creatures, then those who claim that God had made all things by necessity might have persisted obstinately in their error. We have heard how immediately on the first day, lest his works should have long remained hidden, he removed any obscurity. Clarity, among other things, was wanted, and he removed any shadow of darkness by instituting the light and separating light from darkness. Besides, there was a mixture of waters, that is, of the air and of the element water. For by the term "water" we understand the finer elements. Those waters were disturbed by the blowing wind of the Lord. Therefore on the second day God made the expanse, a kind of partition, that we call the firmament. The clear waters he lifted up above the firmament, but the others he wished to be under the firmament, and thus he seemed to be removing the imperfection. And as he commanded by his Word, so it was done. Moreover up to that time the land was not yet cleansed of the waters, nor had it

80 Cf. Eph. 1:20-2:6; Phil. 3:20 f.

densioribus & crassioribus. Etiam illa maxime in salutem hominum, propter quos omnia, condita sunt, quae in suum statum erant instituenda. Legimus igitur tertiam distinctionem, qua aquae iubentur secedere in locum suum, & terra sic prominet ex aquis.

Et dixit deus: Congregentur aquae sub coelis in locum unum, ut uideri possit arida, factumque est ita.

Voluit deus, quemadmodum supra audistis, ut decreuit ab aeterno secum: omnia enim uerbo dei subsistunt. Aquae iam terram obtegunt, quae sub coelo sunt. Dicis: Quomodo in unum locum aquae congregantur? Necesse ut terra prodiret: de fine igitur quaerere. Et dicunt quidam tunc ualles esse factas, quum nulla necessitas cogat, ut sic loquamur: sufficit solum imperium domini. Arida, ut fiat apta semini & ornatui. Nam quandiu aquae terram obtegunt, inepta est ad salutem hominum & procreationem frugum. Non sunt autem haec obiter cogitanda. Psalmus 23. habet: Domini est terra & plenitudo eius, orbis terrarum & uniuersi qui habitant in eo: Quia ipse super maria fundauit eam, et [14r] super flumina praeparauit eam. Magnum plane miraculum est terram considere in medio mari, & ad ipsa flumina, sicque solo uerbo domini seruari. Philosophi arbitrantur se habere iustas rationes, dum dicunt omnia grauia descendere, & levia sursum ire. Sed quid dicent illi, cum objiciemus eis: Nubes grauiores in coelo pendent supra aërem leuiorem? Scio quid objicient: Coelestem uirtutem, uel uim solis haec ita disponere. Tametsi haec solutio nouam quaestionem habitura est. Respondeant de aquis maris rubri, quae longe

received its adornments, for it was as yet covered over with the denser and harsher waters. That too was done chiefly for the well being of humankind, for whom everything that was about to be established in its own place was created. Now, therefore, we read about the third separation, by which the waters were decreed to withdraw into their own place, and the land thus stands out from the waters.

[9] And God said, let the waters under the heavens be gathered into one place, that dry ground should be able to appear, and thus it was done.

As you heard above, God willed, just as he had decreed from eternity within himself, that all things subsist by the Word of God. The waters under the heaven were then covering the earth. You ask, "How are the waters gathered in one place?" It was necessary so that the land should emerge; seek [to understand it], therefore, from the purpose. Some say that valleys were made at that time. Although no necessity compels us that we should speak in this way,[81] the sovereignty of the Lord suffices. Dry, that they might be fit for planting and development. For so long as the waters cover the land, it is not fit for human habitation and the propagation of crops. Things ought not to be considered merely in passing. Psalm 23 [24:1] says: "The earth is the Lord's and its fullness, the world and all who live in it. For he himself established it above the seas and prepared it above the flowing waters."[82] Clearly it is to be considered a great miracle that the land is positioned in the middle of the sea and in the streams themselves, and is thus preserved by the word of the Lord alone.[83]

The philosophers think they have good reasons to say that heavier things descend and lighter things rise. But how will they respond when we object against them that the heavier clouds hang in the sky above the lighter air? I know what they will reply: "A heavenly power, or the power of the sun makes it so." This solution notwithstanding, a new question is to be considered. They ask about the waters of the

81 Oecolampadius's point is that while there is no proof that the valleys were so made, nevertheless the fact can be established on the basis of God's power as revealed in this text.

82 Oecolampadius's Latin text here departs slightly from the Vulgate.

83 The comments here reflect the conviction, widely shared, that since water is lighter than earth only an active miracle prevents the seas from rising up and covering the land.

eminentiores sunt terra, ut historici tradunt: Vnde est quod terram Aegyptiorum non perdunt & inundant? Nisi ex solo dicto dei, qui posuit mari terminum suum, ita ut salua sit terra, & possit proferre suum fructum. Hinc uidere licet simul & diuinam sapientiam & bonitatem. Quamuis dicat, In unum locum: & postea, maria, nihil refert. Varietas nominum marium est a uicinis littoribus, ut dicimus, Aegaeum mare, Persicum, Indicum, Atlanticum, Germanicum, Tyrrhenum, Ionicum, & alia etiam nomina habet, quae hic adducere non est opus. Apparet in his rebus quanta sit uis diuini uerbi, cui recte omnia tribuuntur. Et cum dicit: Factumque est ita, iterum innotescit nobis diuina potentia.

Et uocauit deus aridam terram, & collectionem aquarum uocauit maria, & [14v] uidit deus quod esset bonum.

Terram, quae generali illo nomine appellatur, nunc uocat aridam, aptam semini & ornatui. Terra dicitur, siue apta sit ad semen suscipiendum, siue non, ut in primo uersu audistis. Ita etiam lacus & aliae congregationes aquarum maria dicuntur apud Hebraeos. Nos non dicimus maria, nisi quae in oceanum fluunt, uel quae sinus suos habent. Et iterum testatur se esse dominum, cum rebus iuxta suam proprietatem nomina imponit. Approbauit etiam hoc Deus. Supra de triade mysterium explicatum est. Videre dei est approbare. Adijcere illud possumus: Quemadmodum bonus artifex, cum perfecit opus suum dat illi nomen & laudat: ita etiam perfecto opere, deus uidit quod bonum esset, & approbat. Iterum contra Manichaeos locum habetis qui infamabant bonas dei creaturas.

Et dixit deus: Germinet terra herbam uirentem, que seminificet semen, lignum frugiferum, faciens fructum iuxta speciem suam, cuius semen in semetipso sit super terram, & factum est ita. Et prodire fecit terra herbam uirentem, seminificantem iuxta speciem suam, et arborem facientem fructum, cuius semen fuit in semetipsa iuxta speciem suam, & uidit Deus quod esset bonum. [15r]Factamque est uespera, & factum est mane dies tertius.

Red Sea, which are far higher than the land, as the historians hand down: How is it that the land of the Egyptians is not destroyed and flooded? [It would be] save only for the command of God, who imposed on the sea its limits so that the earth might be secure and able to bring forth its own fruit.[84]

Here it is fitting to perceive at the same time both the divine wisdom and goodness. Although the text says "in one place," it matters not that it afterwards speaks of "seas" [i.e., in the plural]. The various names of the seas come from the neighboring shores, so that we speak of the Aegean Sea, the Persian, Indian, Atlantic, German, Tyrrhenian, Ionic, and also other names, which there is no need to list here. In these things it is made apparent how great is the strength of the divine word, to which rightly all things are attributed. And when he says "and thus it was done," the divine power is again made known to us.

[10] And God called the dry place earth, and the collection of waters he called seas, and God saw that it was good.

The earth, which generally is called by that name, he now calls dry, fit for planting and development. What is called earth is either fit for receiving seeds or it is not, as you heard in the first verse. The Hebrews also call lakes and other bodies of water "seas." We call only the ones that flow into the ocean or have their own gulf a "sea." Again he shows himself to be the Lord, when he names things according to their own qualities. God also approved this. Above the threefold mystery was explained. For God to "see" is to approve. We can add that in the same way that a good craftsman, when he has completed his work, gives to it a name and praises it; so also with this work complete, God saw that it was good and approved it. Again, you have this text against the Manicheans who defame God's good creatures.

[11] And God said: Let the earth sprout living vegetation that will bear seed, the fruit bearing tree that makes fruit according to its own kind, whose seed in itself may be upon the earth, and so it was done. [12] And the earth made living vegetation burst forth, yielding seed according to its own kind, and the fruit bearing tree whose seed was in itself according to its own kind. And God saw that it was good. [13] And there was evening, and morning, the third day.

84 Cf. Job 38.

Audiuistis rerum distinctiones, quomodo quaeque ordinata sint per sapientiam dei, nunc eandem admirari licet. Ab infimo orditur, & terram quae caeteris elementis inferior est, primo ornat. Ita enim solemus nonnunquam infirmis rebus aut membris maiorem honorem impendere. Vt autem uideas quare iusserit aquas abire, in bonum hominibus id factum est. Quamuis herbae bestijs ordinatae in cibum sint, ut psaltes canit, tamen ante diluuium homines herbis usos esse innocuo cibo constat. Etiam herbae usum habent in re medica. Nemo illa parua contemnat, quia admodum necessaria sunt nobis, ut agnoscamus dei sapientiam, & gratias agamus. Terram hic uocat in genere, quae gramina & frutices teneras producit, quaeque, etiam sua incrementa accipiunt, ut crescant in caules solidos, & in gramina quae possunt ferre semen. Etiam haec est benedictio domini, etsi nondum ita uocet, tamen domini donum est. Quod deus iussit ab initio, hoc etiam hodie operatur. Sunt qui oculos tendunt in naturam, & deum non cogitant, quasi non omnia in ipso fiant: sed hi quidem longe errant. In ipso sumus & mouemur.[10] Scimus non passerem de arbore posse cadere, sine uoluntate patris. Ideo illa bene meminerimus, quia qui[15v]dam non putant omnia uim sibi datam a deo, sed suas operationes solas habere, sicque dei operationem seponunt: inde fit ut maior hominum sit impietas & ingratitudo. Nam si sciremus deum ubique praesentem suis donis, utique maiorem illi exhiberemus reuerentiam. In Ioanne habemus: Pater meus usque hodie operatur, & ego operor.[11] Portat omnia uerbo uirtutis suae.[12] Quod qui recte secum expendit, certe cum magna gratitudine deo seruiturus est. Iussit dominus, & omnia parent: solus miser peccator deo non obtemperat: cui tamen ratio data est ideo, ut illum agnoscat, & eius beneficia, nihilominus obluctatur solus ad suum maximum malum. Neque putes deum usque hodie non operari,

10 A marginal annotation here refers the reader to Acts 17[:28].

11 A marginal notation here refers the reader to John 5[:17].

12 A marginal notation here refers the reader to Hebrews 1[:3].

You have heard about the separation of things, how it was fitting that those things, which were put in order through the wisdom of God, are now also to be regarded with wonder. It starts from the lowest, and the earth, which is inferior to the other elements, he adorns first of all. Just so we are accustomed sometimes to give more attention to fragile things or members.[85] Now you see why he commanded the waters to withdraw: it was done for the good of humankind. Although the plants were ordained as food for the beasts, as the psalmist sings,[86] nevertheless prior to the flood it is certain that humankind in [the state of] innocence used plants as food. Herbs also have uses in medical matters. No one treats these small things with contempt, because they are very necessary for us so we should acknowledge the wisdom of God and give thanks. It is called earth here generally because it produces grasses and tender shoots, and also because they receive their own increase so that they may grow into solid stalks and grasses which are able to bear seed. This also is a blessing of the Lord; even if it is not yet called that, nevertheless it is a gift of the Lord.

What God commanded from the beginning he also performs today. There are those who look at nature and do not consider God, as if all things do not happen in God. But these are greatly in error, for "in him we exist and move." We know that a sparrow cannot fall from a tree except by the will of the Father.[87] Therefore we do well to remember these things, because some do not think that their strength was in every respect given to them by God, but that they rely on their own strength alone. Thus they disregard the working of God, whence it is that the impiety and ingratitude of humankind become even greater. For if we know that God is everywhere present in his gifts, then we shall exhibit a greater reverence toward him. In John we have: "My Father is working up to the present day, and I am working too." He upholds all things by the word of his own power. Therefore whoever within himself considers this rightly surely is going to serve God with great gratitude. The Lord commands, and all things obey. Only a wretched sinner would not submit to God. So whoever has been given reason to acknowledge him and his benefits and still fights against it, does so only to his own greatest harm. Nor should you think that

85 Perhaps this is an allusion to I Cor. 8:9-13.

86 See Psalm 104:14.

87 See Matthew 10:29.

& conseruare omnia. In psalmo id clarum est, qui dicit: Aperiente manum suam omnia implebuntur ubertate.[13] Placuit etiam hoc opus deo. Si tibi illud parua res uidetur, quod deus condidit, tamen deo, cuius sapientiae nihil potest comparari, illa opera placuerunt. Nos magna gratitudine illa suscipere debemus.

Factaque est uespera.) Vt supra de uespera, quae concludit diem, & mane quod concludit noctem, intelligere etiam hunc locum debetis. Deus expectauit sequentem diem, cum potuisset uno die absoluere omnia. Sicque tertio die ab aquis terra liberata est. Nunc consequenter ostendit, quomodo etiam reliqua elementa ornauit: & [16r] incipit a coelo ipso. Quamuis magna claritas in coelo sit, tamen pulchrius reddit in hominum solatium, quo magis bonitatem suam in creaturis declaret ac communicet. Miremur igitur sapientiam & prudentiam dei, qui omnia in pondere & mensura fecit.

Dixit uero deus: Fiant luminaria in firmamento coeli, & distinctionem faciant inter diem & inter noctem, & sint in signa, & in certa tempora, & in dies atque in annos. Et sint in luminaria in firmamento coeli, ut lumen praebeant super terram, & factum est ita. Fecit autem deus luminaria magna, luminare maius in dominium diei, et luminare minus in dominium noctis, & stellas. Posuit eas deus in firmamento coeli, ut lucem praeberent super terram. Et ut dominarentur in diem atque in noctem, & distinctionem facerent inter lucem & inter tenebras: & uidit deus quod esset bonum. Et fuit uespera, fuítque mane dies quartus.

[16v]Procedit primo imperium dei, ex quo cognoscimus eius potentiam. Psalmo 18. habemus: Coeli enarrant gloriam dei, & opera manuum eius annunciat firmamamentum.[14] Ita in multis alijs locis Dauid, quoties animum suum uolebat extollere ab istis uisibilibus, deum considerabat.

13 A marginal notation here refers the reader to Psalm 144 [145:16].

14 I read here "firmamentum" for "firmamamentum."

God today is not working and upholding all things. In the Psalm it is clear, where it says: "By opening his hand will all things be satisfied with plenty."[88] This work also pleases God. If to you it seems a small thing that God created, nevertheless those works pleased God, to whose wisdom nothing can even be compared. We ought to receive those things with great gratitude.

The evening came.) You should understand this text like the one above, concerning the evening that concluded the day and the morning that concluded the night. God waited for the next day, even though he could have completed all things in one day. Thus on the third day the land was freed from the waters. Appropriately, Moses now shows how God adorned the remaining elements, and he begins with the heaven itself. However great may be the splendor in heaven, still more beautifully it renders solace to humankind, by which his own goodness is better announced and communicated. Let us wonder at the wisdom and foresight of God, who fashioned all things in weight and measure.[89]

[14] Then God said: Let there be lights in the firmament of heaven, and let them make the distinction between day and night, and let them be for signs, and for fixed seasons, for days and years. [15] And let them be for lights in the firmament of heaven, that light might shine forth on the earth. And so it was done. [16] And God made [two] great lights, the greater to govern the day, the lesser to govern the night, and the stars. [17] And God placed them in the firmament of heaven, so that they would provide light upon the earth, [18] and that they should rule in the day and in the night and make a distinction between light and darkness. And God saw that it was good. [19] And there was evening and morning, the fourth day.

God's first command comes forth, from which we become aware of his power. In Psalm 18 [19:1] we have: "The heavens tell the glory of God, and the firmament makes known the works of his hands." So also in many other places, David was contemplating God whenever he wanted to lift up his heart by means of those visible things.

88 See Psalm 145:16.

89 Again, Wisd. Solom. 11:20.

Luminaria.) Hoc praecipue contra Iudaeos dicitur & Aegyptios, qui astra colebant, & tribuebant illis uim aliquam, cum uidissent quae orto sole & luna contingebant. Sunt alij Peripatetici, qui intelligentias stellis adiungunt: & sunt qui angelis stellis attribuunt. Ne autem stellas animatas faciamus, ut Platonici asseruerunt, hunc locum bene expendite. Nam inde postea homines ad idololatriam prouocati sunt, & deum qui est omnium conditor, dereliquerunt. Angeli spiritus ministratiorij sunt, hominibus ad omne bonum ordinati, ut in epistola Hebraeorum clare patet.[15] Dices: Nónne supra facta est aliqua distinctio? Inter lucem facta est. Omnino dicunt quidam solem & stellas eiusdem naturae esse cum luce illa, quae primum fuit creata, sic tamen quod lux illa sit aliquanto magis condensata, ita ut homo magis potuerit internoscere inter diem & noctem, & ut habeat noctis & diei solatia. Nocte signa uel astra nautis uiam ostendunt, praeterea his qui ambulant noctu: tamen discrimen diei & noctis est, ut sit labor & [17r] quies. Neque hic habent astrologi ut suam uanitatem comprobent. Certum ex cursu signorum quaedam esse, quae tempus serendi, nauigandi, secandi arbores, &c. ostendunt, ut in Ecclesiaste habemus.[16] Concessit enim etiam hoc homini deus, ut iuxta obseruationes tempo-

15 A marginal notation here refers the reader to Hebrews 1[:14].

16 A marginal notation here refers the reader to Ecclesiastes 3[:1-8].

Lights.) This is said principally against the Jews and the Egyptians, who worshiped the stars and attributed to them a certain power, since they had observed that some things were contingent on the solar and lunar cycles. There are other philosophers[90] who assigned intelligence to the stars, and still others who considered them to be angels. Lest we should make the stars animate beings, as the Platonists assert, consider well this text. By these [stars] human beings were afterwards provoked to idolatry, and thus to forsake God, the creator of all things. The angels are ministering spirits, appointed to humankind entirely for good, as the epistle to the Hebrews plainly shows. You might say: "Was not some distinction made above,[91] when the light was made?" Some say that the sun and all the stars are of the same substance as that light that was first created, but that nevertheless that light was somehow greatly condensed, in order that humankind would be able to distinguish between day and night, and that they might have the consolations of night and day. In the night the stars are signs that show the way for sailors, as well as for those creatures who walk at night. Still, the distinction between day and night is given [primarily] that there might be [a time of labor] and [a time of] rest. Nor do the astrologers have here something to justify their empty pride. They show that it is certain from the movement of these signs when is the time to plant, to sail, to prune trees, as we have in Ecclesiastes.[92] For God also has conceded this to humankind, that they should accomplish their work by observations of the

---

90 Although Oecolampadius refers to the Peripatetics here, I take his reference more broadly, i.e., to the opinions of unnamed philosophers.

91 I.e., between the sun, the moon, and the stars, in Genesis 1:3: "Let there be light." Oecolampadius continues here to consider the nature of these various kinds of light.

92 Oecolampadius notes here that through Scripture Christians already have this knowledge, which the astrologers claim as their own.

rum & signorum, quae in coelis lucent, opera sua perficiant. Hyades magis pluuiales sunt, quam caeterae stellae.

Certa tempora.) Vel stata tempora, ut sunt nouilunia, e quibus Iudaei sua festa, paschae, pentecostes, scenopegia designant, quae certis diebus seruare debebant, sic ut semper deo grati essent. Ex cursu lunae metimur annos & menses, ut humana negotia melius possint consistere. Porro ut hinc discamus artem uenandi, & dicamus, quales nam futuri sint olim, qui nati sunt sub Mercurio uel Marte, an fortunati uel non, hoc plane vanissimum est: abducit enim illud ab fiducia uera quae in deum est. Etsi maxime dicamus astris uirtutem esse datam, tamen scimus omnia ita astris data, ut a deo omnia regantur. Nam si assuefacti fuerimus sermoni prophetico, audiemus dominum prohibere pluuias: & ita apparet, nihil absque eius nutu contingere. Proinde effectus illi ad salutem hominum impediuntur, neque sunt homini cogniti. Cum non satis agnoscamus quae ante oculos & pedes sint, quomodo illa examinabimus quae supra nos sunt? Neque de numero planetarum & [17v] cursu omnes conueniunt, ut Rabi Mose inducit. Videamus nos in primis quaenam sit uoluntas dei, quomodo deus uult suis operibus uti, & ne adoremus illa, neque abutamur illis.

times and signs which appear in the heavens.[93] The appearance of the seven stars of Taurus,[94] for example, indicates greater rainfall than the other stars.

Fixed seasons.) Or set times, like the new moons, from which the Jews marked out their festivals, i.e., Passover, Pentecost, Feast of Tabernacles, which on certain days they were obliged to observe so that they would be grateful to God. From the course of the moon are measured years and months in order that human affairs might be better established. But far from it that we should learn from these things [i.e., the sun, moon, and stars] the right time for hunting, or what sort of things will come to pass in the future, or whether those born under Mercury or Mars will be fortunate or not — clearly, this is the greatest vanity for it leads away from the true faith, which is in God. Even if we say that great power has been given to the stars, still we understand that everything was *given* to the stars, so that all things may be ruled by God. For if we have become familiar with the sermons of the prophets, then we will hear that the Lord holds back the rains, and thus it is certain that nothing comes to pass without his nod. To the same degree as those things done for the well-being of humankind are obscured, they are also not recognized by people. Since we do not acknowledge things that are right there in front of our eyes and before our feet, how shall we consider the things that are above us? Neither are all things arranged by the number and course of the planets, as Rabbi Moses alleges.[95] Let us consider above all what is the will of God and how God wants his works to be used, so that we should neither worship nor abuse them.

---

93 For astrological thinking in medieval Christendom, see Lewis, *Discarded Image*, cited above. More broadly, see Hilary M. Carey, "Astrology in the Middle Ages," *History Compass* 8/8 (2010): 888-902. For the views of Oecolampadius's friend and fellow humanist reformer Philip Melanchthon, see Stefano Caroti, "Melanchthon's Astrology," in *'Astrologi Hallucinati': Stars and the End of the World in Luther's Time*, ed. Paolo Zambelli (Berlin/New York: Walter de Gruyter, 1986), pp. 109-21.The limits of astrology for Oecolampadius become immediately apparent, however, in what follows here.

94 I.e., the constellation Hyades, referred to here by its feature that resembles the head of a bull.

95 I.e., the medieval Jewish philosopher and Torah scholar, Rabbi Moses Maimonides (d. 1204), with whom Oecolampadius here indicates his disagreement.

Posuit.) Id est, uoluit esse: non ita fixit: nam suum cursum habent. Ita etiam posuit hominem in hortum uoluptatis.

LECTIO

Singularem dei sapientiam considerauimus supra in dispositione rerum uniuersi, quandoquidem deus omnia in suo ordine optime collocauit: neque solum collocauit bene, sed etiam ordinauit, tam terram quam coelum. Vltra eandem sapientiam magis licebit intueri, una cum bonitate dei. Bonitatem uidemus, quandoquidem communicatiua est suis. Proprium est boni, ut se communicet. Deus optimus omnibus se communicat, cum uidemus omnes res ab ipso conditas maxime utiles. Et fit semper progressus ad perfecta ab imperfectis, in quo fontem omnis essentiae cognoscimus. Nunc autorem etiam uitae agnoscamus. Nihil est quod suum esse non a deo habeat. Hactenus non legimus de aliquibus quae uiuant. Nam de coelo, terra, aquis &c. audiuimus: sunt gramina quae terra producit & frutices, etsi illa diximus uiuere, uitam tamen habent solam uegetatiuam. Non uera illa uita est, quae solum in ipsa sensatione cognoscitur.

[18r]Et dixit deus: Reptificent aquae reptile animae uiuentis, & auem quae uolitet super terram, in facie firmamenti coeli.

Benefacturus igitur homini, quem creaturus erat deus, ornat aërem auibus, aquas piscibus, partim in cibum hominis futura, partim ad gloram dei demonstrandam cessura. שרץ plus est quam producere, significat enim cum multitudine reptificare, Vuurblen, sicut uidemus aceruum formicarum plurimarum, sicque abundantiam hoc uerbo commendauit. Et ex eodem uerbo dei & virtute qua omnia conduntur, reptificant aquae, ut sciamus quantum sit dicere dei.

Animae uiuentis.) Multitudinem animae uiuentis: & ita Graecus interpretatus est: pluralem enim numerum ponit ἐξαγαγέτω τὰ ὕδατα ἑρπετὰ ψυχῶν[17] producant aquae reptilia animarum uiuentium, quod aliquanto clarius est dictum. Syllepsis est, numerus singularis in plurali

17 The text cited here appears to be identical to the Septuagint (at Genesis 1:20).

He placed.)[96] That is, he willed it to be, not that he [physically] set them in place. For they have their own course. In the same way, he placed humankind in the garden of delights.

READING

Let us reflect on the singular wisdom of God shown above in the disposition of the things of the universe, how indeed God set all things in their own very best order, for God did not merely set things out well, but he also ordained them, as much on earth as in heaven. Beyond that, this same wisdom may be better understood as one with the goodness of God. We see the goodness of God, seeing that he has imparted it to his own. It is a characteristic of the good that it should impart itself. The most excellent God imparts himself to all things, since we see that everything made by him is most useful. And progress is always made from imperfection to perfection, in which we recognize the source of every essence. Let us now acknowledge the author of life. There is nothing that has not received its own being from God. Thus far we do not read about anything that lives. We have heard about heaven, earth, the waters and so on; there are the grasses and fruits the earth produces, and although we might have said that they are alive, nevertheless they have only vegetative life. It is not that true life, which is recognized only in sensation itself.

[20] And God said: Let creeping living animals teem forth from the waters, and the bird that flies above the earth, in the face of the firmament of heaven.

For the future benefit of humankind, which God was about to create, he adorned the air with birds and the waters with fish, partly for food for the coming human race, and partly to clear the way to show the glory of God. In Hebrew *sheres* [teeming, swarming things] means more than just to produce. It signifies even more to teem forth, to swirl, even as we see here a great multitude of many forms, an abundance commended by this word. From the same word and power of God by which all things had been made, the waters also teem forth in order that we might know how powerful God's word is.

Living animals.) A multitude of living animals. And so the Greek translates it, for it uses the plural number, *exagageto ta udata erpeta psuchon,*

96 Oecolampadius seems to depart here from his own Latin biblical text and to refer instead to the first Latin word, "posuit," in verse 17 of the traditional Latin, i.e., Vulgate, text.

comprehenditur. Audistis duplices aquas, quaedam tenuiores, at aër superius, nomine aquae comprehensus, & fere pro eodem elemento hic accipiuntur. Eundem diem habent aues & pisces in creatione.

Firmamenti.) Vel extensione coeli κατὰ τὸ στερέωμα. Hac ratione dicitur, quod solent aues [18v] uolitare in aëre. Et coelum aliquando pro aëre capitur, inde uolucres coeli, id est, aues quae in aëre uolitant. Non nunquam res a uicinitate nomina sortiuntur: ita aër propior coelo quam aquae, nomen coeli sortitur.

Et creauit deus cetos magnos, & omnem animam uiuentem & motabilem quam repere fecerunt aquae iuxta speciem suam, & omnem auem pennatam iuxta speciem suam, & uidit deus quod esset bonum.

Egreditur piscium auiumque magna copia, item magnae belluae maris, quas deus ne homini noceant, procul arcet, ut sunt balenae & delphines. Et sunt multo plura genera piscium marinorum, quam animalium terrenorum: & fere non est genus animalis super terram, cui non respondeat marinum eiusdem fere generis, ut lupus marinus, canis marinus, cancer, asinus, &c. Est autem benedictio dei, quod eius fauore in tot periculis crescant & multiplicentur.

Animam uiventem.) Id est, omne animal quod uiuit. Assuescite modum loquendi scripturae, quae animam uocat etiam eam, quae non est rationalis: quandoquidem in animalibus brutis animam uiuentem dicit. נפש non pro spiritu hic, sed pro anima quae uegetatur, et nutritur accipitur. Animam inquam quae agitat se, et repit, [19r] quam aquae produxerunt in speciem suam. Omnia a principio condita sunt. Et similiter iam quod ad aërem attinet, uolatilia adsunt in genere suo. Etiam deus approbauit hoc opus suum, ut bonus artifex. Et iam inueniemus aliquid noui, quod in caeteris non inuenimus.

"let the waters bring forth living reptiles," which is much more clearly said. This is a syllepsis, where the singular number is expressed by the plural. You have heard already of two waters which are finer, with the air being above, which are included under the name of water, a certain one thinner, but the air higher, and they are commonly received here as the same element.[97] On the same day birds and fish were created.

Of the firmament.) Or on the expanse of heaven, *kata to stereoma*. This is said because birds fly in the air; and "heaven" is sometimes understood as "air." Hence, they are the winged creatures of the heavens, that is, birds that fly in the air. Sometimes names are assigned from what is nearby. Air is nearer to heaven than to water, so it is given the name of heaven.

[21] And God created great sea beasts, and every living and moving soul which the waters made to teem forth according to its kind, and every winged bird according to its kind, and God saw that it was good.

A great abundance of fish and birds proceeds forth, and great sea monsters, which God keeps at a far distance lest they harm humankind, as in the case of the whales and dolphins. And there are many more types of marine life than of land animals. Indeed, there is hardly a genus of land animal to which there does not correspond almost the same type of marine life, such as the sea wolf, sea dog, the crab, the sea horse, and so on. But it is the blessing of God, that by his favor they might increase and multiply even among so many dangers.

Living soul.) That is, every animal that lives. Get used to the scriptural way of speaking, which calls by the name "soul" (*anima*) even that which is not rational, since he says there is a living soul in brute animals. The Hebrew word *nephesh*, "living creature," is taken here not for the spirit, but for the soul, which is animated and nourished. I say that it is the soul which moves itself and teems, and which the waters produced according to its kind. Everything from the beginning was made. Likewise also for what keeps to the air. The winged creatures exist in their own kind. God also approved this his work, like a good craftsman. And now we will discover something new that we have not found in other things.

---

97 Oecolampadius refers here to the heavenly spheres, mentioned above.

Et benedixit illis deus, dicens: Fructificate & augescite, & implete aquas in fretis, & auis multiplicetur in terra. Et fuit uespera, fuitque mane dies quintus.

Benedicere dei, est dare uirtutem crescendi & multiplicandi: Quod mox postea exponit per uerba, facite fructum, in maribus uel fretis, id est, in fluminibus & omnibus collectionibus aquarum. Haec est benedictio dei, quod per tot milia secula non corrumpantur, sed permaneant. Ita deus in initio benedixit illis rebus. Neque hoc dixit de herbis & graminibus, quae terra postea sua sponte productura erat. Iterum apparet quod ea quae sensum uitae acceperunt, a deo honestatem accepisse, id est, benedictionem: in quo uidemus benignitatem & sapientiam dei, qui ea ex nihilo creauit. Vnde aquae hanc foecunditatem habent? Vnde aër dabit aues? Nónne diuinam sapientiam agnoscimus una cum eius benignitate, quae talia in usum humani generis creauit & conseruat?

[19v]Et dixit deus: Producat terra animam uiuentem secundum speciem suam, iumentum, reptile & bestiam terrae secundum speciem suam, & factum est ita.

Nondum contentus benignitate suae est deus, quamuis creasset multa quae hominem possent oblectare, multaque in cibum hominum ordinasset, uoluit tamen etiam creare nonnulla, per quae homo exerceretur, & nonnulla quae homini administrarent necessaria. Dicit igitur: Terra producat animal uiuum in sua specie, iumentum & reptile. Et ita diuidit animalia ista in tres species: in animalia domestica, ut sunt oues, boues, porci: deinde in reptilia, ut sunt dracones, & alia quae terra profert: tertio in bestias terrae, ut sunt leones, tigri, lupi, &c. Posset quis admirari, quasi illa cederent in malum humani generis, creare leones & lupos, & id genus perniciosa animantia. Sed si homo perstitissit in sua innocentia, etiam dominus fuisset illorum, & magis cognouisset suam potestatem, & quantum boni a domino accepisset, ut imbellis resistere possit illis, uel solo uerbo. Postea audiemus illa animalia nomina accepisse ab ipso Adam. Etiam Noah postea iussit

[22] And God blessed them saying: Be fruitful and increase, and fill the waters in the sea, and let the birds be multiplied on the earth. [23] And there was evening and morning, the fifth day.

The blessing of God is his giving of the power of increasing and multiplying, which is immediately afterward put forth through the words, "be fruitful," in the seas or channels, that is, in rivers and in every body of water. This is the blessing of God that through so many thousand ages should not be undone, but remain. Thus in the beginning God blessed those things. Neither was this said regarding the vegetation or seeds, which would afterwards be produced spontaneously by the earth. Again it appears that these things that received the sensate life have received an honor from God, that is, a blessing, in which we perceive the kindness and wisdom of the God who made them from nothing. Whence do the waters possess this fecundity? Whence will the air produce birds? Do we not recognize that the divine wisdom is one with his kindness, which created and preserved so many things for the use of the human race?

[24] And God said: Let the land produce the living creature according its kind, animals, creeping things, and beasts of the earth according to their own kind. And thus it was done.

God is not yet content with his kindness, although he had already made many things able to delight humankind and had ordained many things for the food of humankind. Nevertheless, he wished also to create a number of things through which the human being might be exercised, and a number of things that provide human necessities. Thus it is said, "let the land produce living animals according to their own kind, animal and reptile." And so he divided those animals into three kinds: in domestic animals, like sheep, cows, and pigs; then in reptiles, like snakes and other things that the earth brings forth; thirdly in beasts of the earth, like lions, tigers, wolves and so on. One might react in amazement, as if those things were done to the detriment of the human race, the creation, that is, of lions and wolves, and all kinds of dangerous animals. But if humans had persisted in their own innocence, they also would have been lords over those animals and would better have recognized their own power and how much good they had received from the Lord, so that they should be able to stand before those unaggressive animals, even by the word alone. Later we will hear that those animals received their names from Adam himself. Also

animalia ire in arcam, sine aliquo nocumento. Verum quandoquidem deus praesciuit hominem peccaturum, ideo & illas bestias condidit ut exerceatur homo, & ut timeat deum. Pueris opus est uir[20r]gis et terriculamentis, quo magis possint erudiri. Atqui singulari prouidentia deus illas malas bestias abire fecit in loca magis deserta, ut procul abessent ab homine, et ut noctu potius pabula quaererent, quam die ipso. Consideret autem homo, quantum nocumentum inferre possent tam crudelia animalia, si deus non prohiberet.

Et fecit deus bestiam terrae iuxta speciem suam, & iumentum secundum speciem suam, & omne quod reptat super terram iuxta speciem suam: & uidit deus quod esset bonum.

Bestias pluraliter ab alis[18] uersum, placet, etsi singulariter in Hebraeo textu ponatur. Nemo putet bestias illas quia nonnunquam sunt perniciosae, non creatorem deum habere. Hoc si recte intelligeremus, multo magis pacifici essemus. Neque nocebunt animalia illa, nisi dispensante domino. Vipera Paulo non nocuit. Actorum 28. Alia animalia, ut equi, asini, &c. ad portanda onera apta sunt. Et iterum deus approbauit has suas creaturas. Hucusque habemus ijs, quae condita sunt ante hominem, sed omnia propter hominem. Iam creatio hominis sequitur.

Dixitque deus: Faciemus hominem in imagine nostra, secundum similitudinem nostram, & dominentur in piscem maris, [20v] & in uolucrem coeli, et in iumentum, & in omnem terram, & in omne reptile, quod reptat super terram.

Quemadmodum rex potentissimus, ubi aedificiuit magnificam ciuitatem, illamque uarijs modis ornauit, tandem praeficit huic ciuitate uirum quendam insignem, cui suam autoritatem confert, qui suam gloriam & benignitatem praedicet: Ita deus tandem hominem cui facit

18 I read "aliis" here for "alis" in the published text.

Noah afterwards commanded the animals to go into the ark, without any difficulties. In truth, seeing that God foreknew that humans would sin, thence he also created these beasts so that human beings might be exercised and that they might fear God. For the young, rods and threats are useful, by which they should be better educated. And yet God in his singular providence made those ferocious beasts depart into the wilderness, so that they should be far off from humankind, and that they should better hunt out their food by night rather than by day. Let one consider well, moreover, how much greater harm there might have been than just savage animals, had God not prohibited it.

[25] And God made the beast of the earth according to its own kind, and the domestic animals according to their own kind, and everything that creeps on the earth according to its own kind. And God saw that it was good.

It is pleasing that others have translated this with the plural "bestias," even if the singular is used in the Hebrew. No one thinks that because those beasts are sometimes dangerous that they were not made by God. If we had rightly understood this, we would have lived in much greater peace. Neither will those animals cause harm, except by the dispensation of the Lord. The viper did not kill Paul (Acts 28). Other animals, like the horse, the donkey and so on, are suited for carrying heavy things. And here once more God commended his own creatures. Thus far we have those things that were created prior to humankind, but in all respects on account of humankind. Now the creation of humankind follows.

[26] And God said: Let us make[98] humankind in our image, according to our likeness, and let them rule over the fish of the sea, and over the birds in the air, and over the animals, and over the whole earth, and over every creeping thing that creeps upon the earth.

Suppose a most powerful king, when he built a magnificent city and adorned it in various ways, finally set a certain outstanding man in charge over the city, and gave to him his own authority, a man who would publicly proclaim his own glory and benevolence. In just this

98 As the printed text reads, "we shall make." I have corrected this to conform to the subjunctive form used below in Oecolampadius's discussion of the text, i.e., reading "faciamus" for "faciemus."

potestatem omnium, etiam condit. Discimus hic praecipuum scopum scripturae, ut in prima lectione monui, spiritum sanctum huc spectare, ut commendet deum patrem. Iucundum etiam est cognoscere ea quae deus propter hominem condidit: sed multo iucundius quanta sint illa quae in ipsum hominem contulit. Ex his enim multo magis benignitatem dei patris cognoscimus. Vide ut magnifice Moses omnia scribit. Extructus est mundus, ut domicilium hominis: ornatus est, locupletatus est: abundantia ciborum, ministeriorumque parata est, ut inde discat maiora sibi apud deum reposita esse bona. Vide igitur priuilegia. Non simpliciter dicit, fiat homo, sed consilio quodam dicit, faciamus hominem.[19] Ita enim seipsum exhortatur & consultat, tametsi apud illum nulla deliberatione uel exhortatione opus fuerit, quia omnia ab aeterno constituta erant: atqui attemperat se nostrae [21r] infirmitati ut uideamus quam uelit nobis optime. Interim elucent ibi clarissima trinitatis testimonia. Et sicut prius dixit, nimirum ad alterum, ita hic illud confirmat pluraliter loquendo. Nec recipere licet quod Aben Ezra dicit נַעֲשֶׂה[20] pro eo quod factus sit: subdit enim, ad imaginem nostram, ubi iterum pluralis numerus clare repugnat eius expositioni. Sed nec audiendi sunt dicentes deum angelis locutum esse, quasi sine illis creauerit minora, & horum consilio maiora, hoc est, hominem. Ita sane pulchre in idololatriam duceremur. Neque more principium plurali numero loquitur, qui consilio seniorum suorum omnia agunt, dicentes: Hoc sic constituimus, scilicet a magnatibus edocti: quibus uerbis

19 This remark suggests that the publisher erred in printing "faciemus," above.

20 The text has this word spelled backwards—an understandable mistake, particularly on the part of the printer, who presumably could not read Hebrew. The error is corrected here.

way God at last made humankind to whom he gave power over all things. We learn here that the chief aim of Scripture, as I advised in the first reading, is to pay attention to the Holy Spirit in order that he might commend [to us] God the Father. It is indeed a joy to know about those things that God made on account of humankind, but even more joyful to know how many good things he brought together in humankind itself. For from these things we recognize the great benevolence of God the Father. Look how splendidly Moses composes everything. The world had been made as the dwelling place for humankind. It was adorned and enriched. An abundance of foods and services were provided from whence he should learn that greater goods had been stored up for him in the presence of God. Just look at all the special favors. He does not simply say, "I shall make humankind," but by a certain kind of deliberation he says, "Let us make man." So indeed he exhorts and consults within himself, even though there would have been no need of exhortation within himself, for all things were established from eternity. But now he accommodates himself[99] to our weakness in order that we might see that he wills for us only the very best.

At the same time the brightest testimonies of the Trinity shine forth here. For just as when he spoke before, doubtless to another, so here he confirms that by speaking in the plural.[100] Nor can we accept what Ibn Ezra[101] says, that the term *na`aseh* refers to that which is about to be made.[102] For the words that follow, "in our image," again use the plural number, which is clearly opposed to his exposition. Nor must we listen to those who say that God spoke to the angels, as if he had made lesser things without them, but now turned for their counsel for greater things, namely, humankind. Thus we would be nobly led into

99 I.e., God accommodates God's own eternal life, God's ways of being and doing, to the finite and temporal being and experience of the human creature. See also the comments on Gen. 1:3, above.

100 Oecolampadius's argument is that God here speaks to God, which he believes testifies to the internal distinctions within the Godhead, i.e., the three persons in the one deity.

101 Also known as Abraham ben Meir or Ibn Ezra (1089-1164). The exegetical work of this Spanish Jew was well known to Christian biblical expositors in the Reformation period, primarily through the biblical commentaries of Nicholas of Lyra.

102 The Hebrew verb is in the first person plural, i.e., "let us make."

arrogantiam cauere uolunt. Quis autem consiliarius dei? In Esaia habetis, Christum angelum magni consilij uocare, qui solus nouit mentem patris.[21] At inuenis alibi deum & singulariter loqui. Verum non oportebat misellos sic refragari: non enim propterea plures deos inuehimus, quia tres personas in uno deo fateamur.[22] Salua maneat scripturae simplicitas, nec nos turbabit Iudaice perfidiae malignitas. Multum nobis tollunt a dignitate nostra, qui ne filium dei conditorem sinant, etiam angelos creatores faciunt. Dicit autem, in imagine nostra. En quanta & hic dignitas. Sed hic interim nobis inuidens satan, obscurat ea quae dicuntur, ne agnita generositate nostra [21v] digne deo uiuamus. Ecce Anthropomorphitae inepti, de quibus Cassianus multa scribit, illi deo os, membra, & oculos, & alia homninis lineamenta ascribunt: contra quam sectam Basilius multa admodum scripsit ad monachos quosdam, quos aegre a simplicitate illa potuit auellere: & plerique ex ijs adeo pertinaces fuere, ut occidi se permitterent, prius quam illum perniciosum errorem abiurarent. Quae hominum pertinacia? Ipsi

21 A marginal notation here refers the reader to Isaiah 9[:6].

22 Reading here "invenimus" for "invehimus."

idolatry.[103] Nor is it spoken with the plural number after the manner of princes, who do everything with the counsel of their advisors, saying, "This we decree," only after having been thoroughly advised by important men. With these words they wish to avoid arrogance. But who has been God's counselor?[104] In Isaiah you read that Christ is called the angel of great counsel, the one who alone has known the mind of the Father. But elsewhere you find that God speaks also in the singular.[105] But he was not required thus to oppose the wretches. For just because we confess three persons in the one God, we need not on that account introduce multiple gods.[106] The simplicity of Scripture should remain intact.[107]

Nor will the malice of Jewish treachery disturb us. They take much away from our [human] dignity who, lest they allow that the Son of God is the creator, actually make the angels creators. But it says, "in our image." Just look what great dignity is here! But here again Satan, looking at us in envy, obscures the things said here, lest we, having recognized our nobility, should live worthily before God. Behold the inept Anthropomorphites,[108] about whom Cassian[109] writes so much, who ascribe to God a mouth, members, eyes, and other human features. Against this sect, Basil[110] writes a great deal to certain monks, whom he was with difficulty able to turn away from that childishness. But many among them were so obstinate that they would allow themselves to be killed before they would abjure that pernicious error. How

103 That is to say, if the one God speaks here only to the angels and not to God's own internally-differentiated self, then Christians, who worship the Incarnate Word as a divine person, would be guilty of idolatry, led into it "nobly" through false exegetical reasoning.

104 Rom. 11:34; cf. Isa. 40:13.

105 I.e., God says "I" instead of "we."

106 In other words, the confession of God as Trinity does not make Christians polytheists.

107 I.e., the expositor should stick to the literal sense of the text.

108 So called because they believed God has human form, i.e., a human body.

109 John Cassian, ca. 360-435.

110 St. Basil of Caesarea, ca. 329-379.

etiam uerbum urgebant IMAGINEM, neque poterant secum concipere mentis intellectum. Sunt deinde Manichae, qui ex substantia dei animam nostram esse dicunt: quod si uerum, iam impeccabilis esset, & per omnia deus. Alij dixerunt imaginem ex eo solum, quod inuisibilis sit anima ut deus: at sic etiam ad imaginem diaboli essemus creati. Alij solum τὸ ἀρχικον, id est, principatum hominis attenderunt, eo quod subditur: Et dominentur in piscem maris & in uolucrem coeli &c. sicut & Paulus imaginem dei uirum uocat, non foeminam.[23] Atqui hic habemus, quod & foeminam deus creauerit cum mare, licet ille prior peccauerit postea, attamen in pari dignitate condita est cum uiro, sicut etiamnum unus in Christo sunt uir & mulier, neque enim haec illo inferior. Augustinus & post eum recentiores, imaginem in mente, ratione & uoluntate considerant, iuxta trinitatis in deo mysterium: sed non ui[22r]dentur mihi acu rem tangere. Longe enim aliter sunt in una deitate pater, filius, & spiritus sanctus, quam haec tria in nobis, ut annotat Graecos Theodoretus. Ipse in hoc malo Cyrillum sequi, dicentem: Effecti sumus nos ad ueram & certissimam imaginem patris, hoc est, ad filium: et in animabus nostris diuina pulchritudo per participium spiritus sancti inesse significatur. Et enim illa est in nobis, sicut ipse filius. Spiritus enim ueritas est, ut Paulus Galatis, qui

23 A marginal notation here refers the reader to I Cor. 11.

great is the obstinacy of humankind? They even insisted on the word "image,"[111] for they were not able to conceive the mental concept.[112]

Then there are the Manicheans, who say that our soul is from the substance of God. If this is true, then it would be without sin and entirely divine. Others said that the image comes only from this, that the soul is invisible, like God. But in that case we would also have been created in the image of the devil. Yet others attended only to *to archikon* (Gk., "the ruler"), that is, to the dominion of humankind, which follows it: "And let them rule over the fish of the sea and the birds of the air, etc."[113]—just as Paul also calls the man the image of God, but not the woman.[114] Still, we read here that God also created the female with the male. Granted that he was superior after she had sinned, nevertheless she was created in equal dignity with the man. Just as even now man and wife are one in Christ,[115] neither is this woman inferior to that man.

Augustine and more recent writers after him see the image in the mind, reason and will, just like the mystery of the Trinity in God. But this does not seem to me to touch the heart of the matter. For the oneness of deity in Father, Son, and Holy Spirit is much different from this threeness in us, as, from among the Greeks, Theodoret[116] notes. In this I prefer to follow Cyril,[117] saying: "We have been made in the true and most certain image of the Father, that is, in the Son." And it signifies that the divine beauty is present in our souls through participation in the Holy Spirit. For that [beauty] also is in us, even as the Son himself [is in us]. For the Spirit is truth, as Paul says to the

111 I.e., they insisted that the word "image" should be understood literally.

112 By "mental understanding" Oecolampadius means something non-physical.

113 These "others" locate the image of God in the "dominion" given to humankind before the fall. That is, the likeness to God consists in the capacity for rule.

114 Here Oecolampadius addresses the question whether in that case the image, can also be ascribed to the woman. The answer he gives seems to grant her that image, in spite of the words of the apostle Paul, cited in the original text.

115 Cf. Gal. 3:28.

116 Theodoret of Cyr, ca. 393-466.

117 Cyril of Alexandria, d. 444.

imaginem foedarant, in deterius prolapsi, dicit: Filij quos iterum parturio, donec Christus formetur in uobis.[24] Et idem alibi: insculpta est homini diuinae naturae imago, inspirato spiritu sancto: ipse enim est spiritus uitae, quandoquidem uita secundum naturam est deus. Non enim aliter quam accepto dono spiritus, diuinae imaginis capaces sumus. Caeterum dum ad filij imaginem configuramur, totius trinitatis pulchritudo in nobis est. Vna enim summa pulchritudo in illis est, ad quam & nos configuramur, obsignemur licet ad filiationem per filium in spiritu. Eusebij sententia placet, qui dicit: ψυχὴ μὲν οὖν λογικὴ καὶ ἀθάνατος καὶ νοῦς ἀπαθὴς ἐν ἀνθρώπου φύσει εὖ μοι δοκεῖ λέγεσθαι εἰκόνα καὶ ὁμοίωσιν ἀποσῴζειν θεοῦ, καθ ὅσον ἄυλος καὶ ἀσώματος νοερά τε καὶ λογικὴ τὴν οὐσίαν συνέστηκέν ἀρετῆς οὖσα καὶ σοφίας δεκτική. [22v] Hoc autem dono spiritus contigit. Certe quamdiu in potentia sumus, nondum est imago dei in nobis, qui actus est. Spiritus igitur est opus. Vnde & recte Origenes, τὸ κατ εἰκόνα αἱ πράξεις χαρακτηρίζουσι.[25] Sicut portauimus, inquit apostolus, imaginem terreni, ita & portemus imaginem coelestis.[26] Terreni imaginem portauimus iuxta carnem uiuentes, propensi ad peccatum, & mortem, quae inde aduecta perpeti cogimur: portabimus nunc coelestis, iuxta spiritum uiuentes, nacti firmitatem ad sanctificationem, & ex morte reditum ac renouationem ad incorruptionem & uitam aeternam. Vide quot bona simul affert imago? Immaterialitatem in anima,

---

24 A marginal notation here refers the reader to Gal. 4[:19].

25 The citation is from Origen's *Selecta in Genesim*. See PG 12, col. 96, line 14.

26 A marginal notation here refers the reader to I Cor. 15[:49].

Galatians, who had defiled the image and fallen into worse condition: "Little children, for whom I am in labor a second time until Christ is formed in you." Likewise elsewhere: The image of the divine nature has been engraved on humankind, when the Holy Spirit was breathed in.[118] For he himself is the Spirit of life, since God is life according to [his very] nature. For in no other way than by receiving the gift of the Spirit are we able to bear the divine image. When we are conformed fully to the image of the Son,[119] then the beauty of the entire Trinity is in us. For the sole highest beauty is in them [i.e., the persons of the Trinity], to which [beauty] we are also conformed, provided that we are sealed into sonship through the Son in the Spirit.[120]

The opinion of Eusebius is pleasing, who says: "Rather does the rational and immortal soul and the impassible mind in man's nature seem to me to be rightly spoken of as preserving an image and likeness of God, inasmuch as it is immaterial and incorporeal, and intelligent and rational in its essence, and is capable of virtue and wisdom."[121] This comes about, however, by the gift of the Spirit. Surely as long as we are in the process of becoming, the image of God, who is fully realized, is not yet complete in us.[122] Therefore there is need of the Spirit. Whence Origen also rightly says that "the image is shown in actions." The apostle says: "Just as we have borne the image of the earthly man, so also we should bear the image of the heavenly man." While living according to the flesh we have borne the earthly image, inclined toward sin and death, and we are compelled to carry it to the full. Now we will bear the heavenly image, living according to the Spirit, having obtained strength for sanctification, brought back from death for renewal in incorruptibility and life eternal.

---

118 This seems to have been said in anticipation of the life breathed into Adam in Gen. 2:7.

119 Cf. Rom. 8:29.

120 See e.g., Gal. 4:5-6; Rom. 8:14-17.

121 Eusebius of Caesarea, *Praeparatio Evangelica,* Book III, Ch. 10. ET from volume 1 of *Preparation for the Gospel,* trans. Edwin Hamilton Gifford (Oxford: Clarendon, 1903), p. 116.

122 Oecolampadius is relying here on the scholastic distinction between *potentia* and *actus,* i.e., between the incompleteness associated with potency and the fullness of actuality. Human being has potential, but the being of God is fully realized, i.e., pure act.

rationem, uirtutem ac sapientiam, adeoque immortalitatem. Si autem opera carnis operamur, non erit in nobis εἰκόν imago dietatis, sed potius carnis: sed si opera spiritus. Hoc igitur attendentes, facile licebit uidere unde sit uera sanctimonia. Interim hic licebit uidere disputationem de Libero arbitrio. Plane ut apud Ecclesiasticum habemus, principio habuit homo liberum arbitrium, & deus dedit homini possibilitatem faciendi, neque illud negamus, neque praeiudicat diuinae electioni. Deus dedit homini rationem, ut possit eligere, quid bonum quidúe malum: & dedit spiritum ut possit bene agere. Anima Adae libera ab huiusmodi affectionibus erat, neque obnoxia carni, ut nunc est, et propensior erat ad bonum [23r] quam ad malum, nisi postea sua ignauia sibi ipsi incommodasset: sed posteaquam prolapsus est in peccatum, obscurata est imago illa & pulchritodo ablata, sicque facultas ablata est agendi bonum. Nam licet nunc deus homini concedat aliquam notitiam, quid sit agendum, siue per legem, siue per Euangelij uerbum praedicatum, non tamen uires tales addit, quales habuit Adam: ideo nostris uiribus non tantum ualemus, nisi per Christum reformemur. Vbi autem spiritus sanctus nobis concessus fuerit, tunc satis alacres erimus ad bona opera. Videmus etiam uirtutes quae sunt in deo. Ipse sanctus est, iustus, misericors, ueritas, & iustitia ipsa. Homo igitur non est natus ut indulgeat gulae, ebrietati, & corporalibus uoluptatibus, sed ad coelestia bona contemplanda: foueat innocentiam, exprimat omnibus modis Christum. Et ubi haec indepti fuerimus, tunc restituetur nostra imago. Alij hoc pluribus egerunt, dum laborauerunt quomodo restituenda sit memoria, quomodo ipsa mens & uoluntas: sed ex ipsis operibus nostris licet facile uidere, qualis sit cuiusque character. Character sit dei uel bestiae, necessum est. Vbi huiusmodi dignitas characteris dei est in homine, ubi uita est aeterna.

See how many benefits are included in the image? Immateriality in the soul, reason, virtue and wisdom, and even immortality. If, however, we do the works of the flesh,[123] the "eikon" or image of the deity will not be in us, but rather that of the flesh; but if the works of the Spirit...[124] Those who attend to this will easily see where true holiness comes from. At the same time here one will find a dispute over free choice. Clearly, as is written in Ecclesiasticus,[125] in the beginning humankind had freedom of choice, and God gave humankind the possibility of making a choice. We will not deny that, but neither should one prejudge regarding divine election. God gave reason to the human so that he might be able to choose between good and evil, and he gave the Spirit, too, that he should be able to do it well. The soul of Adam was free from any kind of disposition, neither was it liable to the flesh as it is now, and it was more inclined to the good than to evil, except that afterwards by its own faintheartedness it would cause difficulties. After he had fallen into sin, however, the image was obscured, the excellence lost, and thus, too, the capacity for doing good. For although God now concedes to humankind some idea of what is to be done, either through the Law or through the preached word of the Gospel, nevertheless he does not impart [to us] such great powers as Adam possessed. Therefore we are not so strong in our endowments [i.e., as was Adam] except when we are renewed through Christ.

But when the Holy Spirit has been granted to us, then we will be ready enough for good works. We see indeed the virtues that are in God. He himself is holy, just, merciful, the truth, and justice itself. So the human being is not born that he should yield to the appetite, to drunkenness, and to bodily desires, but for the contemplation of heavenly things. He should maintain innocence, that he might imitate Christ in every way. And when we shall have acquired these things, then our image will be restored. Others have done this in many ways, when they struggled so that memory, mind, and will should be restored. But from one's own works one may easily observe the quality of one's character. Our character is either that of God or of the beasts; it's

---

123 Gal. 5:19-21.

124 An allusion to Gal. 5:16 ff. Oecolampadius seems to have intentionally left off the rest of the thought, leaving his hearers/readers to fill it out for themselves.

125 Ecclus. 15:14.

Vita autem aeterna est Christum agnoscere: neque agnoscemus illum, nisi per spiritum dei.

Et dominentur.) Hic additur dominium super omnia [23v] animantia, quae sua potestate potuit subigere. Caeterum nunc per Christum non minorem potestatem habemus, imo plus accipimus, quam per Adam amiseramus. Bonis & electis omnia in bonum eueniunt, mors & uita, alta & profunda, Cephas et Paulus nostra sunt, nos autem Christi. Ita homo rebus omnibus fit superior, & admirabilis, ut nec Danielem leones, nec pueros ignis, nec Iudaes mare, nec Paulo uipera nocere poterat, & credentibus uenena nihil nocent, etsi biberint illa. Vnde etiam dicit bene Ambrosius: Tolle incredulitatem, quia magis ea timenda est, quam praesentissimum uenenum. Sic etiam Paulus admonet ad Ephesios scribens: Renouamini spiritu mentis uestrae, & induite nouum hominen, qui secundum deum creatus est, in iustitia, & sanctitate ueritatis.[27] Et ad Colossenses cap. 3. Induentes nouum hominem, qui renouatur in agnitione dei secundum imaginem eius, qui creauit eum, ubi non est masculus & foemina, Graecus & Iudaeus, circumcisio & praeputium, Barbarus & Scytha, seruus et liber, sed omnia in omnibus Christus. Qui cupiunt igitur liberi esse & dominari in mortem, in infernum, studeant ante omnia, ut conscientiam suam reparent, & ut illa serena sit omnem diligentiam adhibeant. Hocque erit dominium longe amplius & melius, quam Adam unquam habuit.

27 A marginal notation here mistakenly directs the reader to Ephesians 3. The correct citation is Ephesians 4:24.

inevitable. Wherever such dignity of the character of God is present in the human being, there is life eternal. Life eternal, moreover, is to know Christ, and neither do we know him, except through the Spirit of God.[126]

And let them rule.) Here is added the dominion over all the animals, which he is able to subjugate to his own power. Yet now through Christ we have no less power, indeed we receive more than what we lost through Adam. For good men and for the elect, everything works out for the good, death and life, heights and depths.[127] Cephas and Paul are ours, but we are Christ's.[128] Thus humankind became superior over all things, and more wonderful, so that the lions could not harm Daniel;[129] nor the fire, the young men;[130] nor the sea, the Jews;[131] nor the snake, Paul.[132] And among believers poisons cannot kill, even if they drink them.[133] Ambrose has said it well: "Away with unbelief, for higher powers should be feared more than the most powerful poison." Thus also Paul admonishes the Ephesians when he writes: "Be renewed in the spirit of your minds, and put on the new man, who is created according to God in righteousness, and in the sanctity of truth." And to the Colossians, in chapter 3[:10]: "Put on the new man, who is renewed in the knowledge of God, according to the image of he who created him, where there is not male and female, Greek and Jew, circumcision and foreskin, Barbarian and Scythian, slave and free, but Christ is all and in all."[134] Whosoever, therefore, desires to be free and to have dominion over death and hell, let them above all strive to renew their own conscience and apply themselves diligently to set it at peace. This will be by far a fuller and better dominion than Adam ever had. For the grace

126 Oecolampadius discussion of the significance of the image of God here comes to its Trinitarian conclusion: the knowledge of God is given in Christ, through the Holy Spirit. To the specific point here, see I Cor. 12:3.

127 An allusion to Rom. 8:28.

128 Cf. I Cor. 1:12.

129 See Daniel 6.

130 See Daniel 3.

131 An allusion to the Exodus.

132 Acts 28:1-6.

133 See Mark 16:18.

134 Oecolampadius's mention here of "male and female" is a conflation of Paul's words in Galatians 3:28.

Nam gratia per Christum concessa, longe amplior est quam [24r] damnum per Adam inuectum. Etiam homini peccatori creaturae seruiunt, quanto magis, si homo perstitisset in sua innocentia? Vellem etiam uos hoc animaduertere, quandoquidem homo sic honestatus est a deo, & ornatus, ut etiam nos proximos in magno honore haberemus, honorantes in fratribus nostris imaginem dei. Vtique grauiter peccant, qui proximum offendunt, & prasertim eum, cuius est tanta dignitas apud deum. Vnde nimirum homicidium & odium iure maxima abominatio coram deo est, offenditur enim imago dei. Et dum impij saeuire non possunt in deum, saeuiunt in imaginem dei, sed uae illis. Nota autem, ut mihi apparet, & assentit Cyrillus, non est hic facienda distinctio inter imaginem & similitudinem. Secundum similitudinem enim, exponendi gratia adiectum est: quasi dicat: Tunc aderit imago, si uera fuerit similitudo, utpote si misericordiam, patientiam, ueritatem, charitatem, iustitiam, sanctitatemque dei imitamur & in nobis exprimimus. Proinde septuaginta non uerterunt secundo, ad similitudinem nostram, sed solum καθ' ὁμοίωσιν, id quod Hebraeus dicit כִּדְמוּתֵנוּ. Porro צלמ nequaquam Hebraeis figuram corporalem sonat, sed iuxta Rabi Mose Aegyptium, perfectionem internam, utpote intellectum, תואר enim figura et qualitas est. Item Adam, id est, homo, collectiuam significationem habet, unde in plurali [24v] subditur, dominentur, & non dominetur. Item quod dicit, reptile super terram, ne intellige solos serpentes, sed etiam alias feras, id est, quicquid calcat terram.

that has been granted through Christ is greater than the injury brought on through Adam.[135] Even now the creatures serve sinful humankind; how much greater would that have been had humankind remained in its innocence? I really wish you would pay attention to this, seeing that humanity is so honored and endowed by God that we should show great respect to our neighbors, honoring in our brothers the image of God. Surely they sin gravely who harm a neighbor, and especially one who has such dignity before God. Hence it is no wonder that murder and hatred are rightly the greatest abomination before God, for they offend against the image of God. So while the impious cannot rage against God, they rage instead against the image of God. But woe to them! Note well, however, that as it seems to me, and Cyril agrees, a distinction between image and likeness is not to be made here. Indeed, "according to our likeness" is added for the sake of explanation, as if he should say that the image will appear when a true likeness has been developed, namely, when we imitate the mercy, patience, truth, love, justice and sanctity of God and express them among ourselves. Hence the Septuagint does not translate it with a second phrase,[136] but uses only *kath homoiosin*, "according to likeness," what the Hebrew calls *demuwth* ["likeness"]. Moreover, the Hebrew term *tselem* ["image"] is never used by the Hebrews for a bodily figure, but according to Rabbi Moses of Egypt[137] for internal perfection, namely understanding, for [the Hebrew word] *twar* means a shape or characteristic.[138] Furthermore, Adam, that is the human being, has a collective signification, whence it is said in the plural "let them rule," and not "let him rule." So also where it says "that creeps on the earth" you should understand not only snakes but also other beasts, i.e., whatever presses close to the earth.

---

135 Cf. Rom. 5:12-21.

136 I.e., the Septuagint Greek translation uses one word to translate two Hebrew words because they are understood as synonymous.

137 I.e., Maimonides.

138 *Twar* means "look" or "appearance." Oecolampadius seems to be saying that the "image" and "likeness" (*tselem, demuwth*) mentioned here in Genesis denote an internal spiritual or intellectual quality rather than a physical one. If it were the latter, then the Hebrew term would have been *twar*. Here he is clearly following the discussion of the image and likeness in Maimonides' *Guide for the Perplexed*, ch. 1.

Accesserunt omnia animantia postea ad Adam. Vnde רמש pro רמס id est, calcat, dictum uidetur, cognatae enim sunt literae ש & ס.

Creauit itaque deus hominem in imagine sua, in imagine dei creauit eum, masculum & foeminam creauit eos.

Videtis Mosem iterum atque iterum hanc summam hominis dignitatem in medium proferre, nimirum ut profunde inculcet in mentes nostras. Ita ut deus statuit, sic fecit, creauit, & nihil omisit. Quamuis deus ut omniscius, sciret peccaturos Adam & Euam, & futuram maximam ingratitudinem, nihilominus perrexit in creatione. Igitur si quid culpae & mali in homine, deo non ascribatur. Et quod iterum repetit, In imagine dei, ideo facit, ut maior nostra sit culpa, si hoc non seruemus perpetuo in memoria nostra. Atqui quomodo hominem condiderit solum in genere hic praemisit, sequenti capite id latius declaraturus est. Sed ut scias foeminam non fuisse exclusam ab hac dignitate, addit: Masculum & foeminam. Sic etiam in Christo neque mas neque foemina. Itaque dum Eua non peccaret, par dignitas erat Adae & Euae, quia illa etiam spiritum Dei acceperat. Sicut di[25r]xit, In principio creauit deus coelum & terram, & postea singula latius declarat, ita & hoc loci facit. Vide nunc aliam dignitatem hominis.

Et benedixit illis deus, dixitque ad eos deus, fructificate & augescite & implete terram, atque subijcite eam: & dominamini in piscem maris, & in uolucrem coeli, & in omne animans, quod reptat super terram.

Accedit alia dignitas homini per benedictionem, qua & coniugium honestatur, ac quodammodo iuxta uerbum dei praecipitur, sicut postea patebit: & dominium terrae, et quae in illa sunt, conceditur. Et sic homo immortalis, rationalis, iustus, & rectus conditus, accepta liberi

Afterwards all the animals approached Adam.[139] Whence the Hebrew word spelled *Resh-Mem-Shin* ["creeps"] seems to have been used in place of the Hebrew word spelled *Resh-Mem-Samech* because the letters *Samech* and *Shin* are interchangeable.

[27] Thus God created the human being in his own image, in the image of God he created him, male and female he created them.

You see Moses repeatedly mentions this highest dignity of humankind, no doubt in order to impress it deeply on our minds. Thus, God acted and created just as he intended, and he left nothing out. Although God as omniscient would have known that Adam and Eve would sin, as well as their great future ingratitude, nevertheless he went on with the creation. Therefore, whatever guilt and evil is in humankind should not be ascribed to God. The words "in the image of God" are repeated so that our guilt might be all the greater if we do not keep this perpetually in our memory. Although how he created humankind is treated here only in general, in the next chapter it will be explained more fully. But so that you should know that the female was not excluded from this dignity, he adds: "male and female." So also in Christ there is neither male nor female.[140] Therefore until Eve had sinned the dignity of Adam and Eve was equal, because she too had received the Spirit of God. Just as the text said, "in the beginning God created the heaven and earth" and then later explained the particulars more fully, so also it is done in this place. Observe now another dignity of humankind.

[28] And God blessed them and said to them, "Be fruitful and increase and fill the earth, and subdue it. Rule over the fish in the sea, the birds in the air, and over every living thing that creeps upon the earth."

Another dignity is added to humankind through the blessing with which marriage is adorned and in a certain way it is anticipated according to the word of God, just as afterwards will be made plain, when dominion over the earth and everything in it is granted. And so when the human race had been created immortal, rational, just and upright, and had received the possibility of free choice, it was established as

139 That is, they all came to Adam to receive their names. See below in the comments on Gen. 2:19.

140 Gal. 3:28.

arbitrij possibilitate, dominus rerum instituitur. Benedictionem illam accipe ut supra. Gratia dei est, qua homo multiplicari possit. Non est, ut cogitemus his uel illis uerbis dominum esse usum, etsi propheta adiungat uerba docendi gratia. Benedixit, id est, ualde liberaliter concessit gratiam iustificandi. Neque solum Adae, sed etiam suae posteritati. Et hic nihil de malis bestijs dicit, sed de piscibus & auibus, etsi etiam pro futura sint illa animalia homini.

Et dixit deus, ecce dedi uobis omnem herbam seminantem semen, quae est in [25v] superficie universae terrae, & omnem arborem, in qua est fructus arboris, & quae seminet semen, ut sint uobis in escam. Sed & omni bestiae terrae, & cuncto uolatili coeli, atque omni illi, quod reptat super terram, in quo est anima uiuens (dedi) uniuersum uirorem herbae in cibum, & factum est ita.

Ut deus benefecit animae homini, quam ad imaginem suam condidit, ita externum hominem quoque sua solicitudine adiuuit, & nihil deesse uoluit. Innocentem & innocuum cibum primo proposuit, nempe herbas & legumina, & fructus arborum. Quamuis autem non prohibuerit carnes in cibum, ostendit tamen fuisse aurea secula, & hominem & feras innocuis cibis fuisse contentos, miramque fuisse pacem: sicut & Esaias sub Messia praedixit, lupum agno fore compascuum, & uitulo ursum. Nec homini solum praeuidit deus, sed etiam animalibus propter hominem. In sequentibus clarius illa habebitis.

Et vidit deus omne quod fecerat, & ecce erat ualde bonum: & facta est uespera, fuitque mane dies sextus.

Iam quia erat homo, qui poterat donis concessis uti iterum deus ut artifex opus suum laudauit, approba[26r]uitque, et nondum fecisse poenitet. Et nos uidentes dei beneficia, ore & opere gratias agamus, testantes quod omnia bene fecerit, quae in sex diebus condita sunt: maxime autem ualde bona omnia, quia erat homo, qui ex uisibilibus illis, ad contemplandum & laudandum deum surgere poterat.

lord of things. "Receive the blessing," just as above.[141] It is the grace of God by which humankind may be multiplied. It is not, as we might think, that the Lord used these or those words, even if the prophet added words for the sake of teaching. "He blessed," that is, he most liberally granted the grace to be justified. And not just to Adam, but to his descendants as well. Also here it says nothing about the wild beasts, but about the fish and birds, although in the future the other animals would also be useful to humankind.

[29] And God said, "Behold, I gave you every plant bearing seed which is on the surface of the whole earth, and every seed bearing tree in which there is the fruit of the tree, so that they should be food for you. [30] But also to every beast of the earth, and to all the birds of heaven, and even to every thing that creeps upon the earth in which there is a living soul, I have given all green vegetation for food." And thus it was done.

Just as God blessed the souls of humankind, which he made in his own image, so also he assisted the external human being with his own care, for he willed that nothing should be lacking. He first set forth innocent and harmless food: herbs, legumes, and fruit of the trees. Although he did not prohibit eating flesh, nevertheless he showed that it was a golden age when humankind and the beasts were content with harmless foods. And there was an amazing peace. Just as Isaiah preached concerning the Messiah, that the wolf will share the pasture with the lamb, and the bear with the calf as well.[142] Nor did God provide only for humankind, but also, on account of humankind, for the animals. In what follows you will have that more clearly.

[31] And God saw all that he had made, and behold it was very good. And it was evening and morning, the sixth day.

Now because there was the human race that was able to make use of the gifts given, God again as the greatest craftsman praised and approved his own work, and he did not yet regret making anything. And seeing the benefits of God, let us give thanks in word and deed, bearing witness that he made all things well that were created in the six days, but especially because man was by far the best thing of all, who was able to rise up from those visible things in order to praise and contemplate of God.

141 See Gen. 1:22 above.

142 See Isa. 11:6-10.

CAPVT II

Et perfecti sunt coeli & terra, & omnis exercitus illorum.
Ne putemus aliquid ociose in sacris literis dictum esse, quemadmodum nihil in creaturis dei absque singulari ratione conditum est.

Perfecti.) Videntur illae repetitiones esse superuacaneae, sed non sunt. Indiget enim nostra paruitas, ut egregia dei beneficia iterum atque iterum inculcentur, ne ingrati scilicet simus, & ne deum infamemus, ut quidam fecerunt. Itaque nihil est quod desideres. Perfectissimus artifix, perfectissimus opus absoluit. Vult dicere: Quaecunque in coelo & terra existunt, ea condita sunt tanta sapientia, ut nihil sit quod inde quaeratis. Neque praeterea expectandi sunt alij quidam immortales mundi, de quibus philosophi uane disputant: iam perfecti sunt, homine scilicet condito. Sex diebus exactis, homine condita nihil iam superat, ut iterum aduertas omnia homini esse creata.

[26v]Exercitus.) Vel omnis militia eorum. Aduerte uerbum hoc, de militia coeli, praesertim cum in prophetis tam saepissime occurrat. Neque solum intelligimus astra, ut quidam, qui tantummodo ad corporalia oculos conuertunt, sed etiam angelos ipsos. Ideo dominus zebaoth, tam eorum qui in coelis sunt, quam qui in terris, siue corporeae creaturae sint siue coelestes: quia Christus est dominus, angelorum, & uere dominus exercitum. Magnifico autem nomine utitur Moses, quo maiorem nobis spem in deum addat, qui tam egregia propter nos condita esse intelligimus. Sunt angeli administratorij spiritus, sicut supra dixi, propter eos qui salutem consequuntur. Heb. 1. Imo omnis

CHAPTER 2

[1] And the heavens and earth were completed, the whole host of them.

We should not think that anything in the sacred letters has been said idly, just as none of the creatures of God were made without a good reason.

Completed.) These repetitions seem redundant, but they are not. For our smallness requires that the extraordinary blessings of God should be impressed on us again and again in order that we should neither be ungrateful nor defame God, as some people do. And so you lack nothing. The most perfect craftsman brought to completion the most perfect work. He wants to say: Whatsoever exists in heaven and earth, these things were made with such wisdom that there is nothing beyond them that you should seek. Nor hereafter should certain other immortal realms[143] be sought after, concerning which the philosophers vainly dispute, because things were undoubtedly completed with the creation of humankind. Since humanity was created in exactly six days there was now nothing left to do. Once again you should recognize that all things were created for humanity.

Host.) Or all the armies of them. Attend to this word regarding the armies of heaven, especially since it very often appears in the prophets. We understand here not only the stars, like certain men who turn their eyes only to bodily matters, but also the angels themselves. Therefore he is the Lord of Hosts, those in heaven as much as those on earth, whether they be corporeal creatures or heavenly. For Christ is Lord of the angels, and thus truly the Lord of hosts. Moreover Moses uses this magnificent name, with which he brings us to greater hope in God, who we understand to have made so many wonderful things on our account. As mentioned above, the angels are spirits who minister for the sake of those who are pursuing salvation. (Hebrews 1) Indeed, every creature in the heavens or on earth will render service—whether

143 It is unclear what Oecolampadius refers to here by "immortal realms." The point of the sentence, however, is clear, namely, to underscore the uniqueness and finality of God's one creation indicated by the phrase "were completed."

creatura, siue in coelis, siue in terra sit, bonis in bonum seruiet, malis in malum. Perfecti igitur sunt coeli & terra.

Consummauitque deus in die septimo opus suum quod fecerat: & quieuit in die septimo, ab omni opere suo quod fecerat.

In diem septimum malim legere, quam in die. De six diebus auditum est, quid singulis deus operatus sit: nunc de septimo agit, in quo deus cessauit ab operibus. Nomen sabbati a quiete deducitur. Hic non pauca occurrunt admonenda. Deus enim, licet natura sua sit efficacissimus, ita tamen operatur, ne unquam fatigari queat, [27r] neque illi quiete opus, imo quietus est. Nam operatur, & dum operatur quiescit, quandoquidem sola sua uoluntate & uerbo rem omnem perficit. Si ipsam diuinam naturam attenderis, dies ille septimus nunc semper durabit. Nos iuxta nostrum modum intelligendi septem dies facimus, apud ipsum tamen uno momento quodammodo comprehenduntur. Non possumus diuina illa nostris corporeis comparare. Apud Ioannem habemus dictum: Pater meus usque modo operatur, & ego operor.[28] Hic: Quieuit. Illa facila possunt conciliari. Quieuit deus, ne noua opera conderet. Operatur, quia dedit illam uirtutem rebus parturiendi fructus suos, ut initio decreuit, quae omnia suo uerbo contingunt. Ita in ipso sumus & mouemur. Quidam ex nostris, etiam aliqui ex ueteribus, uoluerunt occasionem inde colligere contra Iudaeos, quasi die septimo aliquid fecerit, & quasi die septimo cessauerit: sed non est modus loquendi: uult dicere: Die septimo omnia parata sunt. Marcus Euangelista habet, Sabbatum non esse nisi propter hominem, & ita filium hominis etiam dominum esse sabbati: igitur & sabbatum propter hominem.[29] Discamus hinc quid nobis die sabbati faciendum sit, nempe ut quiescamus a nostris operibus malis, & reficiamur in deo. Summa dignitas nostra, si eo peruenerimus. Die septimo deus quieuit, nos autem nullam quietem inuenimus, nisi relictis [27v] omnibus operibus huius mundi, quietem inueniamus. Nam hoc dicere uoluit, ut si agnouerimus omnia propter nos condita esse, & deum nobis bene

28 A marginal notation refers the reader to John 5[:17].

29 A marginal notation refers the reader to Mark 3.

to the godly in their doing of good, or to the wicked in their doing of evil. Therefore the heavens and earth were completed.

[2] And on the seventh day God finished his own work that he had done, and he rested on the seventh day from every work that he had done.

I would prefer to interpret here [that God finished his own work] "on" instead of "during" the seventh day. Concerning the six days it has been heard what God had effected on each one. Now it sets forth a seventh day on which God ceased from the works. The noun "Sabbath" is taken from "rest." Here there come to mind not a few admonitions. For God, granted that his own nature is most effective, nevertheless works so that he neither becomes weary nor needs sleep—and yet, he still rests! For he works, and while he works he rests since he accomplishes everything by the power of his will and word alone. If you will attend to the divine nature itself, that seventh day [of rest] will now ever endure. We fashion the seven days according to our way of understanding, but with God they are in a way enclosed in a single moment. We cannot compare these divine things to our own corporeal realities. In John we have the saying: "My Father works up to now, and I am working." But here it says: "He rested." These can easily be reconciled. God rested, in that he would not make any new works. He works, because he gave things that power of bringing forth their own fruit, as he decreed in the beginning, all of which comes to pass through his own Word. So in him we exist and move. Certain ones among us, even some of the ancients, wanted to take an opportunity here against the Jews, as if on the seventh day he had made something, and then also he ceased on the seventh day. But that is not [the text's] way of speaking. It wishes to say that by the seventh day all things were ready. Mark the Evangelist says "The Sabbath does not exist except on account of humankind, and thus the Son of Man is also Lord of the Sabbath, and the Sabbath is given for humankind."[144] Here we learn what ought to be done by us on the Sabbath day, namely that we should rest from our evil works and be renewed in God. It is our highest dignity if we shall have arrived at this place. On the seventh day God rested, but we find no rest unless we leave off from all the works of this world. For he wishes to say that if we realize that everything was made on our

144 The marginal annotation is incorrect here. The quotation is actually taken from Mark 2:27-28.

uelle, quod in ipso ueram quietem requisituri simus. Quandiu oblectamur in istis rebus inferioribus, & satiari non possumus, recte terra nobis non perfecta est, & uidetur nobis deum nondum perfecisse opus suum, quia nos non quiescimus.

Et benedixit deus diei septimo, & sanctificauit eum, eo quod in eo quieuisset ab omni opere suo, quod creauit deus ut faceret.

Quod ad diem septimum attinet, expedit homini qui uarijs occupationibus adstrictus est, ut unum diem sibi eligat, in quo magis se exerceat in precibus, & magis oblectetur in deo, quam caeteris diebus. Scimus Christianorum sabbatismum esse perpetuum, ut abstineant a peccatis & sceleribus, quae deum offendunt: sed certum tempus est laborandi. Deus benedixit diei septimo, nimirum nobis illum segregauit, & admonuit, ut si illum domino santificaturi sumus, quod benedictione illius non priuemur. Vera quies ab externis operibus, ut gaudeamus in domino, & oblectemur: quia omnia propter nos facta sunt, & sabbatum etiam illud propter hominem constitutum est ne quis putet nos Iudaizare. Sci[28r]mus quae sit conscientiarum libertas, sed interim attendimus etiam infirmitatem populi. Vtinam omnis multitudo perpetuum sabbatismum obseruaret, & nemo inuideret. Sed quoniam illud nondum assequi licet, saltem impetremus ut aliquem diem infirmo populo concedant hi, quorum interest, quem deo consecrent. Non ut alios dies intendamus uanitati & ijs rebus quae contra deum sunt: sed unam eam ob causam petimus, quo peculiariter deo seruiamus: idque requirit fides. Et nisi hoc fecerimus, parum fidei in nobis esse ostendemus. Putamus deum non posse nos nutrire, nisi in singulos dies laboremus? In quo quidam maxime peccant, qui nullam quietem

account and that God wishes us well, then we should seek true rest in him. So long as we delight in inferior things we cannot be satisfied and the earth has not been rightly completed for us; and so it seems to us that God has not completed his own work, because we are not at rest.

[3] And God blessed the seventh day and sanctified it, because in it he had rested from all his own work, what God had created and made.

That which pertains to the seventh day is expedient for the human being, tied up with various occupations, that God should choose one day for him in which he should exercise himself more greatly in prayer, and take delight in God more than on other days. We know Sabbath observation is perpetual among Christians, in order that they should abstain from sins and wickedness that offend God. But the time for working is fixed. God blessed the seventh day and without doubt set it apart for us, and he admonished us that if we would sanctify it to the Lord, then we would not be deprived of its blessing. It is true rest from external works, so that we might rejoice and take delight in the Lord.[145] For all things have been made on our account, and, lest anyone should think that we Judaize,[146] even the Sabbath was established for humankind.

We know what liberty of conscience is, but at the same time we should pay attention to the weakness of the people. If only the whole multitude would keep the Sabbath perpetually and no one would refuse. But since of course this is never achieved, we at least request that those whose concern it is[147] would grant a certain day to the weak people, which they might consecrate to God. Not that we would intend other days for foolishness and those things which are opposed to God, but we seek that one day that we might reserve specially for God, and faith requires this. And if we do not do this we show that there is little of faith in us. Do we think that God cannot feed us unless we work every day? Some sin greatly in this matter, for they allow no rest

145 Cf. Heb. 4:10.

146 Here the term refers to a legalism (in this case the assertion that civil authorities should institute an official Sabbath day) that could be construed as Jewish. The assumption, widely shared among sixteenth-century Christians, is that Judaism teaches salvation by works, Christianity salvation by grace.

147 I.e., the civil magistrates.

& uacationem ministris & iumentis permittunt, quasi deus non posset eos alere, nisi continui sint in laboribus. Paulus Heb. 3. & 4. pulchre alludit ad sabbati diem, quare ille obseruandus sit summa diligentia: & dicit, ut possimus ingredi in requiem &c. Aliud mysterium etiam hic eruendum, quod frequenter sancti commemorant. Quo die homo conditus, eodem & Christus passus, nempe sexto, & sabbato in sepulchro quieuit. Ita deus etiam tunc quieuit ab omnibus operibus suis, cum iam in cruce clamasset, omnia esse consummata, nimirum ea quae ad salutem humani generis attinebant: eamque sepulturam & quietem exprimere conuenit. Si cum Christo sepulti sumus, cum illo iure etiam quiesci[28v]mus. Necesse moriamur huic mundo, & sic quiescamus cum illo, ut resurgamus in gloriam & nouitatem uitae. Erit olim sabbatismus omnium creaturarum, tunc & nos resurgemus in gloriam incorruptibilem. Benedixit denique deus diei septimo propter nos, ut iure benedicamur, si illum seruemus. Nemo igitur diem illum infamet, quasi sit maledictus & execrabilis. Scitote tempus illud, quod deo uere consecrandum est, non in hypocrisi peragendum esse, sed in sanctificatione, ut deo placeamus.

Istae sunt generationes coelorum & terrae cum crearentur, in die cum faceret dominus deus terram & coelos. Et omnem plantulam agri, antequam esset in terra, & omnem herbam agri antequam germinaret: quia non pluere fecerat dominus deus super terram, nec erat homo qui coleret humum.

Hic infert nouum caput, & quae antea in genere dixit de dignitate humani generis, illa nunc magis illustrat, & speciatim enarrat, nempe quanta deus bona homini exhibuit, & quomodo deus hominem uoluerit uiuere cum magna uoluptate & securitate. Voluit enim hominem quiescere in deo, & praeterea nihilominus laborare in paradiso. Vt igitur hanc narrationem ingre[29r]diatur, plantationem horti docere instituit, in quo homini laborandum erat, & in quo ambulaturus erat feliciter Adam. Vt autem uideatis qualiter hortus iste plantatus sit, prius

or time off for servants or beasts of burden, as if God were not able to support them unless they work all the time. Paul in Hebrews 3 and 4 sweetly alludes to the Sabbath day and why it ought to be observed with the greatest diligence, and he says that we will be able to enter into that rest, and so on.

Another mystery ought to be brought up here, one that the saints often mention. The day when the human being was created was the same day, of course, that Christ suffered, the sixth day, and he rested in the tomb on the Sabbath. So God also then rested from all his works when on the cross he cried out, "Everything is finished!"[148] Doubtless these are things that pertain to the salvation of the human race, and it was fitting to portray it both as the grave and as rest. If we have been buried with Christ, with him also we rightly rest. We have to die to this world and thus rest with him in order for us to rise into glory and newness of life. This will one day be the Sabbath rest of all creatures, when we too rise up into glory incorruptible.[149] Therefore God blessed the seventh day on our account, that we might rightly be blessed if we keep it. Therefore let no one bring this day into disrepute, as if it should be cursed and detestable. Understand that the time that is to be truly consecrated to God should not be kept in a hypocritical way, but with holiness, that we might please God.

[4] These are the generations of the heavens and earth, when they were created, on the day when the Lord God made earth and heavens. [5] Before every plant in the field was in the earth, and before every herb of the field had sprouted, because the Lord had not yet caused it to rain on the earth, there was not a human who could till the soil.

Here begins a new chapter, and the things previously spoken in a general way concerning the dignity of the human race are now made clearer and related more particularly, both how many good things God presented to humankind as well as how God wished humankind to live in great delight and freedom from care. For he wished humankind to rest in God and thereafter nevertheless to work in paradise. Therefore as he introduces this story, he sets up to explain the planting of the garden where humankind was to labor and in which Adam

148 See John 19:30.

149 Cf. I Cor. 15:50 ff.

ostendit omnia quidem alia esse creata, sed horti istius plantationem nondum esse plantatem hoc modo, & monstratam, etsi arbores conditi prius fuerant. Distinguit etiam paradisum ab alia terra, ut supra pulchre separauit aridam ab aquis, & a maribus: praeterea aquas quae sub coelo &c. Ita inuenietis pulchre distingui paradisum a terris, ut uideat homo sibi distribui locum multo amoenissimum & frugiferum, in quo possit omnibus modis refocillari & beatus esse animo & corpore. Audistis hominem ad imaginem dei creatum, utpote rationalem, qui in supernis & coelistibus uersare debet. Sed ex puluere homo: corpori suo labor adiunctus, uerum cum labore felicitas. Neque talis labor fuit, qualis hodie agricolarum est.

Coelorum.) Videtis, iterum in memoriam inducit generationem coeli & terrae, & istae repetitiones uobis admonitionum loco sint. Scito omnia illa esse a deo condita, & non a seipsis posse subsistere. Quod dicit, Generationes coelorum: scias modum esse loquendi scripturae. Sunt quidam qui a termino generationis & natiuitatis abhorrent, & non abhorrent si legant, Generationes coelorum & terrae. Vnde apparet homines illos po[29v]tius ad contentiones natos, quam ad ueritatem inquirendam: & praeter omnem necessitatem pugnant cum alijs, ut aliquid uideantur nosse. Certum, quando de diuinis rebus loquimur, ualedicimus omnibus rebus corporeis. Et qui hanc regulam negligit, non dubium illum in multis errare, & perperam sentire.

בהבראם) Hebraei unica he litera subscriptione hireck, magnum mysterium colligunt, nempe mundum esse praesentem & futurum: sed incertiora sunt argumenta. Nos plane credimus & uidemus mundum esse praesentem, & alium etiam credimus.

Plantulam.) Omne uirgultum fecit iuxta suam rationem seminale: non eo modo quemadmodum nunc in terra nascuntur, sed a nouo ipse condidit uirgulta, & ita omnem herbam campi priusquam germinaret.

was to walk about happily. Moreover, in order that you might see how that garden was planted, he first shows all the other things that were created, but [then] shows that the planting of this garden was not done in this way, even if the trees had been created beforehand. For he distinguishes the [garden of] paradise from the other land, just as above when he deftly separated the dry land from the waters and the seas, and just as afterwards he separated the waters that were under the heaven, etc. Thus you find that the paradise is beautifully distinguished from the lands, so that the human being should see that he was assigned to a place with great beauty and fruit bearing trees, a place in which he could be revivified in every way and happy in both body and spirit. You have already heard that humankind was created in the image of God, namely, as a rational being who should dwell in the heights of heaven. But humankind was also from dust. Work was joined to the body, but to labor, happiness. Nor was this a hard labor like farmers' work is today.

Of the heavens.) You see here that he again brings to mind the generation of the heavens and earth; the repetitions here are an admonition for you. You must know that all things were created by God and could not subsist from themselves. When it says "the generations of the heavens," you should know that this is a scriptural way of speaking. There are some who shudder at the terms "generation" and "birth." But if they read "the generations of the heavens and the earth" they do not shudder. Whence it appears that those people were born more for arguing than for seeking the truth. They fight with others beyond all necessity, so that they might seem to have known something. Certainly, when we speak about divine matters we bid farewell to all corporeal realities. Whoever ignores this rule will no doubt err and think wrongly about many things.

Behibar'am.[150] The Hebrews infer a great mystery from this one letter *he* with the *hirek* subscription, i.e., that the world certainly is present and future. But these [philological] arguments are uncertain. We for our part believe this completely, and we see that the world has a present while we have faith also in its future.

Plant.) He made every plant grow according to its own seminal reason,[151] not in that way by which they are given life in the earth today,

150 Hebrew, "in their being made."

151 Oecolampadius is borrowing from Augustine here. For "seminal reasons" in Augustine's understanding of the creation, see TeSelle, *Augustine*

Sic Deus principio terram condidit & ordinauit, ut uideatis quô sermo tendat, & quô respiciendum sit, nempe ad plantationem paradisi. Alia terra ornata est in solatium hominis, et solo dei uerbo omnia opera facta sunt, neque id tribuas imbribus, aut laboribus hominum. Hocque praeuenit Moses hac particula, quia dominus nondum super terram pluerat, & homo non erat. Vult dicere: Deus illa omnia suo uerbo produxit et sua uirtute, quae postea fieri coeperunt, cum superne terra acciperet pluuiam & foecunda fieret: postea autem homo deputatus [30r] est ut terram ipse coleret: a principio uero fuit culta solo uerbo domini.

Et uapor ascendebat de terra, & irrigabat uniuersam faciem humi.

Alij nebulam dicunt ascendisse. Initio quidem terra non est compluta, postea autem in salutem hominum, ut terrae nascentia seruarentur, deus creauit ut terra irrigaretur ex uaporibus, id est nubibus pluuijs. Graeci habent πηγὴ δὲ ἀνέβαινεν ἐκ τῆς γῆς, & fons de terra ascendebat: quam fontem alij oceanum putant, quod permeatus subterraneos, & per uenas omnem terram irrigat, & quod sic fontes producat. Eusebius Philonem adducit, qui synecdochicôs exponit fontem pro fontibus. Certum in paradiso quatuor flumina praecipua fuisse: et terra etiam uaria flumina habuit & fontes. Veteres ex Hebraeis & LXX. exposuerunt, de fonte.

but instead he made anew plants and likewise every herb on the plain before it sprouted. Thus God in the beginning made and ordered the earth, so that you should see what he is aiming at and what ought to be regarded at this moment, namely the planting [of the garden] of paradise. The other land was adorned for the consolation of humankind. And all these works were accomplished by the Word of God alone, so you should not attribute them to the showers of rain or the efforts of humankind. This Moses anticipates with this particular bit of information, that the Lord did not yet have it rain on the earth, and there was not yet a human being. He wished to say that God by his word and power produced all those things that afterwards began to be made, i.e., when the earth received rain from above and became fruitful. Afterwards, however, humankind was assigned to care for the earth. But at the beginning it was cultivated by the word of the Lord alone.

[6] **And a vapor used to arise from the earth and irrigate the whole face of the land.**

Others say that a fog had arisen. For indeed in the beginning the earth was not rained upon, but afterwards, for the good of humankind and in order that the produce of the earth should be preserved, God created [it] so that the earth would be irrigated by means of a vapor, that is, by a rainy mist. The Greek says *pege de anebainen ek tes ges*, "a spring ascended from out of the earth." Some think this spring was the ocean that penetrated under the earth and irrigated the whole land through fissures that produced springs. Eusebius mentions Philo who takes the singular "spring" as a synecdoche for the plural "springs." Certainly in paradise there were four main rivers, and the land had still other rivers and springs. The older writers among the Hebrews as well as the Septuagint understood it as speaking about a [singular] "spring."

---

the Theologian, pp. 217-18. According to TeSelle, Augustine believed that God made living things in their "seminal reasons" before they had yet appeared on the earth. That is, in the beginning all living things were created "virtually, in their causes, that is, in the seeds by which they would subsequently be consolidated as organisms." (p. 218) The appearance of these living things then takes place over time, as the "seminal reasons" embedded in matter at the beginning gradually unfolds in history.

Formauit quoque dominus deus hominem puluerem de humo, et insufflauit in nares eius flatum uitae, factusque est homo in animam uiuentem.

Quia dixerat antea, neque pluerat, neque homo erat, iam deus ordinat etiam hominem, qui colat terram. Nam homo de terra assumptus est. Illud admodum diligenter describit, ut nostrae humilitatis simus memores. Poteramus felices esse, nisi Adam lapsus esset. Hocque excelsos [30v] ceruices merito humiliabit. Neque simpliciter dicit, fecit hominem: sed plasmauit dominus & formauit hominem, instar figuli. Non solum de luto homo formatus est, sed de puluere, quia puluis terra soluta est. Graeci habent χοῦν λαζὼν[30] ἀπὸ τῆς γῆς. Non carnem factam, uel compactam accepit homo, sed puluerem, ne superbiat in conditorem.

Insufflavit.) Id est, dedit homini uitam. Hebraei ita exponunt, quod intelligendum sit, quod deus fecerit corpusculum illud de terra sic, ut uiueret. Malo in hoc imitari Graecos, attendentes quod caeteris animantibus dictum est, & sic hominem generosiore factum putant. Et Paulum 1. Cor. 11. huc allusisse certum est. Neque possumus negare

30 I read here λαβὼν instead of λαζὼν as found in the printed text.

[7] And the Lord God formed the human being from the dust of the soil, and breathed into his nostrils the breath of life. And the human being was made a living soul.

Because it says that previously it had not rained and there was no human being, now God ordains also the human being to inhabit the earth. For the human was taken from the earth. And this he quite diligently describes in order that we should be mindful of our humble origins. We could have been happy, had Adam not fallen. And this will rightly humble even the most exalted [among us]. Nor does the text simply say that he made the human being, but that the Lord molded and formed the human being like a potter. The human was made not only from the clay, but from dust, for dust is nothing but dissolved earth. The Greeks have here *choun labon apo tes ges*, "taking dust from the earth." The human being did not receive [his body from] flesh, whether molded or compacted,[152] but [from] dust, lest he be excessively proud before the Creator.

Breathed into.) That is, he gave man life. The Hebrews expound this so that it should be understood that God made that human body in such a way that it should live. But I prefer here to imitate the Greeks who, listening carefully to what was said about the other animals, think that the human was made more nobly. And Paul in 1 Corinthians 11 has surely alluded to this. Nor can we deny that the human being is made much more nobly than the other animals. Not that the human

---

152 The question that lies behind the mention of "molded" or "compacted" flesh here seems to be that of the fittedness of the body of Adam for immortality. For the notion of "compacted flesh" see the Pseudo-Clementine Recognitions, Bk. 2 ch. 7, where the writer offers a history of Simon Magus (cf. Acts 8:9-24): "This Simon's father was Antonius, and his mother Rachel. By nation he is a Samaritan, from a village of the Gettones; by profession a magician yet exceedingly well trained in the Greek literature; desirous of glory, and boasting above all the human race, so that he wishes himself to be believed to be an exalted power, which is above God the Creator, and to be thought to be the Christ, and to be called the *Standing One*. And he uses this name as implying that he can never be dissolved, asserting that his flesh is so compacted by the power of his divinity, that it can endure to eternity. Hence, therefore, he is called the *Standing One*, as though he cannot fall by any corruption." English translation taken from the Ante-Nicene Fathers, vol. 8. Available at: http://www.ccel.org/ccel/schaff/anf08.vi.iii.iv.vii.html. Accessed 14 October 2012. Underlining mine. I thank John Thompson for pointing this out to me.

hominem multo nobiliorem esse conditum quam alia animantia: non quod sit homo de essentia diuina, sed est modus loquendi apud Hebraeos. Spiramus dei dono. Per Christum datur spiritus dei, qui nos uiuificat.

LECTIO

Multa quidem bona audiuimus, quae deus in hominem collocauit. Incomparabile, quod ad imaginem suam creauit illum, & in seipso requiem fecit, in deo inquam: ita ut quamuis omnia propter hominem condita sint, homo tamen non in creaturis, sed in ipso creatore beatitudinem & ueram quietem inueniet: & sic quidem internus noster homo beatus est. Quo[31r]niam autem conditi sumus ex corpore & anima, etiam deus uoluit corpori honestissimum locum & delicatissimum assignare, cui similis in uniuersa terra non inuenitur: & hunc locum admodum magnifice describit.

Plantauit quoque dominus deus hortum in Eden ab Oriente, & posuit illuc hominem quem finxerat.

Non est ut pueriliter imaginemur deum arripuisse ligonem, & instar hortulani plantasse hortulum quendam: tota enim ista regio Orientalis supra modum frugifera et amoena erat: unde etiam recte appellari potest, hortus uoluptatis. παράδεισος Graeca vox est, & nihil aliud sonat, quam hortus apud nos. Similiter apud Hebraeos עדן hortus dicitur. Quidam עדן nomen loci putant, & a uocabulo nomen regionem sortiri. Verisimilius est Mosen per hanc dictionem uoluptatem uelle insinuare, ut in eo loco esset homini magna uoluptas, & in quo meras corporis uoluptates inueniret. Apud Ezechielem prophetam & alios, hortus dei, et delitiarum hortus inuenimus, per quod sanus intellectus huius loci aperitur.

Plantauit.) Id est, singulari cura fecit hortum, quem deputauit in usum hominum. Quo iterum agnoscimus, quanti deus fecit hominem, quem creauerat, cui optima quaeque in utilitatem condita sunt. Porro de paradiso ad[31v]modum uariae opiniones fuerunt. Origenistae spiritualem fecerunt nobis paradisum, quia legunt arborem scientiae boni & mali, arborem uitae & mortis: & quoniam nulla arbor tantae

is from the divine essence, but this is a Hebraic way of speaking. We breathe by the gift of God. The Spirit of God is given through Christ, who brings us to life.

READING

We have heard about the many goods that God established for humankind. It is incomparable that he created him in his own image, and made him to rest in himself, I mean, in God. In that way, no matter how much all things were made for humankind, nevertheless the human being should find blessedness and true rest not in created things but in the Creator himself. And in this way indeed our inner human being is blessed. But because we have been created of both body and soul, God also wished to assign a most distinguished and luxurious place for the body, the likes of which was not to be found in the whole earth. And this place is now described most magnificently.

[8] And the Lord God also planted a garden in Eden from the east. And he placed there the human being he had made.

We should not childishly imagine God to have taken hold of a hoe and then like a gardener to have planted a garden. For that whole region of the east was an extraordinarily lovely and fertile area and thus can rightly be called a garden of delights. The Greek says simply *paradeisos,* "paradise," and that means nothing other than what we call a garden. Likewise with the Hebrews the garden is called "Eden." Some think that "Eden" is the name of the place, and that the name of the region is taken from the place. More likely Moses wants to insinuate through the word "delight" that in this place humankind enjoyed the greatest delight and discovered the pure delights of bodily existence. In the prophet Ezekiel and others we find both "garden of God" and "garden of delights," through which the proper understanding of the place is found.[153]

Planted.) That is, he made with remarkable care the garden that he assigned for the use of humankind. In this we recognize again how distinctively God made humankind, whom he had created and for whose advantage all the very best things were made. In the past there were many opinions regarding the paradise. The Origenists made for us a spiritual paradise, for they read about the tree of the knowledge

153 See Ezekiel 28:11-19.

efficaciae sit, ut homini tribuat uitam & scientiam, quae a deo proprie dantur, ideo putarunt hortum esse spiritualem, & ibi homini promissas spirituales delitias. Sed ut uana relinquenda est illa opinio. Fuerunt deinde alij, qui satis cognouerunt allegoriam non habere hic locum, & necesse esse, ut historiam certam habeamus, & hi locauerunt nobis paradisum in quibusdam locis sublimibus, & non obnoxijs hisce uicissitudinibus & uarietatibus, quae sub aëre contingunt: in qua sententia sunt Beda, Theophilus, & alij quidam. Neque hanc opinionem recipere licet, pugnat enim manifeste ipse textus: quia legimus de istis quatuor fluminibus, quorum ortus plerique cogniti sunt, & certum est per quas terras fluant. Proinde ex fluminibus ipsis licet animaduertere, ubinam terrarum ponendus sit paradisus. Igitur relictis illis opinionibus, certius quiddam amplectamur, nempe illum ipsum locum Assyriorum, uel supra Assyriam, in cuius circuitu huiuscemodi flumina uidentur, qui locus etiam prae alijs fertilis & amoenus est, & tunc quoque ab initio maiorem sortitus benedictionem propter hominem. Illum ipsum dico esse locum, de quo dominus loquitur, qui & paradisus [32r] est: etsi postea propter peccatum hominis suam quoque gloriam & benedictionem amisit aliqua ex parte, & terra incepit dare spinas et tribulos, ut postea sequitur, obnoxia maledictioni. Nam uidebimus hanc opinionem satis quadrare & non esse impiam, imo etiam plurimum fidei nostrae inseruire. Sic enim cognoscimus, quandiu deo recte seruierimus, etiam elementa & terram & omnia homini seruire: ubi autem inobedientes deo facti fuerimus, omnia quoque suum ministerium iusto dei iudicio nobis negare, id quod in posterioribus magis liquebit. Quidam multa annotarunt de paradiso, sed illa sufficiant. Videamus curam dei erga humanum genus.

Hortum Eden.) In horto omnes hominis sensus reficiuntur, oculi uiridarijs pascuntur, aures uolucrum cantu mulcentur, nares odoratu fragrantium herbarum opplentur, gustus quoque fructuum dulcedine magnam uoluptatem adfert. Sunt & molles loci, in quibus quiescere, & lassa membra refocillare licet. Proinde locum omnibus delitijs affluentem, paradisum recte appellabimus. Hinc etiam illud nomen translatione dictum arbitror, pro loco refrigerij & gaudij beatorum, quod anima latronis reducenda in paradisum fuerat. Nam non opus habet

of good and evil and the tree of life and death, and because there is no tree that provides life and knowledge (which are properly granted by God), they therefore concluded that the garden was spiritual, a place where spiritual delights were promised to the human race. But this opinion is to be discarded as vain.

Then there were others who well knew that this place is not an allegory, and that it is necessary that we have here reliable history. These men located paradise for us in a certain sublime place free from the changes and variations that occur in the weather today. Of this opinion are Bede, Theophilus, and certain others. Neither can this opinion be received, for it clearly contradicts the text itself. We read of four rivers, whose sources are known to many, as well as the lands through which they flow. Hence from the rivers themselves it may be estimated where paradise ought to be placed. Those other opinions aside, more likely we should embrace that one place of the Assyrians, or above Assyria, in whose borders the rivers are seen, and which is also a more fertile and lovely land than others, and which even from the very beginning was appointed as a land more blessed for human habitation. I say that this is the place of which the Lord spoke, which is also paradise, even if afterwards on account of human sin it also lost in some measure its original glory and blessedness, and the land began to bring forth thorns and thistles, as afterwards follows, from the guilt of the curse. For we will see that this opinion squares up sufficiently with the text and is not impious, indeed it even supports many elements of our faith. For thus we also recognize that the elements, the earth, and all things would have served humankind as long as we would have served God rightly. But when we had become disobedient to God, then all [these] things also denied to us their own services, [and that] by the just judgment of God, as will be made clearer in what follows. Some have said more about the paradise, but let that suffice here. Let us now consider God's care for the human race.

Garden of Eden.) In the garden all the human senses are invigorated; the eyes take in the trees, the ears are soothed by the singing of the birds, the nostrils are filled with the scent of fragrant herbs, and the sense of taste, too, produces great delight with the sweetness of fruits. There are also soft places in which to rest and relieve tired limbs. So this place overflowing with every delight we will rightly call paradise. Hence I also consider the name to have been said here by transference, i.e., for a place of rest and joy for the blessed, much as the soul of the

huiusmodi corporalium locorum solatijs pius, cui sola spiritualia suam saturitatem & delitias exhibent. Tametsi praeterea nequaquam negauerim in[32v]corporea loca inueniri. Voluit Christus polliceri latroni perfectum gaudium & insigne, ut esset secum in paradiso, ubi iam nullus amplius doloribus locus, ut supra hanc terram. Inde etiam facilius poterimus exponere, quod Paulus se raptum dicit quodammodo in tertium coelum.[31] Neque satis aptum corporalia illa transferre in alium locum. Quandoquidem homo sic conditus, quantum ad corpus attinebat, decebat ut honestior illi esset habitatio.

Oriente.) Alij ab initio habent, sed malim ab Oriente dici, ut scriptura loquitur, respiciens ad Hierusalem. Aliqui putant in agro Damasceno, uel in terra promissionis Adam conditum, deinde in aliam regionem translatum, quae paradisus dicta: sed relinquo illa tanquam incerta.

Et fecit germinare dominus deus de humo omnem arborem, quae concupiscibilis erat uisui, & commoda in cibum, & arbor uitae erat in medio horti, atque arbor scientiae boni & mali.

Hic plane uidetis, quare Paradisus hortus uoluptatis dicatur. Erant omnigenae arbores illic plantatae, aspectu iucundissimae, & fructus esui suaues, & gratissimi saporis, et haec seruiunt humanis corporibus. Adiungit:

Arbor uitae.) Hoc est, in hoc horto uolebat deus ho[33r]minem etiam probare, ut postea audietis, an agnosceret deum conditorem suum. Veteres interpretati sunt, quod iuxta illam arborem homo scientiam boni & mali acceperit, quia ibi aperti sunt oculi eius post peccatum, & sic ab euentu arborem illud nomen sortitum esse: non quod arbor per se possit scientiam boni & mali praestare. Sic legimus aquas

---

31 A marginal notation here refers the reader to II Cor. 12[:2].

thief [on the cross] was about to be led into paradise.[154] The upright man does not need for comfort this kind of corporeal space, for to him spiritual things alone produce his fulfillment and delights. Moreover I would in no way deny that immaterial places are to be found. Christ willed that perfect joy and honor be promised to the thief so that he should be with him in paradise, a place where even now there are no more sorrows, as above this earth. Whence we are able to expound even more easily what Paul says about himself, that he was somehow lifted up to the third heaven. Nor are those physical things suitable to be carried over into another place. But since humankind has been so created, it is fitting that, with respect to the body, there should be a more honorable dwelling place for it.

From the east.) Others have "from the beginning," but I prefer to say "from the east," as the Scripture says with respect to Jerusalem. Some think Adam was created in a field near Damascus, or in the promised land, and then carried into another region that is called paradise.[155] But I leave these opinions as uncertain.

[9] **And the Lord God made every tree to sprout forth from the ground, which was desirable in appearance and agreeable for food; and the tree of life was in the middle of the garden, as well as the tree of the knowledge of good and evil.**

Here you see plainly why the paradise would be called a garden of delights. Trees of every kind were planted there, most agreeable in appearance, and pleasant fruits for food with the most pleasing taste, and all these for the sake of the human body. The text adds:

Tree of life.) That is, in this garden God wished also to test humankind, as you will afterwards hear, to see whether they would acknowledge God as their creator. The ancients have explained that at that tree humankind received the knowledge of good and evil, because there their eyes were opened after sin, so that the name for the tree was chosen from the event, not that the tree itself could provide the knowledge of good and evil. We understand in the same way the "water of contradiction," because in that place the Jewish people were reproached

154 See Luke 23:43. The paradise mentioned in Luke is thus brought to bear on the question of the meaning of paradise in Genesis 2.

155 This is the opinion of a.o. Peter Comestor, *Historia Scholastica* (ed. J. P. Migne, *Patrologia Latina*, 198: 1007A).

contradictionis, quia ibi populus Iudaeorum obiurgati fuerunt Mosen & Aaron. Item fons iuramenti, non quod fons iuruerit, sed quod ibi iuratum sit. Et similia multa loca in scripturis obuia sunt diligenti lectori. Sic eandem ob rationem uolunt hanc arborem dictam esse, boni & mali scientiae arborem. Deus praeceptum posuit, ut mox patebit, ne homo comederet de illa arbore. Vere fuit arbor, sed non habebat huiusmodi efficaciam per se, tametsi una eademque consideratione fructus illius poterant uideri. Theodoretus cum hunc locum explanat, similem locutionem esse dicit de baptismo, quod per aquam regeneremur: non quod aqua illa per se sit maioris efficaciae, quam alia aqua, sed quia iuxta hanc aquam regeneramur dato spiritu sancto. Eadem locutio de coena dominica est, & corpus dominicum appellamus. Sic quoque arborem uitae intelligimus, non quod arbor uiuificare possit, quod proprium diuini spiritus est. Si caro non uiuificat, caro inquam Christi, seposita diuinitate, sed spiritus est qui ui[33v]uificat, multo minus nec ulla arbor. Erat ista insignum posita, ut si quidem homo obediens inuentus fuisse, abstinuissetque a ligno uetito, propter obedientiam suam potuisset comedere de arbore uitae, et sic diuino munere immortalis fieri. Iam autem deus sic ordinauit hominem, ut haberet unicum magistrum, cui omnino adhaerere debebat, nequaquam fidens suae rationi: neque in hisce rebus aliquid tentare debuit, nam hoc, ut audietis, homini potissimum est a deo praeceptum. Et sic etiam ab initio uidemus, ut consistat uera iustitia, nempe ex fide, ut credamus uerbo dei, neque sectemur nostrae infirmitatis somnia: nam hinc omne malum processit. Et illa principio describit antequam mandata

by Moses and Aaron.[156] Another example: "oath spring," not because the spring would make an oath, but because in that place he made an oath.[157] And there are many similar places in the Scripture that are obvious to the diligent reader. For the same reason they want this tree to be called the tree of the knowledge of good and evil. God put in place a command, as will be made clear below, that humankind should not eat from that tree. It truly was a tree, but it did not have within itself that kind of power, even if by one and the same consideration its fruit was visible. Theodoret explains that with this text what is said here is like what is said concerning baptism, i.e., that we should be reborn: not that the water itself is somehow more efficacious than other water, but that within this water we are reborn by the giving of the Holy Spirit. The same manner of speech is used of the Lord's Supper, when we call it the body of the Lord. So also we understand the tree of life, not that the tree itself was able to vivify, for that ability belongs to the divine Spirit alone. If the flesh does not vivify—even the flesh of Christ apart from the divinity—but only the Spirit, then how much less some tree?[158] That tree was set up as a sign that if humankind had been found obedient and had refrained from the forbidden tree, on account of their obedience they would have been able to eat of the tree of life and thus by a divine gift to have become immortal. For God had already ordained that the human being should have only one teacher to whom he should adhere in all things, and that he should neither trust in his own reason nor put God to the test in these matters, for this, as you will hear below, was most firmly commanded to the human being by God.[159] Thus we see how even from the very beginning true righteousness is established, namely by faith, in order that we might believe the word of God and thus not follow the idle dreams of our weak nature, for from this source every evil proceeds. And he describes those things in the beginning, before he gives the commandments. For

---

156 See Numbers 20:13.

157 Gen. 21:30-31. The Hebrew for "oath spring" is Beersheba, a reference to the place where Abraham and Abimelech made a solemn agreement respecting Abraham's sole right to the use of a well he had dug there.

158 Cf. John 6:63. Oecolampadius's insistence that the tree in itself did not have the power to vivify parallels his insistence on a spiritual understanding of the Lord's Supper.

159 Cf. Mt. 23:8.

ponat. Nihil autem omnino omittere uoluit deus, quod uel ad fertilitatem, uel ad uoluptatem loci pertineret. Ideo sequitur:

Et fluuius egrediebatur de Eden ad irrigandum hortum, & inde diuidebatur, & erat in quatuor capita. Nomen unius Pison, ipse est qui circuit totam terram Hauilah, ubi est aurum. Et aurum terrae illius est bonum: est quoque ibi bdellium & lapis Onychinus. Nomen uero fluuij secundi Gihon: ipse est qui circuit totam terram Aethiopie. Porro nomen fluuij tertij Hidaekel, [34r] & hic uadit ad orientalem plagam Assyriae: & quartus fluuius est Euphrates.

Dicit quatuor fuisse flumina praecipua in paradiso, Gangen, Nilum, Tigrim & Euphratem: quorum capita trium noscuntur, de Nilo dubitatio fuit. Si autem consulueris historicos de Nilo, quamuis incerta sit eius origo, & bene expenderitis quid scribant, uidebitis & eius ortum. Nam certum aduersas origines habere haec flumina, Nilus enim a meridie mare mediterraneum influit, Tigris a Septentrione, Ganges ab Oriente properat in mare. Inspice tabellam, & uidebis quem locum nobis scriptura commendet: nam quandoquidem ista flumina notiora sunt etiam alioqui in scripturis, tametsi quidam uariant inter Pison et Gihon, malui nostros sequi. Neque me impedit siue Troglodytarum, siue Arabiae felicis regionem, ad quam properat Ganges, influat: nihil omnino id adimet nostrae sententiae. Inuenimus etiam Nilum transire terram Aethiopiae, antequam per cataphracta, quae uocantur καταδōπα,[32] defluat in Aegyptum.

32 This appears to be a misprint of the Greek word καταφρακτοὶ.

God wanted to omit nothing at all that pertains either to the fruitfulness or to the delight of that place. And so it follows:

[10] And a river used to flow down through Eden for irrigating the garden, from whence it was divided into four headwaters. [11] The name of the first was Pison, and it went through the whole land of Havila, where there is gold. [12] The gold of this land is good, and there is also bdellium and onyx. [13] The name of the second river is Gihon, which is the one that runs through the whole land of Ethiopia. [14] The name of the third is Hidaekel, which goes to the eastern part of Assyria. And the fourth river is the Euphrates.

It says that there were four main rivers in paradise: the Ganges, the Nile, the Tigris, and the Euphrates. The headwaters of three of these are known, but that of the Nile is uncertain. If you consult the historians concerning the Nile, however uncertain its origin may be, and if you carefully consider what they write, you will also see where it comes from. For it is sure that these rivers come from opposite origins, just as the Nile flows from the south into the Mediterranean sea, the Tigris from the north, and the Ganges from the east rushes into the sea. Check the map and you will see the place the Scriptures indicate to us, since these rivers are well known elsewhere in the Scriptures. Notwithstanding that some differ regarding the Pison and the Gihon, I prefer to follow our own authorities. Nor does it hinder me if it should flow into the region of the Troglodytes or "happy Arabia," toward which the Ganges rushes.[160] That in no way contradicts our opinion. For we learn that the Nile crosses the land of Ethiopia, until through the cataracts of the Nile river,[161] which are called *katadō-*

160 The *Antiquities* of Josephus (Bk. 1, ch. 15) describe the descendants of Abraham by his wife Keturah (see Gen. 25: 1-6) as inhabiting the land of the Troglodytes or Arabia the Happy.

161 Oecolampadius seems to have in mind the story of the man who, after the defeat of Antony by Augustus, served as the first Roman prefect of Alexandria, i.e., Caius Cornelius Gallus, and who later led his Roman army beyond the "cataracts" (waterfalls) of the Nile, near to the border of Ethiopia. Since the cataracts impeded ships from traveling any further up the Nile, they could be thought of as a kind of "armor" ("cataphract" = "armored soldier") protecting the river's upper reaches. In *The Wars of the Jews* (Bk. 4, ch. 10, para. 5), Josephus reports that the cataract of the Nile "cannot be sailed over," and explains that this is considered one of the natural fortifications of Egypt, meaning that it is difficult to invade from the south.

Praeterea maximas esse diuitias in Arabia & India fere omnibus constat. Scribit Moses ibi aurum optimum esse, & Onychinum gemmam, quae speciem refert unguis: & paucis gemmis ibi commemoratis, ostendere uult terram istam locupletissimam esse & ditissimam. Sunt qui ex illis fluminibus uarias allegorias in[34v]uehere conantur. Alij quatuor Euangelistas, alij quatuor doctores Ecclesiae inde eliciunt: cauete ab illis nugis. Multo tutuis est inde discere, deum bene uoluisse homini, & huius mundi opes dedisse, ut fruamur illis in gloriam eius. Exploditur etiam hic haeresis illorum, qui bonas dei creaturas infamant, & qui iustitiam ab externis aestimant, cum uera iustitia intra nos sit. Ego contentus sum historia ipsa, quandoquidem benignitatem dei commendat. Gihon flumen praecipitat seipsum & circuit terram Aegypti. Tertium flumem Hideckel, & apud Graecos & Latinos Tigris uocatur, a uelocitate & rapiditate nomen habens, supra Assyrios fluit. Etiam Mesopotamia nomen habet, quod sit media inter duo flumina, quae fluunt inter Assyriam &c. Fluuius quartus est Euphrates. Ita omnibus modis latitudo istius terrae nobis describitur, ne putemus paruum esse locum, in quem deus Adam posuit. Et terra ista, quam dominus homini destinauerat, fuit frugifera omnino. Euphrates sicut Nilus inundat. Parum cedit Assyria fertilitate Aegypto.

Tulit itaque dominus deus ipsum Adam & posuit eum in hortem Eden, ut coleret & custodiret ipsum.

Initio noluit deus hominem esse otiosum, quod bene hic obseruandum est. Hebraicum עבד magis perti[35r]net ad culturam agri, & ad operationem, quam ad inhabitationem: quamuis Latini sic loquantur, & colere pro inhabitare accipiant. Omnino homo oblectaturus erat sese plurimum, et potuisset, si perstitisset in innocentia sua.

pa, it reaches Egypt. Besides, it is agreed by almost everyone that the greatest riches are found in Arabia and India. Moses writes that the best gold is there, and the onyx gem, which bears the appearance of a claw,[162] and you recall other lesser stones there, for he wishes to show that that land was most wealthy and productive. There are some who try to bring in different allegories for these rivers. Some bring forth the four evangelists, others the four doctors of the Church.[163] Avoid such trifles. It is much safer just to know that God wished humankind well, and that he gave all the riches of this world in order that we might enjoy them to his glory. Here also is disproven the heretical opinion of those who defame the good creations of God, those who judge righteousness by externals, even when true righteousness is within us. I myself am content with the history, seeing that it commends God's benevolence. The river Gihon hurries itself and goes around the land of Egypt. The third river, the Hidaekel, which is called the Tigris by both the Greeks and the Latins on account of its fierce velocity, runs above the Assyrians. Also, Mesopotamia has its name because it sits between two rivers that flow between Assyria, and so on. The fourth river is the Euphrates. Thus in so many ways the expansiveness of that land is described to us, lest we think that it was a small place into which God set Adam. And that land, which the Lord had prepared for humankind, was altogether fertile. Like the Nile, the Euphrates also floods. Not at all did Assyria yield to Egypt in fertility.

[15] **And so the Lord God took Adam himself and placed him in the garden of Eden, in order that he might cultivate and care for it.**

In the beginning God did not wish that the human being should be idle, which ought to be well noted in this place. The Hebrew word *abad* pertains primarily to the tilling of a field as well to the labor, more than to dwelling in a place, even though the Latins speak so that they use "to cultivate" for "to dwell." The human being was going to delight completely in everything, and he would have been able to do so if he had stood firm in his innocence.

162 The reference here is obscure, but Oecolampadius seems to have in mind the upper shell of a certain sea snail, which was thought to resemble a claw. On the other hand, it may refer to an onyx fern whose leaves resemble a claw while its color resembles the onyx stone.

163 I.e., Saints Ambrose, Augustine of Hippo, Jerome, and Gregory the Great.

Custodiret.) Id est, ut seipsum seruaret custodiendo, ne amitteret tales a deo sibi concessas diuitias. Multae felicitates etiam nobis sunt promissae, quas Christus reddidit sua praesentia. Quemadmodum in Adam nulla solicitudo de rebus futuris erat, ita & nos ubi regenerati per Christum fuerimus, exuemus etiam istam sollicitudinem, & proijciemus in deum spem nostram. Nobis etiam grauissima crux leuis erit per Christum. Erat igitur Adam felix, & poterat in ea felicitate perpetuo manere. Item uoluit deus eum laborare aliquid, ne ociosus esset, sed sine ulla molestia & cura. Nunc labor nobis maledictio est. Adam ut dominus delectatur in horti delitijs, & ita dominus est totius mundi: per hoc enim omnibus modis excitatur homo ad agnoscendam domini beneficentiam. Deinde sequitur, quod praeceptum dominus homini dederit, ex quo discimus quid faciat hominem iustum & iniustum, de quare proximus fusius dicamus.

Praecepitque dominus deus ipsi Adam dicens: De omni ligno horti comedendo comedes. [35v] De arbore uero scientiae boni & mali, nequaquam comedes ex illa: alioquin quacunque die comederis ex ea, moriendo morieris.

LECTIO

Quaerunt hic quidam, cum deus praescierit Adam peccaturum, & expellendum ex paradiso, quare nam illum introduxerit, quare etiam ei praeceptum dederit, quem sciuerat praeuericaturum. Atqui multo tutius foret ab huiusmodi uanis quaestionibus abstinere, quam diuinae maiestati oblatrare. Neque enim est figmenti dicere figulo, quare sic me fecisti? Deus Adae in initio dedit arbitrij libertatem: hoc enim fatentur catholici omnes. In initio inquam dedit, illud tamen non praeiudicat, quin deus operetur omnia in omnibus, a quo ueluti perenni

That he might care.) That is, in order that he himself might preserve it by his care, lest he lose the great riches God had granted to him. Many blessings are also promised to us, which Christ restored by his presence. In the same way that Adam had no anxiety over future things, so also we, when we have been regenerated through Christ, leave aside even this care and place our hope in God. For us even the heaviest cross will be light through Christ.[164] Thus Adam was happy, and he was able to abide perpetually in that happiness. God also wanted him to work at something, lest he should be idle, but without any care or trouble. Now, however, labor is for us a curse. Adam as a lord takes pleasure in the garden of delights, and in the same way he is lord over the whole world. For through this by every means the human being is aroused to acknowledge the beneficence of the Lord. From that it follows that the Lord gave to humankind the precept by which we learn what makes a person just or unjust, about which we next shall speak more fully.

[16] And the Lord God commanded Adam himself saying: "From every tree of the garden for eating you shall eat. [17] But from the tree of the knowledge of good and evil you shall not eat, for in whatever day you shall have eaten from it, in death you will die."165

READING

Since God knew that Adam would sin and be driven out of the garden, some seek here to know why he would have brought him in, and why he even gave a command to him whom he knew would become a transgressor. However, it would be much safer to refrain from such vain questions, rather than to bark out against the divine majesty. It is not for the pot to say to the potter, "why did you make me this way?"[166] In the beginning God gave to Adam freedom of choice; this indeed all Catholics[167] confess. I say he gave it in the beginning, not that he

164 Cf. Mt. 11:30.

165 The phrases "eating you shall eat" and "in death you will die" are an attempt to render in Latin the sense of the Hebrew text. Alternatively, one could translate these as "you shall <u>surely</u> eat" or "you shall <u>surely</u> die."

166 See Romans 9:20; cf. Isaiah 29:16.

167 I.e., "all Christians."

fonte omnia bona fluunt. Illam libertatem homini dedit deus, quod certe multo honestius homini erat, quam si absque omni lege egisset, & quasi absque ratione coactus fuisset ad facienda bona: sic neque uirtus declarata in Adam fuisset, neque ignauia eius manifestata. Porro illius erat, donis a deo tam liberaliter concessis bene uti. Quod peccauit, sua negligentia & ignauia peccauit. Quod autem tantis donis praeditus fuit, & tanta beneficia accepit, diuinae beneuolentiae fuit. Adijcere hoc possumus, quod deus uoluit Adam sibijpsi notiorem redde[36r]re, ut cognosceret quidnam deo deberet, & ut etiam suam fragilitatem agnosceret. Et ideo eius exemplo omnes monemur, licet firmissime stemus, tamen in timore domini ambulemus, & prouideamus ne labamur, iuxta Pauli dictum: Qui stat uideat ne cadat.

Praecepit.) Quia dominus erat, ideo recte praecipiebat creaturae suae. Praecipiebat autem deus rem minime onerosam: praeterea innumera bona concedebat, & ex illis plurimis quendam exiguum censum poscebat, quo agnosceretur esse dominus.

De omni arbore.) Hoc est, magna libertate poteris comedere, et absque periculo, quoties libuerit. Hic uidetis quomodo deus multa bona primo homini concedit. Vult autem etiam indicare dominium suum, ideo praeceptum leuissimum adiungit, quod homo seruare debuisset.

De arbore scientiae.) Audistis unde arbor nomen hoc accepit. Quemadmodum si quis dominus dedisset ciuitati aliquae maxima priuilegia, in signum tamen peteret quotannis non nisi assem, quo agnoscerent ipsum esse dominum: profecto non posset huiusmodi ciuitas conqueri de domino, qui plenam libertatem concesserat, & multa bona, quique nihil repeteret aliud, quam unicum assem. Ita & deus

predestined him,[168] but that God works all things in all, from which all good things flow as if from a perennial spring.[169] God gave that freedom to the man, which certainly was more honorable for him than if he had been driven on apart from every law, as if, that is, he had been compelled to do the good without reason. If that were so then neither would Adam's virtue have been made known, nor would his worthlessness have been brought to light. Again, it was his task to use well the gifts God had so freely granted. In so far as he sinned, he sinned by his own negligence and fault. But insofar as he had been endowed with such great gifts and received such great benefits, it was of God's generosity. We can add this, that God wanted Adam to render himself more esteemed, so that he would know what he owed to God, and that he would also acknowledge his own fragility. And we are therefore warned by his example, that although we ought to stand most firmly, nonetheless let us walk in the fear of the Lord and take care lest we fall, just as Paul said: "Whoever is standing, let him watch lest he fall."[170]

Commanded.) Because he was the Lord, therefore he properly commanded his own creature. However, God commanded something not at all burdensome. After he had granted innumerable goods, out of those many things he asked only for a certain very small tribute, by which Adam should acknowledge that he is Lord.

From every tree.) That is, you will be able to eat with great freedom, and with no danger, and whenever you please. Here you see how God granted many good things to the first man. But he also wished to make clear his own dominion, and so he added the very easiest command, which the man ought to have kept.

From the tree of knowledge.) You have heard how the tree got this name. It is just as if a lord had given some privileges to a certain city, and in return had asked nothing more than a penny each year by which the citizens might acknowledge that he is their lord, so that in this way the city could make no complaint against their lord, since he had granted them complete liberty and many good things and required

168 I.e., God did not predestine Adam to fall.

169 Cf. Jas. 1:17.

170 The marginal notation here refers the reader to Gal. 6. However, Oecolampadius seems to be referring to I Corinthians 10:12, which reads in the Vulgate text: "itaque qui se existimat stare videat ne cadat." Similar ideas are found, however, in Gal. 6. One wonders whether the mistake here belongs to Oecolampadius or to the compilers of the published text.

minimum praeceptum Adae dederat, imo & uires faciendi subministrauerat, si quidem homo uoluisset seruare hoc praeceptum, & ita [36v] etiam immortalitatem assecutus fuisset. Adiungit autem maximum periculum, quod si non uelit id honoris deo dare, saltem periculo suo monitus obediens sit.

Quacunque die.) Hoc est, certissime moriturus es, & nihil certius morte tua. Obijciunt hic, cum Adam nongentos & triginta annos attigerit, quomodo illo ipso die mortuus sit? Respondeo: Est mors corporis, & est mors animae. Quantum ad animan pertinebat, mortuus. Porro quod ad corpus attinet, certissimus erat se moriturum. Nam licet supputes nongentos & triginta annos, & illos confers cum immortalitate, uix eos pro momento habiturus es. Praeterea quando sententia mortis iam pronunciata est, in re is ab omnibus mortuus esse dicitur, etsi adhuc uiuat. Ita etiam certissimum erat Adam, quo ad corpus, mortem nequaquam euasurum. Praeterea dum hic legimus, praecepit de omni ligno &c. uult dicere: Ex omnibus fructibus quos tibi concedo audacter comede, & his ad cognitionem mei excitandus es, uel excitari debes, ut gratus mihi sis, & cognoscas quam tibi sit pernitiosum, si uolueris iuxta rationem tuam ambulare, & tuis uiribus niti. Nam sic edere de ligno scientiae boni & mali, est uelle niti propria ratione, & non credere deo. Statim hic uidemus iustificationem Adae, qualem nam habuerit, & sic nequaquam iustificabimus illum suis operibus. Iustus a deo [37r] conditus est, cum iam nullum opus bonum fecisset. Quid facere poterat cum nondum erat? Porro lapsum uidemus ipsi tribui. Vt autem iustificetur, ex sequenti capite satis clare patebit: sola enim diuina benignitate iustificationem concedi uidebimus.

Et rursum dixit dominus deus: Non est bonum ut sit Adam solus: faciam illi adiutorium quod sit coram eo.[33]

33 Cf. the wording in the Glossa Ordinaria, with the verb in the plural: "Dixit quoque dominus deus: Non est bonum esse hominem solum.

nothing more in return than a single penny. So also God gave to Adam the smallest command, he even furnished the power for doing it; and if the human being had wished to keep this command he would even have gained immortality. God added a great danger as well, so that if Adam did not want to give that honor to God, then at least he would be obedient when he had been warned of the danger.

In whatever day.) That is, you shall most certainly die; nothing is more certain than your death. Some object here that since Adam lived for 930 years, how could he have died on that very day? I answer: there is the death of the body, and the death of the soul. In so far as it pertained to the soul, he died. Moreover, even in what pertains to the body, he was most certain to die. Take 930 years and compare that to immortality and you have hardly a moment. Besides, even now when a death sentence has been pronounced, in fact he is said by everyone to be dead, even while he still lives. So too was it most certain that Adam, with respect to his body, was by no means going to evade death. Afterwards, when we read here that he commanded concerning every tree, and so on, he means to say, "You may eat without fear of every fruit I give to you; by these you ought to be stirred up to recognize me, to give me thanks, and to realize how destructive it will be for you if you wish to walk according to your own wisdom and depend on your own strength." For to eat from the tree of the knowledge of good and evil is to wish to depend on your own reason, and not to trust in God. Immediately here we consider the justification of Adam, and what its character was, for instance, and thus we will never justify him by his works. He was created righteous by God, since he had done no good work yet. What was he able to do when he did not yet exist? Again we see that the fall is assigned to Adam himself. But how he is justified will be made sufficiently clear from the following chapter, where we will see that justification is granted by divine benevolence alone.[171]

[18] Once again the Lord God spoke: "It is not good that Adam should be alone: I will make a helper for him that will be before him."

---

171 Oecolampadius insists here that Adam was created righteous. Because Adam was so made, his righteousness did not depend on later good works for its establishment, that is to say, the first human being was justified before God by grace ("divine benevolence") alone.

Quamuis superiori capite audistis deum masculum & foeminam fecisse, tamen hic clarius dicit conditionem mulieris. Priora generaliter proposita fuerunt &c. Vir non est lapsus, neque praeuaricatus praeceptum dei, nisi per mulierem seductus. Volens igitur deus ostendere, quomodo Adam seductus sit, tempestiue ponit, quomodo mulier condita sit: ne quis obstreperet, Poterat deus non condidisse mulierem, quae cessura esset in tantam pernitiem homini. Hoc igitur praeoccupat, & ostendit illam diuino consilio formatam, & admodum utilem Adae ad conseruationem humani generis, & alias ob causas, &c.

Adam solus.) Omnia alia animantia condita erant cum suis comparibus, nempe mares & foeminae: sed hominem principio deus solum condidit, cui postea etiam aedificauit mulierem, quo magis admiraremur illud opificium, & maior constaret amicitia inter uirum & [37v] uxorem. Id licebit etiam ratione formationis cognoscere. Quidam infamantes coniugum, manifeste blasphemant contra spiritum sanctum, audentes malum pronunciare & dicere, quod deus bonum testatus est. Ecce Eua principio condita, non fuit inferior Adam aliqua ex parte: nam et ipsa diuino spiritu praedita fuit, etiam condita ad imaginem dei. Proinde non erat mala creatura dei, quae in utilitatem uiri condita. Legimus apud Paulum 1. Cor. 7. Bonum est homini mulierem non tangere. Nomen autem BONI nonnunquam commoditatem sonat: estque sententia: Admodum commodum esset homini, si molestia mulierum carere possit, si nullam omnino duceret. Sed quando Eua condita in paradiso, ab initio suae conditionis recta condita est, ut

---

Faciamus ei adiutorium simile sibi." Emphasis added. See, *Biblia Latina cum Glossa Ordinaria*, Facsimile Reprint of the Editio Princeps Adolph Rusch of Strassburg 1480/81, ed. Karlfried Froehlich and Margaret T. Gibson, (Brepols–Turnhout, 1992). p. 23.

As you have heard in the above chapter, God made male and female. Nevertheless here it speaks more clearly about the creation of the woman, which things were set down more generally before. The man would not have fallen, nor would he have transgressed against the command of God, except he was seduced through the woman.[172] God wanted to show how Adam was seduced, and so he set forth at just the right time how the woman was made, lest anyone should object that God should not have created the woman because she made way for such destruction in humankind. He anticipates this and shows that she was formed by the divine counsel, and how she was useful to Adam for the preservation of the human race, and for other reasons, etc.

Adam alone.) All other animals were created with their own mates, namely, males and females. But God made the man alone in the beginning, for whom he later built the woman, on account of which we should more greatly admire the creator and better appreciate the friendship between husband and wife. One may also recognize the reason for her formation. Some defame marriage, clearly blaspheming against the Holy Spirit, daring to pronounce and call evil what God has testified is good. Behold, Eve was created in the beginning and was not in any way inferior to Adam,[173] for she too had been given the divine Spirit and also made in the image of God. Hence, she who had been made for the advantage of the man was not an evil creature of God. We read with Paul in I Cor. 7, "It is good for a man not to touch a woman." The word "good," however, sometimes means "useful." This is therefore the meaning: It would be extremely useful for a man if he could be without the trouble of women, if he were not even thinking about a woman at all. But when Eve was created in paradise, from the very beginning of her creation she was made upright so that she

---

172 The question of Adam's "seduction" is made more difficult by what Paul says in I Timothy 2:14. Note Oecolampadius's comments below, in chapter 3.

173 This is an allusion to the story of Eve's creation out of Adam's rib, recounted below. Oecolampadius apparently wants to reject any insinuation that this manner of creation made her Adam's inferior, an argument that might be made by the defamers of woman and marriage mentioned above. At the same time, Oecolampadius clearly also considers the woman the "weaker part" of the primal couple. See below, chapter 3. I read here the dative "Adae" for "Adam."

minime molestia esset uiro. Nam degenerando quando facta est deterior, excidit a sua nobilitate.

Sit coram eo.) Id est, ut habeat etiam multam commoditatem ex muliere, ad procreandam prolem. Chrysostomus dicit: Cum uir grauioribus curis occupatur, sit mulier ei solatio. Singula quae hic acta sunt, si quis recte expenderit, inueniet multa utilia, quae in honorem coniugij dicta sunt. Deus author est coniugij. Eua in paradiso condita est, Adam extra paradisum. Deus Euam ad Adam adduxit, & principio Adam spiritu prophetico futura mysteria cognouit, ut textus habet. [38r] Non debebat autem deus propter negligentiam Euae, multa alia bona omittere. Ambrosius egregia in hunc locum de bono uniuersitatis non obmittendo, edisserit. Et hoc plane non decebat conditorem omnipotentem, ut in opere suo impediretur per negligentiam unius, ut quae condenda erant posthaberet. Decebat autem Adam principio ut cognosceret secum quam necessaria esset ipsi uxor, & quam utilitatem esset ei allatura.

Itaque formauit dominus deus de humo omnem bestiam agri, & omne uolatile coeli, adduxitque ad ipsum hominem, ut uideret, quomodo appelaret illud: omne enim quod ipse homo uocabat in anima uiuente, illud nomen eius erat.

Causa quare deus adduci curauit animantia ad Adam, haec fuit, ut uideret in omni genere hunc esse ordinem dei, ut per coniugia species conseruarentur, & sic quoque humanum genus multiplicari debere per mulierem, uel adiutorio mulieris multiplicandum. Quamuis interim etiam aliam dignitatem Adae cognoscere licet. Supra dixit Moses, quando conditus sit Adam, ut dominaretur piscibus & uolucribus coeli &c. iam re ipsa declaratur esse dominus. Nam cum omnia ista adducuntur ad Adam, quibus & nomina imponit, certe per hoc Adam cognoscitur omnium esse dominus. Ita Nabucho[38v]donosor cum transtulisset tres pueros in Babel, mutauit eorum nomina, & sic mutatis nominibus in suam gentem transibant, ut ipse dominus illorum

should be the least trouble to the man. For when by falling she was made weak, she lost her nobility.

That will be before him.) That is, that he should have great usefulness through the woman, for the procreation of offspring. Chrysostom says: When a man is weighed down by heavy cares, a wife can be a comfort to him. If one thinks rightly about the particular things that are done here, he will see how many advantages are mentioned in honor of marriage. God is the author of marriage. Eve was made in paradise, Adam outside. God brought Eve to Adam, and in the beginning Adam by the prophetic Spirit recognized a future mystery, as the text says.[174] God was not obliged, however, on account of the [later] negligence of Eve to omit [mention of] her many other good qualities. Ambrose in this place does not omit these excellences but remarks fully on the good of the whole arrangement. Plainly it was not fitting that the omnipotent creator should be impeded in his own work by the negligence of the one, or that the things that were to be made should be esteemed any less. It was fitting, however, that in the beginning Adam should acknowledge how necessary for himself a wife would be, and how she would provide him with assistance.

[19] Therefore the Lord God formed from the earth every beast of the field and every bird of heaven, and he brought them to the man himself in order to see what he would call them. And whatever Adam called each living creature that was its name.

The reason why God took care that the animals be led before Adam was so that he would see in every kind that this was the order of God, that through sexual mating the species would be preserved, and so also that the human race ought to be increased through the woman, that is, it was to be multiplied with the help of the woman. In the meantime one may learn another dignity of Adam. Above, Moses said when Adam was made that he should rule over the fish and birds of the air and so on, and by that very fact he was declared to be lord. For all those were brought to Adam, on which he also imposed names, and by this it is surely recognized that Adam is lord of all. Thus when Nebuchadnezzar brought the three young men into Babylon he changed their names, and by those changed names they were thus transferred into his own nation, so that he himself should

174 Eph. 5:31-2.

esse cognosceretur. Sic hoc loco Adae dominium supra omnes creaturas comprobatur. Insinuatur etiam hic quanta cum securitate tunc temporis uixerit Adam: nam non laedebant illum bestiae, alioqui natura feroces.

Adduxit.) Cum legimus Adduxit, non intelligimus deum crasso quodam modo coëgisse animalia uel aues, sed diuina ipsa uirtus sic ordinauit, ut animalia ista sponte accederent ad Adam, & uolucres coeli conspicuae fierent, & pisces qui in aquis erant adnatarent. Legimus etiam de Eua, quae adducta est uirtute dei sic ordinate, id est, accessit ad Adam. Neque hic opus est, ut ponamus quandam uisionem, quasi Adam uidisset ea, ut prophetae suas uisiones habuerunt.

Igitur uocauit ipse homo nomina cuique iumento & uolatili coeli, omnique bestiae agri: & pro homine non inuenit adiutorium quod esset coram eo.

Hic sub finem huius sententiae, habetis quare omnia alia praemissa sint, & quare aues & pisces &c. adduxerit. Videmus enim neque solum pro impositione nominum adducta esse, sed hac occasione uoluit deus, ut Adam ab initio antequam formaretur mulier, cognosce[39r]ret sibi opus muliere, quam maiori gratitudine in uxorem deberet recipere si illa contingeret. Habemus etiam hoc loco admonitionem non inutilem, sed necessariam, ut curemus ne ita temere coniugia fidelium conueniant rebus non antea praemeditatis, quare nam ducenda sit uxor &c.

Et fecit illabi dominus deus soporem in Adam, & obdormiuit, tulitque unam ex costis illius, et clausit carnem pro ea. Et aedificauit dominus deus costam, quam acceperat de homine in mulierem, & adduxit eam ad hominem illum.

Sic igitur deus formare vuluit Euam consortem uiri mulierem, ut esset arctissima consuetudo, & amicitia inter uirum & mulierem: proinde ex lateribus Adae assumpturus illam, immisit Adae prius soporem ut obdormiret. Quamuis potuisset deus etiam non immisso sopore omni facilitate eadem costam auferre ad Adam, sed noluit. Atqui hoc dei consilium erat, ut quodammodo labore quodam uideatur a uiro

be recognized as their lord.[175] Similarly in this place the dominion of Adam over all creatures is confirmed. Here likewise it is suggested with what security Adam lived at that time, for even the naturally ferocious beasts did not harm him.

Brought.) When we read the word "brought" we should not understand it crassly, as if God had gathered up all the animals and birds, but that the divine power itself ordained it so that the animals themselves spontaneously went up to Adam, the birds of the heavens came into full sight, and the fish in the seas were swimming by. We also read about Eve, that she was brought in thus by the ordained power of God, that is, introduced to Adam. Nor is there need to set this forth as some kind of vision, as if Adam had seen her as the prophets had their visions.

[20] So Adam himself gave names to each animal and bird of heaven and to every beast of the field. And for the man a helper was not found who would be before him.

Here at the end of this sentence you have the reason why all other things were done beforehand, and why the birds and fishes and so on were brought in. Indeed you see that they were summoned not only for the imposition of names, but that on this occasion God also wished that Adam from the beginning, and even before the woman had been formed, would know that she was made for him, and that he would know his own need for the woman, whom he ought to receive with greater gratitude if she should come to be. We have in this place an admonition not useless but necessary, so that we may take care lest the marriages of the faithful be arranged rashly, with matters not thought through beforehand, why a wife should be sought out, etc.

[21] And the Lord God made a sleep fall on Adam. And he fell asleep. And God took one of his ribs out of his side and closed up the flesh there. [22] And the Lord God built the rib he had taken from the man into a woman, and he brought her to the man.

Thus God wished to form the woman, Eve, to be the man's companion, so that there should be the most intimate closeness and friendship between the man and the woman. So he took her out of Adam's side, sending sleep on Adam beforehand. Of course, God could have with all ease done so without putting him to sleep, but he did not want to.

175 See Dan. 1:6-7.

abstractam esse mulierem, et ut iterum illa magis uiro commendaretur. Et ne quis horror uirum obrueret in principio conditionis, tali medio usus est dominus. Necesse est ut hic rationi nostrae ualedicamus, & historiam esse sinamus historiam: deo enim qui sic condidit omnia, hoc quoque facillimum erat, nempe [39v] auferre costam, & pro ea carnem apponere. Nam isto miraculo deus uoluit summam charitatem atque amicitiam nobis commendare, quam coniuges inter se seruare debent: denique docere ut unusquisque coniugem suam pro carne sua agnosceret. Habemus autem ex hoc loco & sequentibus magnum mysterium, quod Apostolus in epistola Ephesiorum capite 5. explanat. Sacramentum, inquit, magnum est, uerum ego loquor de Christo & ecclesia. Nam sicut uir uxorem amat, ita deus ecclesiam, quam suo sanguine redemit, etiam amat. Sic fere mysterium hoc in principio mundi explicatum est, quod Adam secundo mortuo in cruce, uel dormiente, de latere illius sumi ecclesia deberet, cum exiret sanguis & aqua. Certe his symbolis ecclesia congregata est. Christus ad hoc alludit cum dicit: Ego si exaltatus fuero a terra, omnes traham ad meipsum.[34] Porro ecclesia, quae tanto precio redempta est, iure grata esse debet sponso suo Christo, & illum intentius amare. Non auro neque argento redempta est, sed precioso sanguine Christi.

Adduxit.) Vt consideraret eam, quanta pulchritudine & decentia a deo condita esset, quamque congrua suis moribus, et apta suo ministerio esset. Illa etiam saepe repetit, quia hoc est magnum miraculum, ut esset virago, etsi aliud sonet uirago.[35] Nunc prophetiam Adae ponit, qua cognouit, quare mulier sic esset condita, & quam sit ar[40r]cta consuetudo inter mulierem et uirum, nempe ut reputari debeant pro una carne. Proxime illa fusius explicabo.

---

34 A marginal note here refers the reader to John 12[:32].

35 In the margin is the Hebrew word אשה (*ishshah*, woman).

Rather this was the counsel of God, so that it might appear that the woman was extracted from the man with some effort, so to speak, and so that, for her part, she would be commended to the man even more. The Lord made use of such means lest any sort of consternation overwhelm the man at the beginning of [her] fashioning. It is necessary here that we bid farewell to our reason and let the story be the story. For the God who made all things, it was most easy to remove a rib and put flesh upon it. By that miracle God wanted to commend to us the highest love and friendship, which the married ought to preserve between them, and finally to teach each one to acknowledge one's spouse as one's own flesh. We have in this place and the following one a great mystery, which the Apostle explains in Ephesians 5[:32]. "The mystery," he says, "is great, but I am speaking about Christ and the church. For just as a man loves his wife, so God also loves the church, which he redeemed by his own blood." This mystery at the beginning of the world has generally been explained like this: that when the second Adam was dead or "sleeping" on the cross, the church was destined to be drawn from his side when he shed blood and water.[176] Surely by these symbols the church has been gathered. Christ alludes to this when he says: "I, when I am lifted up from the earth, shall draw everyone to myself." Moreover the church which has been redeemed at such a price ought rightly to be grateful to Christ her own spouse and love him more intently. For she has been redeemed not by gold or silver, but by the precious blood of Christ.[177]

Brought.) That he should look at her, made by God with so much beauty and comeliness, and so suitable for his character and fit for his service. He repeats these things frequently, for this is a great miracle, that she should be "Virago," even if "Virago" means something else.[178] Now he sets out the prophecy of Adam, by which he knew why the woman had been made in this way, and how close is the intimacy between woman and man, to the extent that they should be considered one flesh. Next time I will explain all this more fully.

---

176 John 19:34.

177 An allusion to I Pet. 1:18-19.

178 This seems to be a recognition that the *uir* in *uirago* would normally mean "male" or "man." In the Vulgate translation, Jerome had tried to maintain the Hebrew pun *Ish – Issah*, by translating with the Latin *uir – uirago*. But *uirago* means "man-wife." Oecolampadius points out here that this is not really an accurate translation. See also his comments on p. 79.

LECTIO

Soporem missum in Adam, quidam parum aequi matrimonio, significare dixerunt, quod hi qui se iungunt matrimonio, nonnihil declinent a disciplina, & obseruantia uitae sublimioris & angelicae, & propterea consilium istud uocant soporem: in quorum sententia est Ambrosius. Verum si quis uerba quae sequuntur recte expenderit, imo etiam ea quae antecesserunt, uidebit animum Adae aliquo modo illustratum uberiori dei dono. Non enim talis sopor erat, qui eum a diuinis rebus contemplandis impediebat, sed qui carnalia compescebat, & sensum rerum abducentium a deo comprimebat. Praecesserat iam antea consilium uisis omnibus animantibus, & hoc ordinatione dei: unde cogitabat quid de se statuisset deus, et in hac cogitatione existens somnus missus est, & in somno prophetica gratia immissa. Praeterea in paradiso Adam, quando non peccarat, nihil tale ferendum erat, quale post lapsum: de ijs dico, quae ad concupiscentias carnis attinent. Haec autem dicta esse prophetico spiritu Apostolus testatur, & Christus ipse, qui deo uerba illa tribuit. Videmus etiam alios quosdam sanctos uiros propter coniugium diuino munere & prophetico spiritu non esse priuatos. Quis [40v] propius ad deum concessit, quam Moses ipse? Quis Davide magis illustratus fuit? ut taceam de Apostolis, qui in noua lege fuerunt. Itaque uideamus ultra primam omnium prophetiam illam, quam necesse erat non esse uulgarem: igitur interprete Paulo sonabit in Christum & ecclesiam, tametsi pulchre historia praestruatur. Sciatis etiam similia in alijs prophetijs euenire, ut dum quae iuxta historiam uera sunt, nihilominus etiam alia spiritus sanctus illic recondiderit. Quemadmodum plane est uerum serpentem aeneum fuisse exaltatum, & ualuisse sanare ab ictu eum qui illum aspexerat: nihilominus sub ea

READING

Some who have too little patience with marriage have said that the sleep sent upon Adam signifies that those who join themselves in marriage decline in some measure from the discipline and observance of a more sublime and angelic life. Therefore they call this counsel "sleep" which is the opinion, for example, of Ambrose. But if one weighs rightly the words that follow, in fact even the preceding ones, he will see that the soul of Adam is somehow an illustration for the more abundant gift of God. For it was not the kind of sleep that kept him from contemplating divine things but that held in check bodily things and prevented the sensation of anything that would lead [him] away from God. By this time the council where he had seen all the animals had preceded, and this by the ordination of God. Whence he knew what God was about to establish for him, and while in this thought, a sleep was sent, and in this sleep he was given prophetic grace. Besides, in paradise Adam, when he had not yet sinned, would not have considered what he would do after the fall. I am talking about those things that pertain to the concupiscence of the flesh. The Apostle however testifies that these things were spoken by the prophetic Spirit,[179] and Christ himself also assigns those words to God.[180] We also see other saintly men who were not deprived of the divine office and the prophetic spirit on account of marriage. Who was granted greater closeness to God than Moses himself? Who more illuminated than David? I pass over in silence the Apostles, who lived under the new law.[181] And so let us further consider that first prophecy of all, which was necessarily not a commonplace one. Therefore with Paul as interpreter, this text will be heard as pertaining to Christ and the church, even if the history was beautifully prepared beforehand. You should also know that similar things happened to the other prophets, so that while [they proclaimed] things that were true according to history, nevertheless the Holy Spirit also concealed other things within. In this same way it is true that a bronze serpent was lifted up, and was able to

179 I.e., in Eph. 5.

180 Mt. 19:4-6.

181 The interpretation here supports the practice, newly introduced by reformers like Oecolampadius, of clerical marriage. Moses, David, and presumably the apostles too had wives, Oecolampadius avers, but that did not prevent them from living in the closest intimacy with God.

historia Christus patefacit arcanum quoddam delituisse, nempe eos qui in Christum suspensum credituri essent, & oculis animi inspecturi, uitam aeternam habituros, quamuis a serpente, id est, diabolo, morsu letifero fuerint laesi. Proinde ne contemnamus eas allegorias, quas Apostoli interpretati sunt, etsi historia certa sit. His historia docet, primum placuisse deo Euam formari ex costa Adae.

Et ait homo ille, hac uice os de ossibus meis, & caro de carne mea, huic uocabitur uirago, eo quod de uiro sumpta sit ipsa.

Sic quidem nunc placuit deo, ut mulier hac ratione formetur, ex me sumatur, et ex latere meo. Posthac [41r] alia ratio erit, nempe ex coniugio prodituri sunt homines, id est pueri, & propterea istam uolo vocare אשה id est uiraginem. Etsi neque illius uocabuli proprietatem Latinus sermo satis explanat. Significat autem masculam & fortem uirginem. Graeci reliquerunt γυναῖκα. Ita iuxta historiam dignitatem mulieris auditis, quaenam illa, quia de uiro sumpta est. Porro quid futurum posthac sit, praedicit.

Propterea deseret uir patrem suum & matrem suam, & haerebit cum uxore sua, eruntque in carnem unam.

Id est, arctissimum erit inter illos coniugium & uinculum. Quamuis inter parentes & filios magna sit necessitudo, arctior tamen futura est inter coniuges: nam propter coniuges reliquendi etiam sunt parentes. Non quod illis iustus honor denegari debeat, id quod satis cauetur in sacris literis, per illud: Honora patrem tuum et matrem tuam, ut sis longaeuus super terram.[36] Sed sic relinquant parentes, ut propter

36 A marginal notation here refers the reader to Exodus 20[:12].

save anyone who was stricken but then looked to it.[182] Nevertheless, Christ brought to light that a secret meaning was hidden under that history, namely, those who would believe in Christ suspended [on the cross], when they had considered it with their mind's eye, would have eternal life, even though they had been wounded by the deadly bite of the serpent—that is, the devil. Therefore we should not scorn the allegories the Apostles have offered, even if the history is sure. By these things, the history teaches in the first place that it pleased God to have made Eve out of the side of Adam.

[23] And the man said, "This now is bone out of my bones, and flesh from my flesh; she will be called 'virago,' because she has been taken out of the man."

"In this way indeed it now pleased God that the woman was formed in this manner, obtained from me and drawn from my side."[183] Beyond this there will be another reason of course, namely that out of the conjugal relation human beings should be brought forth, children that is. Therefore I with to call her *ishshah,* "virago," even though the Latin term does not make sufficiently clear the properties of this word. It signifies both manliness and vigorous maidenhood. The Greeks leave it here as *gunaika* (woman).[184] Thus according to the historical account you have heard about the dignity of the woman, because she was taken out of the man. He now predicts what the future from then on should be.

[24] Therefore a man will leave his own father and mother and will cling to his wife, and they will become one flesh.

That is, there will be between them the closest conjunction and bond. While [the bond] between parents and children is greatly necessary, that between spouses should be much closer, and on account of their spouses they will even leave their parents. Not that proper honor should not be given to parents, which is stipulated sufficiently in the sacred letters: "Honor your father and mother that you may live long

---

182 Numbers 21:4-8; cf. John 3:14.

183 Oecolampadius here enters into Adam's mind, indicating what he was thinking.

184 I.e., the Greeks do not change this to a less obvious equivalent to the Hebrew original.

amorem parentum, coniugalem amorem non disperdant, quandoquidem humanum genus sic seruari debet. Sunt quidam qui interpretantur hunc uersum eo modo, & dicunt, iam mox ab initio excludi hunc gradum, ne parentes uel pueri cum parentibus rem habeant, & quod iam praeludat diuinus spiritus, futuros quosdam gradus intra quos ho[41v]mo sese continere debeat. Sed hoc relinquimus. Postea in Leuitico tractabimus, quomodo a legitimo matrimonio arceri possint, qui unius carnis esse censentur.

Vxori adhaerebit.) Honesta ratione adhaerebit. Nam si uelit relinquere deum propter uxorem, ut Adam qui noluit suam uxorem contristare, male ageret, idque sana conscientia fieri posset minime. Honeste uiuant, liberos procreent, in gloriam dei educandos. Vna caro sunt, quoniam ex duobus illis prodit unus fructus, tanquam ex una carne. Et uir non habet potestatem sui corporis, neque mulier, ut taceam de unanimitate & concordia, quam alioqui seruare debeant. Sciant se etiam eiusdem nature & dignitatis esse. Talesque erant cum constabat adhuc innocentia. Praeterea ex latere Adae deprompta est mulier, non ex anteriori parte, ne dignior censeretur, neque ex posteriori, ne uilior haberi possit: sed ex latere, ideo ut sit collateralis, & ita ut sit in adiutorium. Et quia haec non tam ad formandos morem pertinent, quam etiam ad constituendas respublicas, apud quas adulterium male audit, negligere haud conuenit. Porro quod ad allegoriam attinet, delibatum est in superioribus. Gaudeamus illius dignitatis nos esse, cuius est Christus. Os nostrum ipse est nosq; ex carne eius, quandoquidem genus humanum assumere dignatus est. Haec summa ecclesiae & nostrorum [42r] omnium dignitas. Qui enim carnem assumpsit nostram & spiritum communicauit, effecit ut cum illo unum simus, Ioan. 17. Natura non possumus unum esse cum patre, sed quia Christus unius naturae nobiscum est, excepto peccato, ita etiam dignitatem suam nobis quodam modo communicauit assumpta nostra natura. Quod dicit, Deseret patrem &c. si de Christo uolueris cognoscere, hoc modo

upon the earth." But married partners should leave parents in such a way that conjugal love does not destroy the love for parents, seeing that it ought to preserve the human race. There are some who interpret this verse to the effect that right from the beginning this step was excluded, lest parents or children with parents would have something, and [they say] that the divine Spirit alludes to future steps from which in the future a man ought to restrain himself. But we let this go. Later we will treat in Leviticus how some can be separated from lawful marriage who are considered to be of one flesh.[185]

He will cling to his wife.) He will cling within reason. For if one should wish to abandon God on account of his wife, just like Adam who refused to sadden his wife, he would act badly, and this could hardly be done with a good conscience. Let them live honorably and procreate children, educating them in the glory of God. They are one flesh, for out of those two comes one fruit just as from one flesh. And the man does not have power over his own body, nor the woman,[186] so that I may leave off any discussion of the unanimity and concord in which they should watch over one another. They also know that they are of the same nature and dignity. They were so excellent when they were still innocent. Moreover the woman was drawn out from the side of Adam, not from a higher part lest she be deemed more worthy, nor from a lower part lest she be able to be regarded as worth less, but from the side so that she would be at his side and so be his helper. Because these things pertain not only to formation in morals but also to the constitution of the state, it is by no means fitting to ignore adultery [when] one hears of it in a society. Again what pertains to allegory has been touched on above. Let us rejoice that we have the dignity of Christ. Our mouth itself and even we ourselves are of his flesh, seeing that he deigned to assume our humanity. This is the highest dignity of the church and of all of us. For the one who assumed our flesh also communicated the Spirit, and so he made it that we should be one with him, John 17. By nature we are not able to be one with the Father, but because Christ is of one nature with us, except for sin,[187] so also he somehow communicated to us his own dignity when he assumed

185 Oecolampadius is referring to the problem of consanguinity here.

186 Cf. I Cor. 7.

187 Heb. 4:15.

accipe: Reliquit Christus synagogam & cognationem suam carnalem, & adhaesit ecclesiae, quae uiuit secundum spiritum: uult denique esse caput nostrum, et nos pro membris habere suis. Si spiritus Christi habitat in nobis, erimus uera dei templa: & qui spiritui illius adhaeret, unus spiritus efficitur cum illo.

Fuerunt autem ambo illi nudi, homo (inquam ille) & uxor eius, & non erubescebant.

Paucula verba sunt, sed admodum praegnantia. Quid referebat dicere Adam nudum, nisi gloriam egregiam contineret nuditas? Nihil deforme erat illis, neque ipsa erubescentia: erant recti, iusti, uestiti innocentia, praeterea non mordebat illos mala conscientia. Felix est innocentia sine uestibus. Neque periculum ibi erat peccati. Ita omnibus modis deus condiderat hominem felicem & securum, tam corpore quam animo.

our nature. When it says, "Whoever will leave his father"[188] etc., if you wish to understand this as concerning Christ, then receive it this way: Christ left the synagogue and his carnal relations, and he clung to the church, which lives according to the spirit. For he wishes to be our head and to have us for his members.[189] If the spirit of Christ lives in us, then we will be true temples of God.[190] And whoever clings to his Spirit, is made to be one spirit with him.[191]

[25] The two of them were naked, the man (that man, I say) and his wife, and they were not ashamed.

There are only a few words, but surely they are pregnant. Why does he turn and say that Adam was nude, except that nakedness encloses an extraordinary glory? In them was nothing deformed, nor shameful. They were upright, just, clothed with innocence; what is more, a bad conscience did not vex them. Innocence is happy without clothes. Nor was there any danger of sin. So in every way God had made humankind happy and secure, as much in the body as in the soul.

---

188 The allusion is to Mark 10.

189 I Cor. 12:12; Eph. 1:22 ff.

190 Rom. 8:9-10; I Cor. 3:16, 6:19.

191 I Cor. 6:17.

[42v]

CAPVT III

In hoc capite tertio describit nobis Moses diuinus propheta lapsum Adae, & quomodo iterum restauratus sit, & quam poenam Adam et Eua luerint propter peccatum, quod perpetrarant contra dei legem.

Serpens uero fuit callidior omni bestia agri, quam fecit deus, & dixit ad mulierem: Etiamsi dixit deus, non comedetis de omni ligno horti.

Ille uersus praemittitur, quo commodius caetera describantur, & ad epicherema pertinet. Indicaturus enim Moses cuius dolis Adam lapsus sit, organum ipsum primo describit, quod daemon elegerat. Serpens astutus est prae omnibus bestijs: caetera animantia bruta sunt, quorum aliqua magis callida sunt aliqua minus. Serpens ille habebat blanditiem quandam, & miram calliditatem, per quam & Euam seduxit. Arbitrantur quidam tunc aliam fuisse figuram serpentis, quam nunc est. Multa sunt etiam genera serpentum: quidam erecto collo uadunt inter reptilia, ut basilisci & coronati serpentes: quidam repunt. Praeterea nullus horror erat Adamo inter has bestias constituto, quia nullum erat peccatum, et saluum adhuc erat dominium Adae in omnes creaturas. Non est ideo magnum miraculum, si Eua collo[43r]cuta est serpenti. Satan deligit sibi huiusmodi blanda organa, ut homines decipiat. Discamus hic ne nostris uiribus aliquid tribuamus. Si Adam securus non fuit in paradiso a satanae suggestu, neque nobis pomittamus ullam securitatem in hoc peccatrici mundo. Videmus &

CHAPTER 3

In this third chapter the divine prophet Moses describes to us the fall of Adam, how he would again be restored, and what penalty Adam and Eve would pay for the sin that they committed against God's law.

[1] The snake, however, was more cunning than every beast of the field that God had made. And he said to the woman: "As if God said that you should not eat from every tree in the garden!"[192]

This verse is spoken as a preface by which the rest of the things would be more fully described, and it pertains to an *epicheirema*.[193] For although Moses is about to indicate by whose trick Adam fell, he first describes the instrument itself that the demon chose. That snake was cleverer than all the other beasts. The other animals were brutes, and some were more skillful, others less. The snake had a certain charm, and an amazing craftiness, through which he also seduced Eve. Some figure that the appearance of the snake was different then than now. There are many kinds of snakes. Some walk upright among the other reptiles, like the basiliscus[194] and the crowned snake. Others crawl. Besides, for Adam, who had been made in the presence of these beasts, there was no dread, for there was not yet sin and the dominion of Adam over all creatures was still intact. So it is no great wonder that Eve spoke to the snake. Satan selects for himself alluring instruments like this in order to deceive human beings. Let us learn from this text lest we attribute anything to our own powers. If Adam was not secure from the suggestion of Satan even in paradise, neither should

---

192 The Latin here, *etiamsi*, suggests an ironic expression through which the serpent seeds doubt in the woman.

193 Aristotle used the term επικέρημα to denote an attempt at a syllogism. Oecolampadius understood it to mean a syllogism in which the proof of the major or minor premise precedes the conclusion. In this case, he means only that Scripture first tells about the instrument by which the fall came about, i.e., the serpent, before it tells how the fall occurred.

194 A type of lizard.

sentimus quotidie uarios astus daemonis: nihil enim astu illius uersutius: hominem qua parte infirmior est, ea aggredi solet, & ita etiam Euam aggressus est. I. Thimot. 2. scribit Paulus, quod Adam non sit deceptus, sed Eua. Illam auertit satan mira astutia a simplicitate sui sensus. Praeterea hunc modum habet satan, ut quammaxime fidei omnium insidietur. Primum in genere nobis suspicionem quandam de deo, quasi non optime nobis uelit, suggerit, & quasi inuideat nobis, uel quasi minus certa sint quae ab illo dicta sunt. Caeterum illud כִּי notate, neque opus est repetere. Id uult dicere: Deus dixit, non edetis de omni arbore horti. Nam Latini hoc nomine utuntur in irrisionibus. Item etiam, si aliquid affirmare uolunt uel reijcere, illud adijciunt, ut bonus scilicet est uir, quasi dicant, minime. Ia eben also ists.[37] Vult igitur satan persuadere, dicendo: Non illa tam certa sunt, ut tu dicis: putas quod prohibeat uobis deus aliquid ex ullis arboribus paradisi? quid illa ad deum? Nunquid esca ad deum? quod intrat in os, non coinquinat hominem. Putatis quod tale aliquid prohibuerit uobis [43v] deus? Haec est astutia diaboli, ut faciat dubitare de uerbo domini corda nostra: & ubi soluerit timorem & fidem, ut putemus uerbum eius non esse tam rigide dictum, facile tunc uincet, quia inuenit nos infirmos, & dubitantes de uerbo domini.

Et dixit mulier ad serpentem, de fructu ligni horti comedimus. De fructu uero arboris, quae est in medio horti, dixit deus: nequaquam comedetis ex ea, neque contingetis illam, ne forte moriamini. Et dixit serpens ad mulierem: Non moriendo moriemini. Sed scit deus, quod ipsa die quando comederitis ex ipsa, aperientur oculi uestri, & eritis sicut dij, scientes bonum & malum.

37 We have here a rare lapse into the author's native German language.

we promise ourselves any security in this sinful world.[195] We see and feel today various forms of demonic guile, for there is nothing more deceitful than his craftiness. He is accustomed to attack mankind in whichever part is weaker, and so also he attacked Eve. In I Timothy 2[:14] Paul writes that Adam was not deceived, but Eve. Satan with remarkable cleverness diverted her from the simplicity of her senses. Moreover, this is Satan's way, so that he can ambush as many of the faithful as possible. First he wants to create in us the suspicion that God does not want the best for us. He suggests that God is somehow jealous of us, or [he tries] at least to make us less certain of those things that have been said by him. Secondly, note the Hebrew *ki* [as though], which there is no need to repeat. He wanted to say that, "God said you cannot eat from *every* tree in the garden." The Latins certainly use this word[196] to denote derision.[197] Likewise they add it if they want to affirm or deny something, such as "*sure* he is a good man," as if to say, "hardly!" (In German:) "Yes, indeed, so it is!" Thus Satan wants to persuade by saying: "Those things are not as sure as you say. Do you think that God would prohibit you from *any* of the trees of paradise? What is that to God? What is food to God? What goes into the mouth does not contaminate a man. Do you think that God would prohibit you from such a thing?" This is the cunning of the devil, that he makes our hearts doubt concerning the word of the Lord. Wherever he shakes loose fear and faith, so that we think that God's word has not been spoken soundly, there he conquers easily, because he finds us weak and in doubt concerning the word of the Lord.

[2] And the woman said to the snake, "We may eat from the fruit of the trees of the garden. [3] However, of the fruit of the tree in the middle of the garden, God said, 'Do not eat from it, neither shall you touch it, lest perhaps you die.'" [4] And the snake said to the woman: "You will by no means die. [5] But God knows, that on the same day when you eat from it, your eyes will be opened and you will be like gods, knowing good and evil."

---

195 I read "promittamus" here for "pomittamus."

196 I.e., "etiamsi." In today's English one might say, "Yeah, like God said you couldn't eat...".

197 That is, when they mean to speak derisively.

Bene expendite uerba ista, & uidete ne imitemini exemplum Euae, quae dicit: Hoc mandatum est dei, qui permisit de lignis ut comedamus, de uno autem isto non permisit. Et addidit: In medio. quasi dicat: Videtur esse aliquo modo preciosior fructus ille. Et iterum addit: Ne attingatis. Quamuis Eua dicere poterat hoc, animo maioris religionis: Dominus dixit, ne edatis, ideo ne attingere uolumus. Ita sapientior uolebat deo esse. [44r] Proinde non est tutum aliquid addere uerbis dei, uel demere. Haec erat ignauia Euae, quae tam statim assensum praebuit serpenti. Nam hoc unum spectauit serpens, si posset Euam eo ducere, ut seduceret, & in dubium uerbum dei poneret: et ita fere omnes peccamus. Nam si hoc certissime persuasum esset, deum uidere omnia, & iudicem esse, & sumpturum rationem de omnibus factis, siue bonis siue malis, non luctaremus nos dicentes in animo, Impune erit peccatum &c. quod Sapientiae 2. cap. describitur pulchre: sed utique cessaremus a peccatis. Hoc quamprimum animaduertit satan in homine, non cessat suis suggestionibus quo tandem id quod instillauit peragatur. Et quia semel scintillam ignis immiserat in animam Euae, iam parat istam incendere. Dicit enim satan: Vana illa uerba sunt, nihil est quod timeas etc. Nisi enim Eua uacilla esset, audacior satan non fuisset factus cum ea colloquendi. Sic ubi nosipsos uincendos dederimus satanae, facile uincit, & maxime tunc gloriatur de nostro interitu.

Oculi aperientur.) Duo facit Satan: timorem soluit, ne a morte sibi timerent, & transgredientibus bona pollicetur, quasi deus inuideat. Mendax est, & ab initio. Aperti quidem oculi eorum sunt, sed in magnum malum ipsorum: & dij non sunt facti, imo animantia. Nonne Adam prius bonum & malum sciuit? alias non scisset [44v] de praecepto. Vult deus ut iuxta uerbum illius agamus. Satan ab obedientia dei abducit, & nosipsos nobis ipsis relinquit. Ex illis pollicitis statim misera Eua seducta est, & uidit quod antea non uiderat. Caeterum

Weigh these words, and consider them carefully, lest you imitate the example of Eve. She said: "This is the command of God, who allowed that we should eat from the trees, except for that one." And she added, "in the middle," as if to say "it seems that this fruit is more precious." And again she added, "neither shall you touch it." Eve may have added this intent on greater piety, as if to say, "The Lord said, 'do not eat it,' so we do not want even to touch it." Therefore she wished to be wiser than God. But it is not prudent either to add to the words of God, or to take away from them. This was the faintheartedness of Eve, that she offered her assent to the snake right away. For the snake focused on this one thing. If he could direct Eve to it he would be able to lead her astray and place the word of God into doubt. Almost all of us sin like this. On the other hand, if we were assuredly persuaded that God sees everything and is the judge, and that there will be a reckoning for all things that have been done, either good or evil, then we would not struggle, saying in [our] hearts that sin will go unpunished, etc., which is splendidly described in Wisdom 2.[198] But let us by all means cease from [our] sins. Satan turns his attention to this as much as possible in his dealings with man, and he does not stop his suggestions until he brings his insinuations to completion. As soon as he has placed the spark of fire in Eve's soul he is ready to ignite it. For Satan says: "Those words [of God] are empty; you have nothing to fear." Had Eve not hesitated, Satan would not have become so bold in speaking with her. Likewise whenever we hand ourselves over to Satan to be defeated, he conquers easily and exults greatly in our destruction.

Eyes will be opened.) Satan does two things. He dissolves fear, lest they fear for themselves on account of death, and he promises good things to transgressors, as if God were jealous. He is a liar, and from the beginning.[199] Their eyes are certainly opened but to their own great calamity. And they are not made gods but, more correctly, mortals.[200] Didn't Adam previously know good and evil? Otherwise he would not have known about the command. God wanted us to do according to his word. Satan led us away from obedience to God and abandoned us to ourselves. By those promises poor Eve was seduced

198 See Wisd. Solom. 2, where the fate of the wicked is described in disturbing detail.

199 John 8:44.

200 Lit., "living beings."

dum haec uel legimus uel audimus, possumus uarias fraudes satanae, quibus humanum genus uexat agnoscere. Primum in externis habet sua organa, habet haereticos, habet hypocritas: Iam per serpentem loquitur, iam per impios & malos homines, qui nos a fide uera abducere conantur. Deinde etiam ipsa nostra concupiscentia, quae in nobis est, uarie tentamur, ut in Iacobi epistola habemus, qui dicit: Vnusquisque tentatur dum a propria concupiscentia abstrahitur & inescatur. Deinde concupiscentia posteaquam concepit, parit peccatum, peccatum uero perfectum progignit mortem. Curandum igitur omnibus modis, ne uerbum dei ablegemus, sed illo constanter inhaereamus. Per Euam quidam intellexerunt sensum: offert enim sese uoluptas sensui nostro admodum delectabilis & grata, mox ubi timor dei ablatus fuerit, maximum periculum est sensibus animi, ut sic peccatum consummatur: de quo uberius crastina lectione.

LECTIO

Audiuimus nuper impostoris antiqui insidias, et quibus arietibus, quibúsue machinis simplicissimos quosque aggrediatur exemplo Euae, maxime ut sum[45r]mum istud bonum, fidem inquam nostram depopuletur: quam ubi a nobis abstulerit, tunc nos totos sibi subijcit. Hoc igitur unicum eius studium est. Quia enim ipse e coelo fuit eiectus, non cessauit quin inuidens homini, ipsum e paradiso fraudibus suis eijceret. Vidimus etiam in Eua nostram fragillitatem, & quam proni ad peccandum simus, & quomodo a concupiscentia nostra tanquam a serpentinis suggestionibus inescamur. Nunc sequitur.

Videns itaque mulier, quod bona esset arbor illa in cibum, & oculis concupiscibilis, desiderabilis quoque esset ipsa arbor ad prudentiam comparandam, tulit de fructu illius & comedit: deditque uiro suo existenti secum, qui & ipse comedit.

Tentationem audistis, nunc poenam uel fructus infidelitatis licet agnoscere. Mox enim amissa fide, etiam innocentiam amisit, & in se sensit illicitos motus, & desideria nocentia. Nam vidit, inquit. Nónne

immediately, and she saw what beforehand she had not seen. Now, as we read or hear these things, we can recognize the various schemes of Satan by which he troubles the human race. First he has his external instruments: the heretics, the hypocrites. Even as he spoke through the snake, so now he speaks through impious and evil men, who try to lead us away from the true faith. Then, too, we are variously tested by the sinful desire within us, as we read in the epistle of James, who says: "Each one is tested when by his own desire he is carried away and enticed. Then after sinful desire has conceived it brings forth sin, and sin when brought to completion produces death."[201] We must therefore take care in every way, so that we do not depart from the word of God but dwell in it constantly.[202] By the word "Eve" some understand "sensation," for pleasure offers itself to our senses as very delightful and pleasing, but as soon as the fear of God is taken away, there is great danger for the senses of the soul, for in that way it is consumed by sin. Concerning that, more in tomorrow's lecture.

READING

We have recently heard in the example of Eve the crafty devices of the ancient imposter, and by what battering rams and siege engines he attacks those who are most simple, chiefly so that he might rob that greatest good, that is, our faith. Once he has taken it from us, then he subjects us all to himself. This is therefore his one desire. For because he himself had been thrown out of heaven he did not cease attacking humankind, seeking by his treacheries to get them ejected from paradise. We also saw in Eve our own frailty, how we are prone to sinning, and how we are enticed by our own sinful desire as much as by the suggestions of the snake. Now it continues.

[6] Seeing that the tree would be good for food, pleasing to the eyes, and desirable for gaining wisdom, the woman took of its fruit and ate. She also gave it to her husband there with her, who himself also ate.

You heard the temptation, and now you can recognize the penalty, or the fruit of faithlessness. For as soon as faith was lost, innocence went with it, and she felt within herself illicit movements, a deadly

201 See Jas. 1:14-15.

202 An allusion to Col. 3:16, or perhaps John 8:31.

etiam Eua ante uiderat? neque caecam illam creauit deus, ut arborem non uideret ante oculos positam, & ut non uideret qui nam, & quam delectabilis fructus in hac arbore. Hoc nemo negat. Sed aliter nunc uidet, aliter etiam antea uidit. Quamuis enim etiam frueretur oculorum munere antea, tamen non impediebatur a diuinarum rerum [45v] consideratione, neque sic delabebatur ad inferiora ista. Nam illud uidere, quod Eua uidit hanc arborem bonam esse ad edendum, insinuat quod iam propensa esse coepit ad res istas inferiores appetendas. Poterat etiam edere, sed absque omni uoracitate uel gula, uel immoderata cupiditate. Iam sensit in se deordinationem quandam uim suam exerentem, & illa ipsa deordinatio hoc loco indicatur. Miro modo Eua expetijt arborem & fructus illius. Considerauit bonos fructus arboris istius, & quam iucunda arbor oculis esset, & sic tota oculis haerebat in illam, & non ab istis creaturis ascendebat ad ipsum conditorem, sed neglecto conditoris praecepto, secuta est suas concupiscentias. Ita desiderabilis arbor probabatur ei, & quod audierat a serpente cogitabat, si posset similis dijs fieri, bonum & malum scientibus. Mendaciter daemon multa promiserat, propterea sperabat tale eximium donum posse aequari se deo, & non curabat, quae deus praeceperat. Hoc postea indicabit Moses de utrisque quomodo oculi amborum aperti sint, sed nondum malam conscientiam, & huiusmodi deordinationes senserant. Supra annotatum est, quare arbor scientiae boni & mali dicta sit, non quod arbor possit aliquid scientiae dare, sed quia praeceptum accepit homo, ne sua ratione fisus uelit uiuere, sed potius iuxta uerbum dei praescriptum omnia agere debere. [46r]

Comedit.) Praecessit tentatio, uicta erat, & ita abiecto pudoris freno, comedit. Ratio haec peccati est, quod nisi poenitentia statim aboleatur, maiora sumat incrementa. Non contenta est Eua, quod ipsa mandatum dei transgressa est, sed etiam in idem peccatum coniugem suum

desire. For she saw, it says. Did Eve not also see beforehand? God did not make her blind so that she could not see the tree set right before her eyes, or on the other hand that she could not see how delectable was the fruit on this tree.[203] This no one denies. But now she sees differently than before. Although she enjoyed the function of the eyes beforehand, nevertheless she was not hindered from the contemplation of divine things, nor did she sink down to those inferior things. For that word "to see," that Eve "saw" that this tree was good for eating, implies that she had begun desiring those inferior things. Beforehand she had been able to eat, but without any voracity, any gluttony or immoderate desire.[204] But now she sensed within herself a certain disorder displacing her own strength, and that disorder itself is revealed by this text. In a remarkable measure, Eve longed for that tree and its fruit. She considered carefully the good fruits of that tree and how pleasant the tree was to the eyes, and thus through her eyes the whole tree held fast in her so that she did not rise up from creaturely things to their creator, but by ignoring the precept of the creator she followed her own carnal desires. And so she approved the tree for its desirability, and she considered what she had heard from the snake, that they would be like gods, knowing good and evil. The demon deceitfully had promised many things, so she was hoping to possess such an exceptional gift as being equal with God,[205] and she did not care what God had commanded. Afterwards Moses will indicate how the eyes of each of them were opened, but they did not yet have a bad conscience, so they did not yet sense their disorder. Above it was noted why it was called the tree of the knowledge of good and evil, not that the tree was itself able to give knowledge, but because man received the command that he should not wish to live by confidence in his own reason, but that instead he ought to do everything in accordance with the word and precept of God.

She ate.) The temptation was over; she had already been defeated, and so, having cast off the bridle of shame, she ate. This is the way with sin, that unless it is immediately put to an end by penance, it advances more and more. Eve was not content that she herself had transgressed

---

203 Reading "quinam" here for "qui nam."

204 Here the internal disorder caused by sin expresses itself in desires that are no longer fully under rational control.

205 Cf. Phil. 2:6.

trahit, & autorem peccati facit. Non enim nocuisset humano generi, si Eua solum peccasset, & Adam immunis peccati fuisset: potuisset deus aliam uxorem condere, illa reiecta. Vbi autem Adam peccauit, peccatum in omne genus humanum descendit. Nullas hic persuasiones adhibet Eua. Legimus simpliciter, comedit Adam, ne scilicet contristaret uxorem suam. Apostolus Adam non seductum fuisse, sed Euam, testatur, ut supra monui. Adam acceperat mandatum a deo, nondum Eua creata, eratque Adam doctor Euae. Nam sic ab initio dominus ordinauit, ut alij alios doceant, ne uerbum suum contemptui esset. Facile igitur potuit imponi Euae, tanquam discipulae, quae illud mandatum acceperat ab homine Adam: sed Adam a domino audierat, propterea peccatum Adae minus excusabile est. Ipsius erat mulierem corripere propter praeuaricationem, et non mox assentire eius suggestionibus. Similiter nulla ratione excusabiles erunt qui aliorum sunt doctores, si ob infirmatitem plebis quae facile seducitur, ipsi quoque eandam uiam ingrediuntur. Neque enim omnino excu[46v]sauit Aaronem, quod populus peteret sibi fabricari idola: nam & ipse debebat populum reprehendere. Ita pastor plebis debet se gerere uirum in his quae spectant, ad gloriam dei, uel promouendam, uel obscurandam. Sic etiam Paulus monet Corinthios, ne sicut Eua in simplicitate sua seducta est, etiam sensus ipsorum corrumpantur. Accepimus iam peccatum, & nunc utrisque peccantibus, audietis quomodo omnis honestas cessauerit, & decor ablatus sit ab eis. Vnde legimus:

Et aperti sunt oculi amborum, & cognouerunt quod nudi erant, & consuerunt folia ficulneae, feceruntque sibi cinctoria.

the command of God, but also drew her own husband into the same sin, and so became the author of sin. For it would not have harmed the human race if Eve alone had sinned and Adam had remained free from sin. God could have created another wife and rejected that one. But when Adam sinned, sin descended on the whole human race.[206] Here Eve employed no persuasions. We read simply that Adam ate, certainly so that he would not disappoint his wife. The Apostle says that Adam was not seduced, but Eve, as I noted above.[207] Adam received the command from God when Eve had not yet been created, so Adam was the teacher of Eve. The Lord ordained it so from the beginning, that some should teach others so that his own word should not be disregarded. Therefore it was imposed readily upon Eve, like a disciple, who received that command from the man Adam. But Adam heard it from the Lord, on account of which the sin of Adam is less excusable. It was his duty to reproach the woman on account of her transgression, and not immediately to assent to her suggestion. Likewise those who are the teachers of others will be by no means excused, if, on account of the weakness of the people who are so easily seduced, they themselves also follow the same path.[208] Nor did it in any way excuse Aaron that the people asked him to make idols for them.[209] For he himself should have held the people back. So also a pastor of the people ought to act like a man in those matters that pertain to the glory of God [and need to be] either promoted or obscured.[210] In the same way Paul admonishes the Corinthians, lest just as Eve was seduced in her simplicity so also their senses might be corrupted.[211] Having heard about sin and that both were now sinners, you will next hear how all their uprightness was left behind and their beauty taken away. Whence we read:

[7] So the eyes of both of them were opened, and they knew that they were naked. And they sewed together fig leaves and made loincloths for themselves.

---

206 Cf. Rom. 5:12.

207 I Tim. 2:14.

208 Cf. James 3:1.

209 See Ex. 32.

210 That is, the people will either listen to him, or they will not.

211 I Cor. 11:3.

Iterum per apertionem oculorum, quia agnouerunt se esse nudos, indicatur pudor illis innatus. Iam uidebant membra sua rebellia rationi, & sic quoque animam aliquo modo esse mortuam intelligebant. Mortua enim mox ut comederunt fuit anima eorum, quia priuata dei gratia: neque tam efficax spiritus dei in illis erat, ut antea, qui moderaret omnia eorum membra. Non enim duntaxat genitalia membria simpliciter hic intelligenda sunt, etsi hoc adducetur ab omnibus, quod prae maximo pudore illa tegerint, sed sensus omnes non obtemperabant rationi, quandoquidem ipsi deo inobedientes fuerant. Ob hanc nouitatem igitur, quam antea in se[47r]ipsis non attenderant, iam erubescunt, uident bonum & malum, uident quid admiserint. Non ignorabant se prius etiam uestitu carere, sed non offendebantur nuditate illa, quia nihil erat unde erubescere poterant. Verum ubi tantam rebellionem inuenerunt in membris suis propter peccatum, inuenerunt se etiam spoliatos exuuijs donis dei. Porro hinc apparet, quod ubi peccatum est, non posse nostris laboribus, nostraque cura nosipsos reparare, sed opus est divina gratia, qua corda purgantur, ut possimus agnoscere peccatum, & id agere quod domino placet. Homo tamen, praesertim peccator, qui multum fidit sua ratione, cogitat quomodo possit suis uiribus se honestare, & abscondere suam turpitudinem, quod iam Moses ostendit, sed id sua prudentia non faciet.

Folia ficulneae.) Aptiora aliquanto ad contegendum folia illa sunt: succinctoria nimirum, ut membra sua tegerent, consuunt. Nuditatem illam antea in se ipsis non agnouerant, quam iam post perpetratum peccatum conspiciunt. Sed uanum erat illud studium contegendi, nam ante oculos domini plus satis conspicui erant. Discamus igitur uires nostri arbitrij, quas iactant quidam, non sufficere, ut si ceciderimus, iterum reparari possimus: opus est deo adiutore. Nam si quispiam potuisset aliquid, nemo magis utique potuisset Adam et Eua, qui tam recti conditi fuerant a deo: sed inuenimus [47v] illos omnino succumbere. Et haec dicta sunt de peccato. Nam nunc deus misertus illorum, uocat ipsos ad iudicium antequam condemnet: deinde condemnat, ut iterum humiliatis concedat gratiam, etiam in hoc ostendens se benignum patrem. Sunt qui illa considerant praeter spem, sed magis

Again through the opening of the eyes, since they knew that they were naked, their innate sense of shame is indicated. For they saw that their own members were rebelling against reason, and so also in some way they understood that their own souls were mortal. For their souls were dead immediately when they had eaten, for the grace of God was lost. Nor was the Spirit of God, who had held all their members in check, as effective in them as before. This should not be understood simplistically as applying only to the genital organs, even if this will be brought up by everyone, since those [organs] ought to be covered out of the greatest shame. But all their senses no longer complied with the demands of reason, seeing that they were disobedient to God himself. On account therefore of this novelty, which they did not experience beforehand, now they were ashamed. Seeing good and evil, they see what they have lost. They were not ignorant beforehand that they were without clothes, but they were not offended by that nudity, because there was within them no source of shame. But when they found such rebellion in their members on account of sin, they found themselves also despoiled of the gifts of God. Hence it is clear that wherever there is sin, we cannot by our own efforts and our own care renew ourselves, but there is need of divine grace, by which our hearts are cleansed so that we can recognize sin and do what is pleasing to the Lord. Nevertheless the human being, particularly the sinner who trusts much in his own reason, imagines that he is able to bring honor on himself by his own powers and to conceal his own shame, as Moses shows here. But he will not accomplish that by his own prudence.

Fig leaves.) Those leaves were somewhat more suitable for covering up. Evidently they sewed together aprons, so they could cover their members. Previously they had not taken note of their nudity, but after sin was committed they caught sight of it. But their rush to cover it over was vain, for before the eyes of the Lord they were more than sufficiently conspicuous. Thus we learn that our powers of free will, of which some boast, do not suffice for us to repair ourselves once we have fallen; we need God as our helper.[212] For if anyone could have done something, there was certainly no one more able than Adam and Eve, who had been created upright by the Lord. But we discover that they succumb altogether. And these things were said regarding sin. But now God has mercy on them. He calls them to a trial before he would pass sentence. Then he passes sentence so that he might give

212 Perhaps Oecolampadius has a Psalm in mind here. See, e.g., Ps. 54:4.

attendere debebant bonitatem dei, qui sciebat morbum nostrum tali remedio indigere, & ut sic cognosceremus peccatum nostrum, & recte humiliaremur.

Et audierunt uocem domini dei deambulantis in horto ad uentum diei, & abscondit se Adam & uxor illius a facie domini dei inter arbores horti.

Vocantur igitur a deo ad reddendam rationem. Ita & nos dum peccamus, putamus deum non uidere, neque attendere nostra peccata: sed ubi peccauerimus conscientia nostra concutitur his arietibus: Quare hoc fecisti? sic & sic, &c. Nam illa obiurgatio erat uox domini dei. Neque uerisimile est, quod uiderint deum hoc modo, ut quidam prophetarum. Ad exponendum hunc locum satisfacit Chrysostomus. Et satis est, si deus ita illorum conscientiam concussit, ut agnoscerent peccatum peractum.

Deambulantis.) Peccator ubique sibi timet. Et est hic ad uesperam diei, uel cum iam dies refrigeraretur. [48r; the page number is mis-marked as 44r] Quidam putant fuisse factum sonitum quendam cum strepitu, qui mentem illorum consternauerit, quique sonitus uox dei fuerit, ut postea in Cain uidebimus, quomodo illorum[38] conscientia sua uexarit. Pessima erynnis[39] est conscientia peccatis polluta. Erat eis horror cum strepitu, uel cum alijs rebus aliquid terriculamenti excitabatur tempore uesperarum. Et mos est scripturae tempus assignare moribus congruum. Nox erat quando Petrus negabat Christum: &

---

38 I read here illorum rather than illum for the printed text's illū.

39 "Erynnis" (Erinyes) is an allusion to the Furies, who in classical mythology stir up madness in those conscious of guilt.

grace to the humbled,[213] thus showing himself to be a kind Father. There are those who consider them beyond hope,[214] but they ought to attend more to the goodness of God, who knew that our disease requires such a cure. In the same way let us acknowledge our sin and so be rightly humbled.

[8] **And they heard the voice of the Lord God walking in the garden in the cool of the day. And Adam and his wife hid themselves from the face of the Lord among the trees of the garden.**

Thus they were called by God to come recover their reason. Just so we also, when we sin, think that God does not see or pay attention to our sins. But whenever we sin our conscience is struck by this battering ram: "Why have you done this?" and so on and on. For that rebuke was the very voice of the Lord God. Nor is it likely that they had seen God, as did some of the prophets.[215] Chrysostom is sufficient for expounding this text. It is enough if God so aroused their consciences that they would acknowledge the sin committed.[216]

Walking.) The sinner is everywhere afraid. Here it is in the evening of the day, or when the day became cool. Some think that he made a confusing sound with a crash that shocked their minds. But whatever was the sound of the voice of God, we will later see in Cain[217] how would it have jolted their consciences. A conscience fouled by sins is the very worst form of madness. Dread came over them at the sound of the crash, or else it was aroused by other frightening things at evening time. And it is the custom of Scripture to assign a time that suits the mood. It was night when Peter denied Christ, and it was cold,

213 I Pet. 5:5.

214 The "them" in this phrase seems to refer to Adam and Eve. Perhaps, however, Oecolampadius was trying to make the broader point about divine goodness for all those who might be tempted to consider themselves "beyond hope."

215 I.e., in a mystical vision. See e.g., Isa. 6:1 ff.

216 This suggests that Oecolampadius understands the conscience as the voice of God heard by Adam and Eve.

217 Gen. 4:6-7.

frigus, quia deficiebat charitas & fides. Ita hoc loci etiam tempus facto bene congruit.

A facie.) Quid faciet peccator? quomodo se abscondet a facie iudicis, qui ubique est, & omnia comprehendit? Iam uident se omnino deprehensos: in arbustum quoddam densius se conijciunt, in quo delitescant, ne uideantur. Iterum magna stultitia illorum apparet in eo quod se occultare conantur a domini facie. Desideria illa denique stulta secuta est magna caecitas, quia non bene sentiebant de deo.

Et uocauit dominus deus ipsum Adam, & ait illi: Vbi est tu?

Emphaticôs est dictum: Vbi ubi? Dominus non per ignorantiam loquitur, quasi ignoret quid actum sit, uel ubit sit, sed ut prouocet eum ad confitendum peccatum suum, & ut agnoscat in quantam sese coniecerit miseriam. Quasi dicat. Quousque te praecipitasti ô Adam? [48v] in quam foueam te coniecisti? ex qua felicitate deiectus es? Non es idem Adam qualis a me conditus fuisti, iam fugis lucem, qui eras dominus totius mundi. Haec sunt uerba dei ad Adam, quibus deus alloquitur suam conscientiam. Neque opus ut de illa externa uoce intelligamus, etsi dominus facile potuerit per angelos uocem talem formare, cui nihil impossibile. Atqui nolumus contendere cum quopiam de illa re. Id enim quotidie experimur in nobis, quod ipse Adam, cum praeceptum domini transgredimur, & agnoscimus etiam quam male egerimus ubi peccatum fuerit impletum. Aliter tamen deus admonet peccatorum, & aliter satan. Deus admonet, ut poenitentia deleamus peccata. Satan admonet & irridet, ut eos quos antea in peccatum seducendo iniecerat, omnino perdat per desperationem. Videtis autem hic pulcherrime hominem internum describi, quomodo secum affligatur,

because he had lost faith and love.[218] Here, too, the time of day fits the deed.[219]

From the face.) What will the sinner do? How will he hide himself from the face of a judge who is everywhere and sees all things? They see that they have been caught red-handed, but then they go into an even denser grove of trees, in which they hide themselves lest they be seen. Again, their great foolishness is shown in that they try to hide from the face of the Lord.[220] Indeed, even to have acted on such a foolish desire was great blindness, for they were not thinking clearly about God.

[9] And the Lord God called out to Adam himself and said to him: "Where are you?"

It is said emphatically: "Where, oh where?" The Lord does not speak through ignorance, as if he did not know what had been done or where he was, but in order to provoke him to confess his own sin and to acknowledge what misery he had brought upon himself. It was as if to say: "Oh Adam, how have you been cast down, thrown into so deep a pit, fallen from such a blessed state? You are no longer the Adam I made; you flee the light, you who were lord of the whole world." These are the words of God for Adam, by which God addressed his conscience. There is no need for us to understand this divine address as an external voice, although the Lord, to whom nothing is impossible, was easily able to form a voice through the angels. But we don't wish to argue with anyone about this matter. For we daily experience in ourselves what Adam felt when we transgress the command of the Lord, and also when we recognize how evilly we have acted whenever a sin comes to completion. For God admonishes us of sin in a different way than Satan. God admonishes so that through repentance we should cease from sin. Satan admonishes and mocks us, so that those whom he threw into sin by seducing them, he now may destroy through despair. Here, however, you see that our inner selves have been most beautifully described, how we are crushed within ourselves and seek

218 See Luke 22:54-62, which reports that Peter was warming himself by a fire when he denied Christ.

219 Note that both time and temperature function figuratively here.

220 Cf. e.g. Psalm 139:7-8; Jer. 23:24.

& ubique quaerat effugia, cum nulla appareant nisi ad deum conuersi fuerimus.

Qui ait: Vocem tuam audiui in horto, & extimui, quia nudus ego, & absconditus sum.

Tardus est Adam ad agnoscendum peccatum suum, & quiduis aliud loquitur, quam ut se reum esse dicat. Vult dicere: Iam praeter morem solitum duriorem te experior, & longe aliam uocem audio, quam hacte[49r]nus. Hinc factum est quod prae timore me sic abscondo: non est amplius mihi talis fiducia, ut sic comparere possim coram te. Audiui iram tuam, quam ferre non possum. Non dicit Adam peccatum suum, quod merito confiteri debebat: unde dominus amplius urget eum ad confessionem peccati, quo tandem misericordiam & remissionem adsequatur. Sic uidetis peccatorem non audere oculos in coelum attollere. Lege Luc. 15. de filio prodigo locum diligenter, & invenies quid peccatorem oporteat facere. Et nisi dominus adiuuet sua gratia ut iterum spem misericordiae dei concipiat, non miserum peccatorem desperare. Nam uidetis Adam quandam deordinationem in se experiri qualem nunquam passus fuit, attamen peccatum suum agnoscere recusat.

Et ille dixit: Quis indicauit tibi quod nudus esses? nunquid de ipsa arbore, de qua praecepi tibi ut non comederes ex ipsa, comedisti?

Ecce tu non fateris peccatum tuum, necesse ut ego tibi illud objiciam. Praeuaricatus es praeceptum meum. Parum quiddam erat, quod mandaueram, nempe de unius arboris fructu ne comederes, cum alia omnia tibi concesserim. Comedisti de hoc uetito fructu: haec praemia tuae ingratitudinis, et fructus tuae inobedientiae, iam nihil in te pulchrum inuenies. Adam nondum senserat [49v] mortem. Et quamuis anima eius gratia dei destituta esset attamen non sensit ipsam mortem, sed incipiebat paulatim erubescere, fugere, trepidare &c. Nam rationem reddere tanto iudici, non parua carnificina est mentis. Vult igitur dominus dicere: Inde apparet unde sint tibi oculi aperti. Nónne antea nudus eras? quae illa noua nuditas? Apparet te

everywhere a way of escape, although none appears until we are converted to God.

[10] And he said: I heard your voice in the garden, and I was afraid because I was naked, so I hid.
Adam is late to acknowledge his sin, and the other things he says only testify that he is guilty. He wants to say, "Now I experience you more harshly, beyond your usual way, and I hear a much different voice than beforehand. Whence it happened that I hid myself out of fear. I did not any longer have such faith that I would be able to appear before you. I heard your wrath, which I am not able to bear." Adam did not name his sin, which rightly he ought to have confessed. So the Lord further presses him to the confession of sin, from which would follow mercy and remission. Thus you see that the sinner does not dare to lift his eyes up to heaven.[221] Read diligently Luke 15 on the prodigal son, and you will find what a sinner ought to do. No wonder[222] if the sinner would despair if the Lord did not help by his grace, so that he might once again grasp the hope of the mercy of God. For you see that Adam experiences in himself a certain disorder that he had never felt before, yet he refuses to acknowledge his own sin.

[11] And He said, "Who pointed out to you that you were naked? Can it be that you have eaten from that very tree from which I commanded you not to eat?"

"Look, you do not admit your sin, so it is necessary that I confront you with it. You have violated my command. It was a small thing that I commanded you truly not to eat the fruit of that one tree, since I had granted to you all the others. You have eaten of this forbidden fruit. This is the reward for your ingratitude, the fruit of your disobedience: you will now find within yourself nothing noble." Adam had not yet felt death. Although his soul was destitute of the grace of God, nevertheless he felt not his own death. But little by little he began to feel shame, to run away, to tremble, and so on. For to give an account before such a judge is no small mental torture. The Lord therefore wishes to say: "From whence and where do your eyes appear to have been opened for you? Were you not already naked? What is new about that

221 Cf. Luke 18:13.

222 Reading "mirum" here for "miserum."

nudum esse ab innocentia et uirtutibus: habe hoc tibi propter peccati praeuaricationem.

Et dixit Adam: Mulier ipsa quam dedisti ut mecum esset, ipsa dedit mihi de arbore, & comedi.

Quamvis iam palam deus obiecerat Adae peccatum suum, per quod volebat illum inducere ad confessionem, quo citius ei misereretur: ille autem non solum non confitetur peccatum suum, sed etiam in sociam suam reijcere studet, imo in deum, qui sibi illam dederat. Vult dicere: Quare non dedisti mihi aliam mulierem, quae honestiora suasisset? Tu autor illius peccati es, quia tu dedisti illam. Quam stulta excusatio sit, facile quis uidet, cum Adam debebat docere uxorem suam, & non uicissim ab illa doceri. Vocem dei, non mulieris audire debebat. Tales etiam plerique hodie inueniuntur, qui audent dicere: Quare dominus corpus mihi dedit tam infirmum, tamque propensum ad peccandum? Neque interim illi expendunt deum etiam promisisse gratiam. Non est igitur ut culpam in illum reijcias, cuius est o[50r]mnis honor et gloria. Haec sunt illa folia ficulnea, id est, friuolae excusationes, quas perpetuo culpis nostris praeteximus. Statim nos excusamus postquam lapsi sumus in peccata, quasi innocentes simus, nunc in hos, nunc in alios culpam reijcientes, cum maxima culpa in nobis sit. Ita profecto nemo statim suam ignauiam agnoscit. Videmus quantum innatum sit nobis philautiae in excusando nostra delicta. Miserares, uolumus iusti et sancti apparere, cum simus insignes peccatores. Haec est illa haereditas, quam ex ipso Adam habemus. Oportet ut quisque agnoscat malitiam humani cordis: illa enim agnita, omne studium emendandae uitae excitabit.

nakedness? It appears that you are indeed 'naked,' bereft of innocence and virtue. Consider this [to have happened] to you on account of the transgression of sin."

[12] And Adam said: "That woman whom you gave to be with me, she gave to me from the tree, and I ate."

God had now openly upbraided Adam, and through that he wished to move him to confession, for which he swiftly would have had mercy on him. However, he not only does not confess his sin, but even tries to put it back on his partner and, even worse, on God himself, who had given her to him. He means to say, "Why did you not give me a different woman, who would have advised [me] more honorably? You are the author of that sin, because you gave her to me." Everyone will easily see what a foolish excuse that is, since Adam was supposed to teach his own wife, and not instead to be taught by her. He should have listened to the voice of God, not of the woman. Today also there are many like this who dare to say, "Why did the Lord give me such a frail body with such a propensity toward sin?" Nor in the meantime do they weigh against this that God has also promised grace. Therefore, you should not place the guilt on him to whom belong all honor and glory. These are those fig leaves, i.e., frivolous excuses, with which we always cover over our sins.[223] We excuse ourselves as soon as we have fallen into sin, as if we were innocent, placing the guilt now on one and then on the other, when the greatest guilt is really in us. Surely no one acknowledges his own laziness right away. We see how much inborn love of self is in us, excusing our faults. Wretches that we are, we want to appear just and holy when we are actually manifest sinners. This is the inheritance we have from Adam. It is necessary for everyone that he should acknowledge the wickedness of the human heart, for that recognition will stir up all zeal for the amendment of life.

---

223 Here is an echo of a long tradition of allegorical reading of this text, where the "leaves" with which the primal couple covered themselves stand for the "excuses" they made for sin. The great pioneer of this exegetical route was Origen of Alexandria. For an English translation of the fragments of Origen's work on this text still available to us, see his *Homilies on Genesis and Exodus*, trans. Ronald E. Heine (Washington, DC: Catholic University of America Press, 1981). Note also Oeolampadius's remarks on Gen. 3:21, below, regarding the "tunics of skin," for which he is also indebted to Origen.

Et dixit dominus deus ad mulierem: Cur hoc fecisti? Et dixit mul[i] er: Ipse serpens seduxit me, & comedi.

Vides etiam quod & ipsa mulier stultam excusationem adfert. Serpens uim non fecit, ideo suae stultitiae illud peccatum debebat ascribere, non serpenti. Ita suis uerbis se incusauit, cum libere peccatum suum debebat confiteri. Vbique per omnem scripturam licebit animaduertere, quoties deus iustitiam exercet, et poenam aliquam intentare uult, primo satis cognitum facit peccatum, propter quod punire hominem deliberat. Sic etiam hoc loco antea expostulauit cum Adam & Eua, et quum rei inuenti sunt, sententiam, quam meruerant facta ipsorum, subiungit. Quam[50v]uis autem illa uideantur esse admodum dura & crudelia, reuera tamen si recte expendantur, sunt misericordiae dei plena. Et iterum licebit agnoscere diuinam beneuolentiam: neque enim deus cum homine egit, quemadmodum meruerat, pro magnitudine peccati. Adam cum omni sua posteritate meruerat totus abijci, totusque condemnari: deus tamen spacium poenitentiae tum illi tum posteritati eius donauit, & de redemptore prouidit, ex mera benignitate, et a nullo prouocatus. Haec igitur cum poenis illis coniuncta sunt. Necesse itaque est, ut misericordiam dei ubique magnifaciamus . Imo si omnia ordine perspexeris quae hic aguntur, uidebis iterum deum cum homine tanquam patrem cum dilecto filio agere, quem inuitus tam dure tractat. Quia enim abusi sumus delitijs paradisi, & nihil profuit nobis omnium rerum abundantia, alia uia erudire nos uoluit deus, nimirum per calamitates & aduersitates, ut sic tandem contemtis istis rebus temporalibus, ad uera bona conuertamur. Videamus igitur sententias illas.

Et dixit dominus deus ad serpentem: Quia fecisti hoc, maledictus es prae omni iumento, & prae omni bestia agri: super uentrem tuum gradieris, & puluerem comedes omnibus diebus uitae tuae.

Primum condemnat deus serpentem a quo tamen [51r] facti rationem non quaesiuit. Neque expostulauerat antea cum serpente, sicut cum Adam & Eva. Longe enim aliud peccatum fuit diaboli, qui per serpentem operatus fuit, quam peccatum uel Adae uel Evae: quia is per malitiam & inuidiam peccauerat, ad obscurandam diuinam gloriam: quod genus peccati fere grauius est, quam ut unquam ueniam

[13] And God said to the woman, "Why have you done this?" And the woman said: "The snake seduced me, and I ate."

You see that the woman also brings out a foolish excuse. The snake did not take her by force, so she ought to have ascribed that sin to her own foolishness, not to the snake. Thus she condemns herself with her own words, while she ought freely to have confessed her own sin. All through the whole of Scripture one can see that as often as God administers justice and wishes to threaten some punishment, he first makes well known the sin on account of which he is considering to punish humankind. So also in this place, before he has remonstrated with Adam and Eve and they were found guilty, he passed the sentence, which their deeds had earned. However much these things may seem harsh or severe, in reality, if considered rightly, they are ripe with the mercy of God. Once again it is right to acknowledge the divine benevolence, for God does not do with humankind what was merited by the magnitude of the sin. Adam together with all his posterity deserved to be completely rejected and wholly condemned. Nevertheless, God gave both to him and to his posterity room for repentance, and he provided for a Redeemer out of pure kindness, and without being prompted. These facts must therefore be held up alongside those punishments. Thus it is necessary that we everywhere magnify the mercy of God. So if you have kept in view the whole order in which these things were done, you will see again that God works with humankind like a father does with a beloved son, whom he treats harshly only with reluctance. For since we abused the delights of paradise and benefited not at all from its abundance, God willed to teach us in another way, through calamities and adversities, and thus also through contempt for temporal things, and so to convert us to the true good. Let us now turn to those sentences.

[14] And the Lord God said to the snake, "Because you have done this, cursed are you above all beasts of burden, above all beasts of the field. Upon your belly you will go, and you will eat dust all the days of your life."

God first condemns the snake, from whom nevertheless he did not ask for an account of his deed. Nor did he remonstrate beforehand with the snake, as with Adam and Eve. For the sin of the devil, who was working through the snake, was far different from the sin of either Adam or Eve. He sinned through malice and hatred, to obscure

mereatur. Etiam olim diabolus eiectus fuit ex angelorum consortio propter suam malitiam. Expediebat etiam homini, & addebat nonnihil consolationis, uideri iam inimicum suum grauiter a deo tractari & puniri. Solemus enim nonnunquam consolationem accipere, quando uidemus eos qui nos afflixerunt, ante oculos nostros male habere. Ideo & serpens principio punitur, & sic aliquid timoris tum Adae tum Euae incutitur, id tamen habebat suam consolationem.

Quia fecisti.) Peccatum serpentis deus non manifestat, utpote rem perquem inuisam et abominabilem. Fecisti tantam rem, illam meam creaturam, propter quam omnia consideram, abduxisti, inuidiaque decepisti. Ausus igitur tantam rem, maledictus sis prae omnibus bestijs. Habebat serpens aliquid praerogatiuae prae caeteris animantibus, quia callidior ערום & in hoc habebat aliquid prouidentiae. Fertur tunc erectus incessisse, & statura regiam dignitatem habuisse prae caeteris animalibus, unde etiam familiarior fuit homi[51v]ni. Quantum exaltatus est serpens, tantum humiliatus est prae omnibus animalibus, ne amplius erigeret se in sublime.

Puluerem terrae.) Non vesceris de alijs fructibus terrae nascentibus, quia occasionem dedisti mulieri ad peccandum: haecque erat condemnationem serpentis. In omnibus illis sententijs uos potestis considerare, quomodo id deus potissimum punit in homine peccatore, quod praecipue auertere solet a deo. Serpens erectus incedebat. Punit igitur illum deus & humiliat, ut ambulet super terram, quia erecte incedendo familiaris fuit homini, et sic decepit. Inuenimus in serpente illam superbiam, quae proprie est Luciferi: in muliere delitias. Econtrario ambo puniuntur, nempe doloribus. In Adam inuenimus ignauiam, quae leuatur laboribus. Quidam illa exponentes asserunt multas allegorias, quas non licet omnino contemnere, modo habeamus historiam. Diabolus abusus est serpente, ideo etiam serpens puniri debuit propter hoc: sed grauior poena diabolo instigitur. Et quae poena est diaboli, ea etiam est membrorum illius, quia aeque illis peculiare est, & abducere simplices a gloria dei, & conspirare contra pios, atque diabolo ipsi.

the glory of God, a grave sin worse than any venial one. At one time the devil was even expelled from the company of the angels on account of his malice. It was also expedient for humankind and added no little consolation to see their enemy already seriously dealt with and punished by God. For we are accustomed sometimes to receive consolation when we see those who have afflicted us punished before our eyes. Thus also in the beginning the snake is punished, and so even as a certain fear came over both Adam and Eve, nevertheless they had their consolation.

Because you have done.) God does not disclose the sin of the snake, inasmuch as the thing was regarded as extremely detestable and abominable. "You have done such a serious thing, you have carried away and hatefully deceived this my creature, for whom I made all things. Since you dared to do such a thing, cursed are you above all the animals." The snake had a certain priority over the other animals, because he was called *awroom,* "cleverer." In this there was an element of providence. It is said that he then walked erect and had a regal dignity of stature above that of the other animals, whence he was also more familiar to humankind. As much as the snake was exalted, just so much he was humbled more than all animals lest he should exalt himself even more to a lofty position.

The dust of the earth.) "You will not eat from the fruits springing forth from the earth, because you have given the woman the occasion to sin." And this was the condemnation of the serpent. In all these words you can consider how God most powerfully punished in sinful humankind chiefly that which accustoms them to turn away from God. The snake walked erect. Therefore God punished and humbled him that he should crawl along on the ground, because in walking upright he seemed familiar to humankind, and thus deceived them. In the snake we find that overweening pride, which is Lucifer's own, but in the woman the pleasure of illicit delight. So the two are punished in contrary ways, though certainly with sufferings. In Adam we find laziness, from which he is released through hard labors. Some expositors bring forth here many allegories, which need not at all be despised, provided that we have the history. The devil has misused the snake, and so the snake also ought to be punished on that account. But the weightier penalty is imposed on the devil. And whatever is the devil's penalty, the same applies to his minions, because it is equally peculiar to them to lead the innocent away from the glory of God and conspire

Terrena illi quaerunt, etsi uideantur sublimia sapere. Sic etiam hi in quibus potestatem suam exercet, puniuntur a deo propter superbiam suam, ut iam non adspirent [52r] ad coelestia, sed solum temporalibus contenti sunt: & dum potiuntur illis delitijs, putant se esse beatos, quod tamen maxime ad eorum maledictionem pertinet, quia fontem omnis boni amiserunt.

Et inimicitias ponam inter te & inter ipsam mulierem, inter semen tuum, & inter semen illium: ipsum conteret tibi caput, & tu conteres eius calcaneum.

Dicitur serpenti, maligne egisti cum homine, praesertim cum muliere, quam inuenisti infirmiorem: tu post hac ab illa uinceris, & ab eius semine. Si etiam naturam rerum spectemus, tale quiddam inuenimus, quod natura abhorreamus a serpente, praesertim muliebre genus illos magis formidat, unde inimicitiae quaedam sunt inter serpentes & mulieres. Illae enim omnino uellent serpentes ablatos, quia insidiantur illis. In serpentibus etiam pestilens uenenum est, quo hominibus molesti sunt. Ipsum semen, id est, humanum genus, conteret caput tuum. Homo sciet infirmitatem tuam, quod contrito capite totus peris, & ita potestatem tuam tollet: tu autem non poteris mox inuadere caput hominis, sed insidiaberis solum calcaneo, quia humi incedes, & non potes te adeo erigere, ut aliquid nocumenti inseras homini. Hebraei habent: Mordebis sibilando pedibus, infundendo ita uenenum in posteriorem partem hominis. Tale [52v] quiddam licet uidere in istis animalibus, quae oderunt humanum genus. Nihilominus longe sublimiora hic commendantur nobis. Videmus enim quod deus non omnino hominem abijcit, quamuis exasperauerit eum, sed potius conatur illum seruare. Iam constitutus homo superior serpente, ut spem concipiat deum sibi bene uelle: & ita constituit deus hominem, ut pater terrenus facit, qui dat filio suo potestatem contra hostes &c. Vnde etiam homo potuit surgere, & maiorem spem de deo habere. Neque

against the pious, just like the devil himself. They seek earthly things, even though they appear to understand the sublime. So also those in whom he exercises his power are punished by God on account of their pride, so that they may no longer aspire to heavenly things but are content with only temporal goods. And when they come to possess those delights, they think that they are blessed. Nevertheless, this certainly results in their condemnation, for they have let go of the fount of all good things.

[15] And I shall place enmity between you and the woman, between your seed and her seed; he will bruise your head, and you will bruise his heel.

This is spoken to the snake, "You have behaved wickedly with humankind, particularly the woman, whom you found weaker. After this, you will be conquered by her, and by her seed." Even now, if we observe the nature of things we find that by nature we shrink back in horror from the snake. Women especially are even more afraid of them, whence there is a certain enmity between snakes and women. They want snakes completely removed, because they lie in ambush for them. In the snake also there is deadly venom, by which human beings are afflicted. "Her seed," that is, the human race, "will crush your head."[224] The human being will know your weakness, because with your head crushed you will be completely ruined, and thus he will take away your power. You, however, will not be able to attack the head of the man, but you will lie in ambush only for his heel, because on the ground you will go and so you will not be able to rise up to strike him with something deadly." The Hebrews have, "You will hurt him while hissing at his feet," which means sticking the poison into the backside of the human being. We see that in all those animals who hate the human race. At the same time, this text commends to us far higher things. We see that God did not utterly reject the man, although he exasperated him, but on the contrary he tries to save him. For humankind was made superior to the snake, that it might grasp hold of the hope that God wishes him well. God established the human being as does an earthly father, who gives to his own son power against enemies, and so on. Whence also the human being could lift himself up

224 Oecolampadius is taking "seed" here as a plural term that refers to all Christians, i.e., one that promises that all Christians will be able to crush the serpent's head. Cf. Romans 16:20.

ibo inficias, quin in hoc uersu consolatio magna sit homini data. Quid magis consolatur nos, quam cognoscere deum nobis bene uelle, & dare virtutem ut hostem uincamus, qui longe damnosior est hostis, quam serpens? Potestas diaboli multo nocentior est quam ullius crudelissimi hostis. Deus igitur qui adest homini contra inimicum minus ualidum, utique contra inimicum magis ualidum non denegabit suum auxilium. Estque sententia: Sint perpetuae inimicitiae inter mulierem & semen illius, id est, contra ipsum diabolum, & eius filios. Nam generatio malorum contra electos dei pugnat, quae organum est diaboli, ut pessundet bonos. Tam contra diabolum ipsum, quam contra membra eius, sunt inimicitiae assiduae fideli homini. Videamus itaque quanta benignitas sit patris, qui nobis sua gratia adest, & adesse uult. Per caput potentiam, pote[53r]statem, & omnem uim intelligimus. Deus dat filijs suis ut possint draconem & basiliscum conculcare: quam potestatem etiam Christus suis discipulis promisit. Illa potestas per gratiam dei datur & nobis, ut conteramus caput inimici. Ille enim non cessabit, quin semper nobis insidietur. Qui mordebit uertunt, sic interpretantur: Poterit carni nocere, & inferioribus partibus, & temporalibus rebus: non autem animae, nisi uelimus gratiam dei omnino contemnere: illamque consolationem ante omnia puto hic commendari. Nec me latet quod recentiores dicunt, de semine Christo esse intelligenda. Licet fit uerum, tamen nullibi ab Apostolis hoc testimonium citatum legimus, cum alia de Christo filio dei adduxerint. Contra Iudaeos pugnaturi, uereor citius irrideamur, quam aliquid efficiamus, si hunc locum citauerimus. Apud pios autem hoc testimonium multum ualet, quia per semen Christum sciunt diabolum sua potestate exutum, imo & penitus uictum. Item quaedam de calcaneo adijciunt, cui satan insidiatus est, quia Christus tentarus & suffixus in crucem. Iudas enim

and hold onto a greater hope in God. I will not deny that great consolation is given to humanity in this verse. What greater consolation is there than to know that God wishes us well and gives us the strength to overcome the enemy, who is really a much more dreadful foe than the snake? The power of the devil is much more harmful than that of even the most bloodthirsty enemy. God therefore, who is present with the human being, will certainly not deny his help against a stronger foe any more than against a weaker one. The meaning is that there should be perpetual enmity between the woman and his seed, that is, against the devil himself and his offspring. For the race of those who are evil fights against the elect of God. They are the instrument of the devil, to destroy good people. For the incessant struggles of the faithful are as much against the devil himself as against his members. Let us consider, therefore, how great is the benevolence of the Father, who is present in us by his grace, and even wants to be there. By the word "head" we understand all power, strength and force. God gives his sons the ability to tread on snakes and reptiles,[225] which strength Christ also promised to his disciples. By the grace of God that strength is also given to us, that we should crush the head of the enemy. For that one will never cease to lie in wait for us. Whoever turns away he will sting, for it is understood that he will have power to injure only the flesh, the lower parts, temporal things, but not the soul, unless we will to disregard the grace of God altogether. In this text, I believe, this consolation is commended above all things. I am not unaware that more recent expositors say that this "seed" is to be understood as pertaining to Christ. This may be true, but nowhere do we read this testimony cited by the Apostles, although they bring in other texts about Christ the Son of God. If we should cite this text to dispute against the Jews, I fear we would more likely be ridiculed rather than accomplish anything.[226] Among the pious, however, this testimony avails much, because they know that through Christ the "seed" the devil has been stripped of his power, indeed, inwardly defeated as well. They add something similar concerning the "heel," for which Satan lies in ambush, because Christ

225 Cf. Mark 16:18.

226 A characteristic expression of exegetical caution of the sort that seeks to defend the Christian reading of the Old Testament by restraining more exuberant Christological readings of the text. As we see in what immediately follows, however, Oecolampadius allows such readings for the edification of Christian people.

qui prodidit Christum, hoc egit incitatus a diabolo: similiter et Iudaei. Quamuis etiam si proprietatem uerbi seminis aduertamus, non ad unum, sed ad posteritatem benedictio in Christo competit. Pulchre spes datur in deo, quod licet digni simus condemnatione, tamen ea beni[53v]gnitas dei est, quae non uult tradere nos hosti, sed facere superiores. Sequitur nunc de Eua.

Ad mulierem uero dixit: Multiplicando multiplicabo dolorem tuum, & conceptum tuum: in dolore paries filios, & ad uirum tuum erit desiderium tuum, & ipse dominabitur tibi.

Scimus quomodo Eua peccauerit imbecillitate infirmior & simplicior, unde impositum ei a serpente. Non legimus quod deus maledixerit Euae, ut etiam postea de Cain: sed illud de terra & serpente legimus: unde sententia ista erat aliquo modo tolerabilis. Vult deus dicere: Nunc aliter te erudiam: quia per delitias istas declinasti a me, & abusus es bonis concessis, mutabo illam uiuendi rationem in aliam tibi utiliorem, ut non tam secure uiuas absque omnibus molestijs. Et mulieri, quae uas est natura infirmius, iuxta Pauli dictum, deus plures afflictiones dedit. Hocque hic est notandum, ut tempore mensium, & quando concipiunt & pariunt. Nonne sic omnis fere uita mulieris laboriosa est? Menses cum patitur, grauida cum est, cum parit, nonne omnia plena dolorum? Dicit igitur: Hanc crucem tibi iniungam, ut posthac maiori diligentia memor sis mandatorum dei. Neque aliam ob causam ea imponit mulieri, quam ut ne posthac sit superba, sed memor suae fragilitatis. Chry[54r]sostomus dicit in hunc locum: Quamuis cruciatus sis habitura in partu, tamen post partum iterum conuerteris ad uirum tuum, & alios pueros paries. Malo aut sic interpretari. Eris sub uiro tuo, illi honorem dabis, ille imperabit tibi, ut postea deus seipsum exponit, quod uir caput sit mulieris. Ita & iuxta

was stretched out and nailed to the cross. For Judas, who betrayed Christ, did this having been incited by the devil.[227] Likewise also the Jews. However, if we also attend to the meaning of the word "seed," the blessing in Christ applies not to one person but to the coming generations. Hope in God is wondrously given, for although we are worthy of condemnation, nevertheless the benevolence of God is such that he desires not to hand us over to the enemy, but to make us the conquerors.[228] Now it continues concerning Eve.

[16] But to the woman he said, "By a great deal I will multiply your suffering, and your conception. In pain you will bring forth sons, and your desire will be for your husband, and he will rule over you."

We know how through weakness Eve, feebler and less intelligent, sinned, which is why the serpent attacked her. We do not read that God cursed Eve, as we see afterwards in [the case of] Cain.[229] But we do read that concerning the earth and the serpent, which is why that opinion was somewhat tolerable. God wishes to say, "Now I will teach you otherwise. Because through those pleasures you fell away from me and abused the goods granted to you, now I will change that way of life into another more useful to you, so that you no longer live secure from all troubles." And to the woman, who, according to the saying of Paul, is by nature a weaker vessel,[230] God gave many afflictions. Here is indicated this: the time of the menses, and when they conceive, and when they give birth. Is not the life of nearly every woman full of labor? When she endures menses, when she is pregnant, when she gives birth, are not all these things full of suffering? Therefore he says, "This cross I enjoin upon you, so that afterwards you should be more diligently mindful of the commandments of God." This was imposed on the woman for no other cause than that she should be not proud, but remember her own frailty. About this text, Chrysostom says, "Although you will suffer in childbirth, nevertheless afterwards you will turn back to your husband, and you will bring forth other children." I prefer instead that it be interpreted this way. "You will be under your husband, to him you will give honor, he will rule over

227 See John 13:2, 27.

228 Cf. Rom. 8:37.

229 Gen. 4:11 ff.

230 An allusion to I Pet. 3:7.

Apostolum non permittitur mulieri loqui in ecclesia, sed subdita sit uiro & tegat caput suum.

Desiderium.) Alij concupiscentia, uel conversio. αποστροφη, auersio ab alijs ad illum in cupiditate quadam, ut sit vir quasi patronus in omnibus rebus mulieris. Et auersio pro conuersio accipitur. Dicit: Antea aequalis marito eras, eiusdem dignitatis, ex latere uiri, & dignitate par, sed iam quia fuisti uiro causa ruinae, in poenam tuam futurum est, ut subdita sis uiro. In sequenti capite habebitis de Abel, quod conuersio eius sit ad Cain, quia Abel non insidiabatur dignitati Cain, ut sciatis etiam hoc eo in loco pertinere ad imperium. Mulier illa est quae peccauit, & sic sunt delitiae in amaritudines conuersae. Sic nobis continget si ab obedientia domini cessemus: immittet cominus uarias aegritudines, ut reuertamur ad eum. Nunc loquitur Adae.

Ad Adam uero dixit : Quia audisti uocem uxoris tuae, & comedisti de arbore, de qua praecepit tibi dicens: non [54v] comedes ex ea, maledicta est humus propter te, in dolore comedes eam omnibus diebus uitae tuae. Et spinam atque tribulum faciet crescere tibi, & manducabis herbam agri.

Alij, In afflictione comedes. Ita Adae improperat tum negligentiam suam, tum etiam ingratitudinem, quod abusus sit benignitate dei. Taxatur etiam ibi magna ignauia Adae: oportebat enim eum strenuum uirum esse, etsi Eua a serpente fuisset decepta. Ipse magister Euae erat, ideo magis strenuum esse illum dedebat. Ipse debebat docere uxorem, quod neglexit, et ex magistro inepto, discipulis ineptus factus est. Vult

you," just as later God himself says that the husband is the head of the wife.[231] So also the Apostle permits not a woman to speak in church; instead she should submit to her husband, and cover her head.[232]

Desire.) Some say this is desire, or a turning back. The Greek term *apostrophe* [indicates] a turning away from other things to him with a certain desire, so that the husband would be like the wife's patron in all things. So "turning away" is understood here as "turning back." He says: "Previously you were equal to your husband, with the same dignity, taken from the side of the man, with equal rank. But now, because you have become the cause of ruin to the man, it will be your penalty that you should be under the man." In the following chapter you will consider Abel insofar as his turning would be towards Cain, because Abel did not scheme to defraud Cain of his [superior] position. Thus you should know that this word in that text also pertains to the authority to rule.[233] The woman is the one who sinned, and so those delights were turned into bitterness. This will happen to us also if we cease from obedience to the Lord. He will send against us various afflictions, so that we might be turned back to him.[234] Now he speaks to Adam.

[17] But to Adam he said, "Because you have listened to the voice of your wife and have eaten from the tree concerning which I commanded you saying, 'Do not eat from it,' cursed is the earth on account of you; in pain you will eat it, all the days of your life; [18] thorns and thistles it will grow for you, and you will eat the vegetation of the field."

Others read this as "in affliction you will eat." Thus he reproaches Adam both for his negligence and also for his ingratitude, because he abused the benevolence of God. He also takes stock here of how great was the faintheartedness of Adam, for it behooved him to be a stalwart man, even if Eve had already been deceived by the serpent. He was Eve's teacher, wherefore greater strength was bestowed on him. He should have instructed his wife, but he failed to do it, and from an

---

231 See I Cor. 11:3.

232 See Eph. 5:22, and I Cor. 14:34-5.

233 I.e., that Abel respected his brother's superior position by virtue of his primogeniture.

234 See, e.g., Deut. 8 passim.

dicere: Fuisti inobediens, uictus es a delitijs, fuisti ignauus spectator prohibitarum delitiarum, maledicta igitur terra. Dominus omnium rerum eras, & terra propter te condita, ut tibi seruiret: sed quia tu non seruiuisti creatori, neque terra tibi seruiet. Et postea subdit: Licet labores & sis strenuus, tamen terra fructum non dabit. Vide quid fecit ignauia tua. Pro delitijs habebis hunc laborem. Poteras in paradiso uiuere felix & immortalis, sed iam laborabis: et si multum laboraueris, tamen non dabit terra fructus quos speraueris. Iam mutabitur tibi paradisus, & pro optimis fructibus dabit tibi spinas et tribulos, ut uix inde sis habiturus foenum terrae, id est, uilem fructum. [55r]

In sudore uultus tui uesceris pane donec reuertaris in humum: ex ea enim sumptus es, quandoquidem puluis sis, & in puluerem reuersurus sis.

Vide quid egeris: delitiae fuissent tibi seruare paradisum, nunc laborabis usque ad sudorem. Maledicti qui Adae iugum excutiunt. Nihil feliciter continget absque labore. Neque solum de labore agricolarum hunc locum intelliges, sed quicquid agit homo quos honestum est, id in scriptura dicitur laborare.

Pulvis es.) Haec erat sententia in Adam, quae & totum humanum genus comprehendit: sed semper quaedam consolatio speranda apud patrem misericordiarum.

LECTIO

Audiuimus heri, quomodo inobedientiam Adae & Euae deus paterna castigatione castigauerit, & pro delitijs paradisi uarias calamitates humano generi immiserit, praesertim mulieri, cui praedicuntur dolores menstrui & partus. Deinde etiam uiro, quamuis laboret in sudore uultus sui, tamen terram fore infrugiferam, ut homo cognoscat, quaecunque terra profert, illa diuino beneficio concedi, et non humano labore acquiri. Postremo memores eos facit suae originis, quod

inept teacher students are made inept. God wants to say: "You have been disobedient, defeated by pleasures, an ignoble beholder of forbidden delights; therefore the earth is cursed. You were the lord over all things, and the earth was made for you, to serve you. But because you have not served the Creator, neither will the earth serve you." Afterwards it follows: "Although you may labor ever so hard, nevertheless the earth will not give its produce. Behold what your sloth has done! In the place of delights you have hard labor. In paradise you could have lived happy and immortal. But now you will work. And even if you work a lot, nevertheless the land will not yield the produce you hope for. Now the whole paradise will be changed for you, and in the place of the best produce it will give to you thorns and thistles, so that only with difficulty will you have the earth's hay, that is, a poor crop."

[19] In the sweat of your face you will eat bread, until you return to the ground; for from it you were taken up, since you are dust, and to the dust you will return.

Look what you have done. It would have been a delight for you to tend the garden, but now you will always labor until you sweat. Cursed are those who shake off the yoke of Adam. Nothing comes to pass easily without hard work. Nor should you understand this text as applying only to labor in the fields, but to whatever things a person does that are honorable, which in Scripture is called work.

You are dust.) This was the sentence passed on Adam, which also applies to the whole human race. There must always be hope for some comfort, however, with the Father of mercies.[235]

READING

We heard yesterday how God punished the disobedience of Adam and Eve with paternal correction, and how in the place of the delights of paradise he sent upon the human race various misfortunes, especially upon the woman, for whom the suffering of menses and childbirth were predicted. Next also upon the man, that however much he should work in the sweat of his face the land would remain unproductive, in order that humankind should know that whatever the earth brings forth is granted by divine benevolence and not acquired

235 2 Cor. 1:3.

talia ferre debeant, donec in terram redeant, de qua sunt sumpsi. Et quamuis illa satis dura uideantur, rectius ta[55v]men remedia commemorantur, quam inter poenas. Deus enim non oblectatur poenis nostris: sed multo magis gaudet, si homo reuertatur a peccatis suis, & sic uiuat. Proinde non parum aberrant sophistae, qui uolunt unicuiq; peccato suam poenam deberi: et ideo solent dispensare satisfactiones, & suas indulgentias confirmare. Dicunt: Adam peccauit, secuta est haec poena mortis &c. Potest aliqua ratione dici poena, nam omnia illa non erant suauia toleratu: sed si quis ita uelit dicere poenam, ut sophistae, quasi satisfaciat Adam pro peccato, plus diuinae iustitiae derogabit, quam addet: unde omnia ista rectius remedia dixerimus, quam poenam. Electis per hanc uitam omnes calamitates non inter poenas numerantur, sed sunt materia certaminis, ut homo seipsum humiliet, & deum agnoscat. Ita poteritis etiam respondere, ubi passim in scripturis legitis, post peccata secutas esse poenas. Propter poenitentiam deus immittit poenas, ut desistamus a peccatis, non quod poenae sufficiant pro peccatis nostris delendis. Sanguis Christi emundat nos a peccatis, non satisfactio nostra.

by human labor. Next he reminds them of their origins, which they ought to keep in mind until they return to the earth out of which they were drawn. And although these things seem hard enough, they are more properly remembered as remedies than as punishments. For God does not delight in our penalties but, much more, he rejoices if a man is turned from his sins and thus lives.[236] Hence the sophists stray not a little, who want for each one to be held responsible for his own penalty for sin, and who on that basis are accustomed to dispense satisfactions and to declare their indulgences.[237] They say that Adam sinned and the penalty of death followed, etc. But this could be called a penalty for a different reason. For all these things were not easily endured. But if one wants to call that a penalty, as the sophists do, as if Adam could make satisfaction for sin, then he will do more to diminish divine justice than to magnify it. Whence we can rightly say that all those things are more remedies than penalty. Among the elect all the misfortunes of this life are not counted as penalties, but are the material of the struggle so that a man might humble himself and acknowledge God. In the same way you will also be able to answer when you read throughout the Scriptures that after sins there are the attendant penalties. God imposes penalties for the sake of repentance, in order that we should cease from sin,[238] not because the penalties suffice to wipe away our sins. The blood of Christ cleanses us from sin,[239] not our [works of] satisfaction.

---

236 See, e.g., Luke 15:10.

237 By "sophists" here Oecolampadius clearly intends not the ancient Greek teachers of philosophy and rhetoric, but the scholastic theologians and their doctrines of penance, according to which some of the penalties of sin remained even after priestly absolution. In medieval scholastic penitential theory, these punishments were to be dealt with through "works of satisfaction," i.e., good deeds done in a state of grace, which would then offset the punishments owing for previous sin. A properly absolved Christian could therefore offer a monetary gift to the church, in exchange for which the church would provide an "indulgence" in remission of some or all of those remaining penalties. This practice was open to serious abuse, as Martin Luther's protest against indulgences in 1517 clearly shows. For a convenient overview, see P. F. Palmer and G. A. Tavard, "Indulgences," in the *New Catholic Encyclopedia*, 2nd ed., Vol. 7 (Detroit: Gale, 2003), pp. 436-441.

238 Cf. I Pet. 4:1.

239 I John 1:7.

Et uocauit Adam nomen uxoris suae Heva, eo quod ipsa fuerit mater omnis uiuentis.

Statim ex hoc uersu cognoscitur Adam accepisse quandam consolationem: nam iterum ut supra prophe[56r]tice loquitur. Quasi dicat Adam: Ecce uideo deum adhuc paterne mecum agere, & non omnem posteritatem simul tollere propter peccatum meum: Nam uxor mea dabit mihi filios, qui etiam ipsi sunt uicturi, & adhuc nobis est spes aliqua uitae, quamuis mortem meruerimus. Potestis etiam hoc cognoscere, quod Adam nomen mulieri imponit post peccatum, & per hoc ostendit se esse dominum & caput mulieris, quae ante peccatum erat consors, & eiusdem dignitatis. Nomina enim alicui imponere, dominij symbolum est. Supra animalibus, non uxori nomina imposuit. Est igitur in hoc uersu prophetice dicto spes quaedam Adae. Si ad allegorias spectare libet, sicut supra, ecclesiam esse uxorem Christi cognoscamus, in qua sola uita nobis conceditur: & qui extra ecclesiam sunt, & charitatem non habent, uitae non sunt participes.

Fecit quoque dominus deus ipsi Adam & uxori eius tunicas pelliceas, & induit eos.

Iterum uidemus diuinam prouidentiam & curam erga humanum genus. Cum iam nudi ambularent Adam & Eva, & erubescerent, obnoxijq; essent uarijs iniurijs, aeris imbribus, rigoribus, caloribus &c deus uestiuit eos. Ibi uarias allegorias sumpserunt: & quidam satis ridicule exposuerunt humana corpora esse pelli[56v]ceas uestes. Hieronymus & alij quidam accipiunt hic argumentum pro tuenda uirginitate contra coniugium, cum tamen deus hoc uoluerit humano generi consulere. Etiam unde has pelles deus acceperit, habent quaestionem: sed libenter ea relinquo, quae nihil aedificant. Omnes pecudes dei erant, ideo facile pelles potuit acquirere, & nuditatem illorum contegere. Sensus est, quod deus dederit eis ingenium, ut pararent sibi uestes. Nam pleraque scripta sunt, & traduntur deo, & solum insinuant ea quae deus homini

[20] And Adam called the name of his wife Eve, because she would be the mother of all the living.

At once from this verse it is seen that Adam had received a certain comfort. For once again, as above, he speaks prophetically. It is as if Adam had said: "Behold, I see that God is still dealing with me paternally, and likewise that he is not taking away all my posterity on account of my sin. For my wife will give to me sons who will also survive, and so there is still hope in us for a sort of life, even though we deserve death." You may be sure that Adam gave the name to the woman after sin and in this way showed himself to be the lord and head of the woman,[240] she who before sin was a partner with equal worth. To impose a name on someone is a sign of dominion. Above, he imposed names on the animals but not on his wife. The hope of Adam is therefore prophetically spoken in this verse. If you like to look at allegories, just as above, we acknowledge that the church is the wife of Christ,[241] in which alone life is granted to us, for all who are outside the church and have not love do not share in life.

[21] The Lord God also made for Adam and his wife tunics out of skin, and he clothed them.

Again we see the divine providence and care for the human race. For because Adam and Eve would have been walking around naked, and would have been ashamed, liable to various injuries, to the rains, the cold and the heat, and so on, God clothed them. Here some take up various allegories, and indeed some have quite laughably claimed that the "tunics of skin" were in fact their human bodies. Jerome and some others accept this argument because they wish that virginity should be held up over marriage, whereas God by this [simply] wanted to look out for the human race.[242] They even question whence God received those skins. But I gladly leave such questions behind, for they do not edify. All sheep were God's sheep, so he was able easily to acquire hides and so to cover over their nakedness. But the sense is that God gave to them the ability to furnish clothing for themselves. For many things have been written and handed down about God, and they only

240 See I Cor. 11:3.

241 See Eph. 5:25-32.

242 I.e., for the individual Christian to decide for either the celibate or the married life.

concessit, ut supra cum audirent deum ambulantem & loquentem &c. Qualis autem illa uox fuerit, dixi. Ita & hic aliquo modo ostenditur, quod deus fecerit homini pelles, cum dederit ingenium faciendi. Vel si iuxta literam illud intelligere uis, non errabis. Iterum spes nostra confirmatur ut bene confidamus, quod deus non sit nos derelicturus. Ne simus igitur nimium soliciti de cibo & potu. Cibum dabit, qui iam uestes dat. Ita in primis hominibus uidemus, qualia necessaria sint omnibus. Victum & amictum habentes, his contenti simus. Legimus denique deum dedisse eis pelliceas uestes, non sericas, uel molles adeo: Nam poenitentiam & asperiorem uitam illis quodam modo insinuare uidetur. Hoc quidam elicere solent. Quid non sperarent post delicta de diuina beneuolentia, quae non solum eos non extinguit, sed etiam noua beneficia confert?[57r]

Et dixit dominus deus: Ecce ille homo fuit quasi unus ex nobis, ut sciret bonum & malum: & nunc ne forte mittat manum suam, & accipiat etiam de arbore uitae, & comedat, & uiuat in seculum.

Sunt qui hunc uersum affirmatiue exponant, & putant si per asseuerationem exponatur, commodiorem interpretationem sic haberi: sed ego malo simplicem sequi sensum. Sunt enim haec ironicos dicta. Neque dedecet deum ad nostram eruditionem quaedam ironice loqui, quemadmodum patres de filijs suis nonnunquam loquuntur: non quod oblectentur stultitia illorum, sed ut cupiant illos erudire. Sic spiritus sanctus etiam hic loquitur.

Ecce ille homo.) Vide quam bene successit Adae, sic praeuaricare praeceptum nostrum: uide quam particeps sit diuinitatis. Non potuisset longius a nobis recedere, quam sic transgrediendo praeceptum meum. Induerat pelliceis Adam, ut cognosceret etiam suam uilitatem: & ita erat comparatus bestijs insipientibus, quorum etiam pelles gestabat. Dicit: Omnino est factus nobis dissimilis, hocque uolebat. Videmus iam iumentis fere inferiorem. Quam male cesserunt homini sua consilia: propterea opus ut aliter erudiamus hunc nostrum filium.

Arbore vitae.) Id est, ne semper sit ita miser, & [57v] tam ignominiosus. Nam si acciperet de ligno uitae quod deus constituerat in paradiso (ut supra de arbore scientiae & boni & mali dictum, cuis fructus prohibitus) potuisset immortalitate potiri. Haec magna misericordia dei. Nos multum horremus mortem, cum finis sit malorum. Non esset optandum ut perpetuo in hoc exilio uiueremus. Vult dicere deus: Hoc homini longe satius est, ut quam remotissime remoueatur ab hoc

insinuate what God granted to humankind, as above when they were hearing God walking and talking, etc. However, as I said, it was a voice of some kind. So also it is shown here that God in some way made skins for them, when he gave them the ability of making them.[243] But if you wish to understand this text according to the letter, you will not err. Here again our hope is confirmed so that we might be well assured that God will not forsake us. Let us not therefore worry too much about food and drink. The one who gives clothing will also give food. Thus we see in the first human beings what sorts of things are necessary for all. We have food and clothing; let us be content with these.[244] For in fact we read that God gave them tunics of skin, not of silk or something soft. Penance and a harsher life seem somehow to be suggested for them. This idea some are accustomed to draw forth. After their fall, what should they not have hoped for from the divine kindliness, since he not only had not killed them but had even bestowed on them new benefits?

[22] And the Lord God said, "Behold, the man has become like one of us, knowing good and evil. Now, lest perchance he should put forth his hand and take also from the tree of life and eat, and live forever."

There are those who expound this text in the affirmative, for they think that if they do so earnestly they will get the most suitable interpretation. I prefer, however, to follow the simple sense. These things are said ironically. Nor is it unsuitable for God to have spoken for our instruction with a certain irony, as fathers also sometimes speak concerning their own sons, not that their foolishness is [meant to be] amusing, but because they want to teach them. Here the Holy Spirit also speaks this way.

Behold the man.) "Look how far Adam has advanced, even to violate our command, and behold how he might share in our divinity![245] He could not have fallen further away from us than by so transgressing my command." He had clothed Adam with skins in order that he should recognize his own lowly state. So also he was compared to the dumb beasts, whose skins he even wore. God says: "He has been made

243 I.e., the ability to make clothing.

244 See Matt. 6:25.

245 I Pet. 1:4.

ligno. Dum dicit: Ne forte manum mittat etc. id est, cum consideratione quadam, & dedita opera comedat. Alias potuisset simpliciter dicere: Ne forte comedat. Estque sententia: Cogitabit quomodo possit perpetuo uiuere, non quam miser sit. Et quamuis summa bona amiserit, nihilominus placebit sibi sua miseria. Non agnoscet se tam miserum, si permiserimus eum in paradiso, unde optabat de arbore uitae, & sic fieri immortalis.

Et emisit eum dominus deus de horto Eden, ad colendum terram, de qua sumptus fuerat.

Eiecit eum deus horto uoluptatis propter suum peccatum. Hic necesse est ut seruemus historiam. Nam antea audiuimus Adam non esse formatum in paradiso, forsan circa agrum Damascenum, uel in aliquo simili loco, deinde translatus in paradisum. Igitur in locum primum, in quo primo conditus fuit emittitur Adam, [58r] & ex loco paradisi mittitur in illam terram, unde sumptus fuit. Terra ista maledicta, proinde in sudore uultus sui laborare cogebatur.

Itaque expulit illum hominem, & collocauit a plaga orientali horri Eden Cherubim, & laminam gladij uersatilis, ad custodiendum iter arboris uitae.

wholly unlike us, and this is also what he wanted. We consider him now almost inferior even to the animals. What evils befell the man through his own counsels! Thus the need for us to teach this son of ours in another way."

From the tree of life.) That is, lest he should always be so wretched and disgraced. For if he had taken from the tree of life that God had established in paradise (as is said above concerning the tree of the knowledge of good and evil, whose fruit was prohibited), he could have become immortal. This is the great mercy of God. We fear death greatly, since it is the end of the wicked. But it was not desirable that we should live forever in this exile. God wishes to say, "This is much better for the man, that he be set as far as possible apart from this tree," while he said, "lest he should put forth his hand," etc.; that is, that after some consideration and dedicated effort he should eat. Otherwise he simply could have said, "lest perchance he would eat." This is the meaning: "He will consider how he might be able to live forever, not how wretched he would be. And even though he will lose the highest good, nevertheless he will gratify himself in the midst of his miseries. He will not acknowledge that he is so wretched if we allow him to remain in paradise, where he would hope in the tree of life and thus become immortal."

[23] And the Lord God expelled him from the garden of Eden, to cultivate the earth out of which he had been made.

God threw him out from the garden of delights on account of his sin. Here it is necessary that we attend to the history. Previously we heard that Adam was not formed in paradise, but perhaps somewhere near Damascus or in another similar place, and then brought into the paradise.[246] Therefore Adam was exiled into that place in which he had first been created; he was sent out of the place of paradise into that land from which he had been taken up. The land had been cursed, so he had to work by the sweat of his face.

[24] Therefore he banished the man, and he placed at the eastern side of the garden of Eden the cherubim and a shining sword turning every which way, to guard the way to the tree of life.[247]

246 Here Oecolampadius accepts an interpretation, which he had considered doubtful in his exegesis of Gen. 2:8, above.

247 I read here "horti" for "horri."

Sic expulit eum deus, ne iterum ingrederetur: id est, suis uiribus nunquam eam felicitatem acquiret quam amisit. Nam constituit ibi ab oriente iuxta paradisum cherubim, & gladium uel romphaeam, ut Graeci uerterunt uersatilem, per tempus uitae adae. Per cherubim quidam angelos intelligunt. Etsi hic dicat fuisse terram illam obseruatam angelorum ministerio, ne Adam ingrederetur, postea tamen non opus erat hac custodia, ne Adam comederet. Dixi nuper de paradiso: ne imaginemur, ut plerique, locum esse ualde remotum, et quasi de altissimo monte descenderit Adam: deinde ut alij narrant, ultra mare positum esse: scriptura enim omnino repugnat. Nam uidemus aliqua flumina, quae obambulant paradisum. Noluit autem deus redire Adam ad illum locum. Et quamuis uere olim illic talis arbor fuerit, postea tamen terra illa mutata fuit, factaque obnoxia maledictioni, & sic felix terra aliud nomen accepit. Simpliciter illum uersum exponere possumus: deus [58v] omnibus modis curauit, ne Adam iterum regrederetur ad eam felicitatem, unde excidit: id est, suis uiribus adsequi uitam aeternam non potuit. Christus promissus uere aperuit paradisum & regnum coelorum. Videt autem Adam ante oculos suos eam regionem, de qua expulsus propter peccatum suum fuit, unde memore esse debuit ex quanta dignitate exciderit: quod etiam nos cogitare oportebit. Sed haec omnia in bonum homini facta sunt: nam longe maior nunc gratia, quam si non praecessisset peccatum. Et ita usque huc descripsit Moses ingenium hominis & dignitatem, & quomodo ob nostram ignauiam praeceptum domini praeuaricamur, & iterum diuina benignitate reseruamur in hac uita, ut nosipsos exerceamus & emendemur. Nunc progreditur ultra in sequenti quarto capite, in quo cognoscemus propositis duorum exemplis fratrum, quod bonorum hominum ingenium, & quod malorum: & qui ueri sunt filij dei, & qui non. Nam Abel ille primus iustus, pulchre deliniabit nobis, quomodo boni in hoc

God banished him, so that he should not again enter in, that is, that he should never by his own powers regain that happiness which he had lost. For he placed there on the eastern side of paradise the cherubim and a sword or a spear, which the Greeks translate "turning back and forth," throughout the entirety of Adam's life. Some understand the cherubim as angels. Even if he says here that the land was watched over by ministering angels lest Adam should come back in and eat, nevertheless afterwards there was no need of this custody. I said above concerning paradise that we should not imagine it, as do many, as a place terribly remote, as if Adam had come down from the highest mountain. Then there are others who say that it was placed beyond the sea. But the Scripture disagrees completely. For we read that there were some rivers that ran through the paradise. God did not wish for Adam to return to that place. And although formerly there was in that place such a tree, afterwards that land was so altered and punished by the curse that this blessed land received another name. We are able to exposit that verse simply: God took in every way such care that Adam could not again enter into that blessedness from which he was utterly cut off. That is, he was not able by his own powers to gain life eternal. The promised Christ truly opened paradise and the kingdom of heaven. Adam, however, sees before his own eyes that region [i.e., paradise] from which he was banished on account of his sin, so he should remember from what great dignity he had been cut off. This it behooves us also to consider. But all these things were done for the good of humankind, for how much greater now is grace than if sin had not come before.[248]

So also up to now Moses has described the innate quality and dignity of humankind, and how on account of our faintheartedness we violated the command of the Lord, and further how by divine kindness we have been spared in this life, in order that we might discipline and correct ourselves. Now he continues into the following fourth chapter, in which we will learn from the example of two brothers that is set forth what the character is of those who are good and those who are evil, as well as who are the true sons of God and who are not. For Abel,

---

248 Cf. Rom. 5:20. This is an echo of Augustine, and of the antecedent Latin tradition generally which can speak of the "happy fault" or "fortunate ruin" of Adam. Here we see one of the elements that identifies the western character of this commentary, in spite of Oecolampadius's intriguing appropriation of the eastern fathers in some places.

seculo habeant: deinde Cain, qui fortunatior in hoc seculo, quales mali sint declarabit. Moses potuisset scribere alias genealogias, & certum est quod Adam initio multos liberos procrearit, quamuis solum hi tres, Cain, Abel & Seth commemorantur. Illi autem soli recensentur nobis in bonum, quia omnia conscripta sunt ad no[59r]stram eruditionem, ut inde emendemur.

the first righteous man,[249] will beautifully sketch for us how the good have it in this age. Then Cain, who was more fortunate in this age, will make known what the wicked are like. Moses could have written other genealogies, and it is sure that Adam in the beginning procreated many children. However, only these three — Cain, Abel, and Seth — are here mentioned. These alone are set forth for our good, because all things have been written down for our instruction that we should thence be corrected.[250]

---

249 Heb. 11:4.

250 See, e.g., I Cor. 10:11, Rom. 15:4.

INDEX

I

J

L

M

O

P

R

S

T